AFGHANISTAN IN TRANSITION
CAROLINE HUDSON FIRESTONE

ISBN: 978-1-61623-416-4 – Hardcover
        978-1-61623-417-1 – Paperback

Library of Congress Control Number: Pending

Caroline Hudson Firestone

        Afghanistan in Transition

To Order: CFirestone@NewHudsonFoundation.org

Printed in China

First Edition

Manufactured by 1st Global Graphics Inc., Irwindale, CA

TO THE COURAGEOUS PEOPLE OF AFGHANISTAN

AND TO

FATIMA GAILANI

Fatima Gailani, Din Mohammad Nazari, and Amima Afzali cutting the ribbon for the four ARCS bungalows.

FOREWORD

The tragic events of September 11, 2001 forced the United States and the international community to take a long hard look at a nation that had endured terrorism breeding on its soil and for far too long suffered unmentionable atrocities under Taliban rule. Admittedly, I was one of the millions who were educated by the nightly news. As I watched Operation Enduring Freedom (OEF) drop bombs on the mountainous terrain of Afghanistan to root out Taliban insurgents on one channel, I learned of the plight of millions of Afghan refugees and the brutality that women endured. I became more interested as each day passed, buying books on Afghanistan's history, going to panel discussions on the future of Afghanistan, reading every newspaper article I could.

One day, I attended a luncheon in New York that featured a guest speaker from Afghanistan. She was a young woman dressed in a stole and floor-length dress who had come to raise money for a girls' school in Afghanistan. She told us that before the Taliban took over she had been a TV announcer. At that time, in 1996, her short hair was uncovered and, like the other Afghan women at the television station, the length of her skirt was to her knees; Kabul was called the Paris of Asia. Shortly after the insurgents had taken over Kabul, they went to her TV station. They ordered all the employees to the main room, where in front of her they killed everyone with their Kalashnikovs. The lead insurgent told her to go home, get her family, go to Pakistan and never return. She took his advice and fled over the border with her family. Recognizing that as an educated woman she could still make a contribution, and even as a refugee help other women left behind, she began crossing back into Afghanistan wearing a burqa to teach women to read and write. This was accomplished by creating a sewing circle, and when anyone knocked at the door the lessons were put under their skirts and the sewing brought out.

As I learned more about Afghanistan and the courageous plight of its people, I decided to write and publish my first book called *Afghanistan Evolving*. It was done to tell of the beauty of a country that was left in ruins—wrought by 25 years of war and regimes that had no regard for the splendor of its God-given natural resources.

After publishing the book, I felt exhilarated and wanted to get even more involved. A friend, Connie Duckworth, a savvy, intelligent woman who had become the first female partner at Goldman Sachs, told me about her involvement with the U.S.-Afghan Women's Council (a public-private partnership designed to mobilize public and private sector resources to empower Afghan women). After many meetings with State Department and Afghan officials, I was asked to join the Council. In the beginning, my projects were giving computers to groups of girls who came to the United States for business education and a tree planting and nursery initiative with the Global Partner-

ship for Afghanistan. I began traveling on a fairly regular basis to Afghanistan to evaluate the work on the ground, to meet with Afghan officials, and to assess for myself the needs of the people. In the process I set up the New Hudson Foundation.

On one of my visits, I met Fatima Gailani. Fatima is the daughter of Pir Sayed Ahmed Gailani, leader of the Qadiria Sufi Order in Afghanistan (the Qadiria Order has one hundred million followers in the Muslim world) and the leader of the National Islamic Front of Afghanistan which fought against the Soviet occupation of Afghanistan in the 1980s. One of her maternal grandfathers was a king who had had 50 wives. Fatima Gailani lived in exile during the Soviet invasion of Afghanistan and acted as spokesperson in London for the Afghan Mujahedeen. She attended the Bonn Conference on Afghanistan in 2001. After her return to Afghanistan she was chosen as a delegate to the Emergency Loya Jirga (Grand Council) of June 2002 and was appointed as a constitution drafting and ratifying commissioner. After Hamid Karzai was elected as Afghanistan's first president in 2004, he offered Fatima Gailani many high-level positions, including ambassadorships and a cabinet post. Rather than taking a lofty position, she chose to be the head of the Afghan Red Crescent Society (ARCS). Like the American Red Cross, ARCS takes care of those who have been displaced by human conflict/natural disasters. However, ARCS also covers the poorest of the poor by providing basic healthcare, shelter and educational services. This was not a highly sought after position, but Fatima felt she could make a real contribution to her homeland by serving in this role. Today, the ARCS is the lifeblood of Afghanistan because of her giving and loving heart, as well as her brilliant management style.

Now that I've told you about my inspiration behind the book, let me tell you a little about the book's content. *Afghanistan In Transition* starts with the present—where Afghanistan stands now. It would be impossible to have enough time to trace the miracle of what brought this country to where it is today. While many challenges still lie ahead, the remarkable progress that has been made over the past eight years is extraordinary. The resilience of the Afghan people is inspiring and the important work they are doing to rebuild their nation into a peaceful, prosperous and democratic nation has worldwide consequences. This book pays tribute to the Afghan people and the amazing work that the Non-Governmental Organizations, the military, donor nations, foundations and private citizens are undertaking to assist reconstruction efforts to ensure that Afghanistan never returns to the dark days of the Taliban.

Perhaps the Afghan proverb—there is a path at the top of even the highest mountain—meaning where there is a will there is a way—underscores best my sentiments about the daunting task at hand and the extraordinary accomplishments already made.

Caroline Hudson Firestone

TABLE OF CONTENTS

*Marco Polo sheep rams (Ovis ammon polii)
in the eastern Pamir Mountains.*

BACTRIAN GOLD

Terracotta Buddha statue from the site of Hadda. The statue was photographed at the moment of unwrapping in the presidential palace, Kabul, 2004.

Balkh, the major city of ancient Bactria, at the foot of the central highlands in northern Afghanistan, is said to have been home to legendary prophet Zoroaster, residing here centuries before the arrival of Alexander the Gr...

AFGHANISTAN'S HIDDEN TREASURES

Afghanistan—at the crossroads of ancient trade routes and great civilizations—was home to some of the most complex, rich and original cultures on the continent of Asia. The exhibition, AFGHANISTAN: Hidden Treasures from the National Museum, Kabul, celebrates the unique role of Afghanistan as a center for both the reception of diverse cultural elements and the creation of original styles of art that combine multiple stylistic materials.

This exhibition highlights the amazing rediscovery of Silk Road treasures from Central Asia, thought to have been lost during decades of warfare and turmoil in Afghanistan. These masterpieces of the Kabul Museum collection remained hidden for 25 years, thanks to the heroism of the Kabul Museum's staff, who had secretly crated them and placed them in the vaults of the Central Bank in the presidential palace. It was only in 2004 that the crates were opened to reveal that these works had survived intact.

The spectacular arts exhibited here show the pivotal role played by ancient northern Afghanistan—Bactria in western sources—as a strategic crossroads for trade and cultural exchange between East and West. Its culture reflects contacts with Greece, Iran, Mesopotamia, India, China and the Eurasian steppes. Bactrian craftsmen absorbed the artistic traditions of these diverse lands and developed their own distinctive style.

The works on view come from four archaeological sites and span Afghan history from its earliest civilization to the time of Rome:

- Tepe Fullol, an original Afghan Bronze Age site dated to 2200 B.C.
- Aï Khanum, a Hellenistic city founded in Afghanistan by the successors of Alexander the Great in the fourth century B.C.

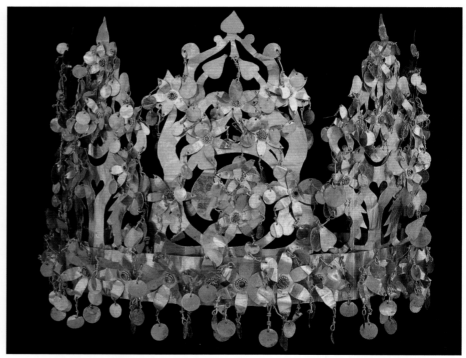

Crown. Tillya Tepe, Tomb VI. Second quarter of the 1st century A.D. Gold, imitation turquoise. 45.0 x 13.0 cm. National Museum of Afghanistan. 04.40.50. This can be separated for travel into five pieces

- Begram, a Silk Road city that flourished at the heart of the Silk Road in the first and second centuries A.D.
- The Bactrian Gold found at Tillya Tepe, where a nomadic chieftain and members of his household were buried 2000 years ago. More than 21,000 stunning gold objects and ornaments, all locally made, reveal a true "Silk Road" art.

TEPE FULLOL AND THE BRONZE AGE

Afghanistan's natural resources—gold, copper, tin, lapis lazuli, garnet and carnelian—drew settlers who brought farming to the fertile foothills of the Hindu Kush mountains more than 6,000 years ago. By the early part of the Bronze Age (ca. 2200 B.C.), an urban culture had developed in northern Afghanistan with its own distinctive style of architecture. Bronze Age towns featured massive fortified buildings with towers constructed of unbaked bricks. This architectural tradition continued for centuries.

As this Bronze Age culture had no known writing, its original name is lost, but archaeologists call it the Oxus civilization, after the Oxus River (modern Amu Darya) that flows through the region. In 1966 farmers near the northern Afghan village of Fullol accidentally discovered a burial cache that contained the first evidence of the Oxus civilization in Afghanistan. The grave contained several bowls, including three on view in the exhibition, which are made of gold that probably came from the Oxus riverbed. Their designs include animal imagery—a boar and bearded bulls (the latter derived from distant Mesopotamia)—indicating that at this early date Afghanistan was already part of an extensive network of trade and cultural exchanges.

The grave goods from Tepe Fullol attest to the existence of elites whose wealth was the result of a very active role in the trade of precious materials, particularly lapis lazuli, that were mined in the nearby mountains of Badakhshan and exported to the major cities of Mesopotamia and further west to Syria and Egypt.

AÏ KHANUM

Bactria, the richest province of northern Afghanistan, attracted the interest of Alexander the Great where he is said to have founded eight Hellenistic cities. The existence of these cities remained a mystery until 1961 when the late Afghan king Zahir Shah was shown a Corinthian capital while hunting in northern Afghanistan and recognized its antiquity.

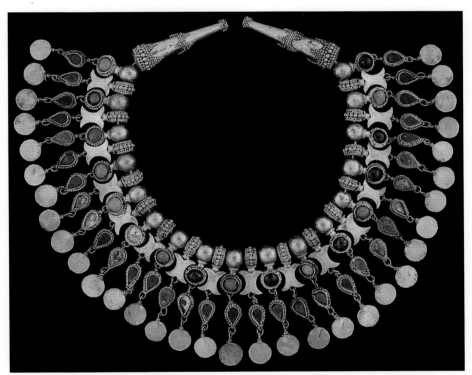

Ornament for the neck of a robe. Tillya Tepe, Tomb V. Second quarter of the 1st century A.D. Gold, turquoise, garnet, pyrite. L 29.1 cm. National Museum of Afghanistan. 04.40.140.

Exploration of the area led to the excavation of Aï Khanum by French archaeologists from 1964 to 1978, which brought to light the best-preserved Hellenistic city of Asia, at the gateway to the nomadic world. Aï Khanum was modeled on a Greek urban plan and was filled with the public buildings

Standing ram. Tillya Tepe, Tomb IV. Second quarter of the 1st century A.D. Gold. 5.2 x 4.0 cm. National Museum of Afghanistan. 04.40.399.

Fragment of a bowl. Tepe Fullol. 2200-1900 B.C., Gold. H 14.9 cm. National Museum of Afghanistan. 04.29.5.

of a Greek city, such as a gymnasium for education and sports, a theater, a fountain and a library with Greek texts. Other structures derive from ancient Near Eastern traditions, such as the royal palace and the temples. The same melding of Eastern and Hellenistic elements is found in the artistic production of the local workshops.

BEGRAM

One of the most remarkable finds in world archaeology was made at Begram in Afghanistan in 1937: the discovery of an intact Silk Road merchants' warehouse from the first century A.D. The warehouse contained a remarkable cache of works of art—glassware, bronzes and porphyry from Roman Egypt; first-century lacquer bowls from China; and ivory furniture ornaments, made in India or locally carved.

Ever since its discovery, scholars have puzzled over the nature of the settlement at Begram. Some believed it to be a city founded by Alexander the Great or his successors in the fourth century B.C. (Alexandria ad Caucasum), which later became the summer capital of the Kushan dynasty.

Minister of Information and Culture Sayeed Makhdoom Raheen (center) turns to Viktor Sari-anidi (left, front) as the inventory team opens the first safe of Bactrian gold in the presidential bank vault, Kabul, 2004. Through Afghanistan's decades of disruption, some 20 or 30 men, the key-holders, were cultural heroes by refusing to talk to anyone about the location of this great ancient treasure. Someone in the 1970s, moved the treasure in six crates—first to the presidential palace, then to a vault under the palace. Key-holders like Omara Khan Masoudi, now the head of the National Museum, and Ameruddin Askarzai, an employee of the central bank, stayed in Kabul because each felt personal responsibility for the safety of Afghanistan's heritage. Mr. Askarzai ignored Taliban threats and even spent time in jail to protect the art. In 2003 the crates were identified but out of reach. Some key-holders were gone, a key had been broken in the lock, etc. It required a presidential decree to allow a locksmith to force entry. Finally, the first box was opened and out poured plastic bags filled with gold appliqués, jewelry and other pieces of gold.

According to this view, the works of art constitute a treasure hoarded or assembled over time by Kushan rulers for their personal use. More recent studies have regarded Begram not as a royal city but as an important trading center on the northwestern edge of the Kushan Empire.

In this view, the finds represent a splendid repository of trade goods, sealed off to protect valuable commodities awaiting further distribution along the Silk Road.

The end of the royal Greek city of Aï Khanum (meaning "Lady Moon") came suddenly around 145 B.C. at the hands of nomads from the northeast, who set fire to the palace and robbed the treasury.

BACTRIAN GOLD

Perhaps the greatest of all finds from Afghanistan's past was found on the eve of a recent civil war. In 1978, a Soviet-Afghan team of archaeologists made an extraordinary discovery: the cemetery of a nomadic family buried in the first century A.D. The graves revealed a stunning treasure of some 20,000 gold objects, consisting of jewelry and luxury items including ceremonial weapons and appliqués. These items were carefully excavated and hidden for safety during the Afghan civil war—and not thoroughly studied until now.

Most of them were inlaid with an astonishing range of materials, available to the local artists, particularly semiprecious stones such as turquoise from Iran, lapis lazuli from Afghanistan and Tajikistan, garnets and amethysts from India, and Baltic amber.

The finds at Tillya Tepe revealed a nomadic culture that was very refined and eclectic. The nomads retained their own imagery—the "animal style" of the steppes—but they also absorbed different elements from works of

Pendant Showing the "Dragon Master" Tillya Tepe, Tomb II. Second quarter of the first century A.D. Gold, turquoise, garnet, lapis Lazuli, carnelian, pearls. 12.5 x 6.5 cm. National Museum of Afghanistan 04.40.109.

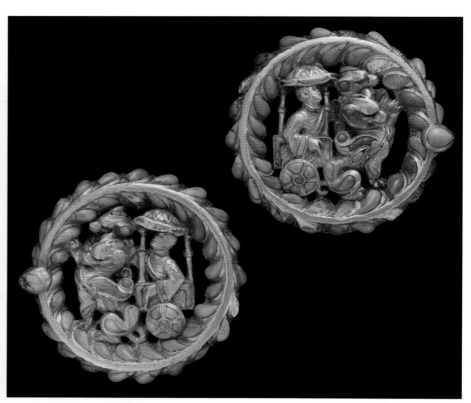

Boot buckle decorated with image of a carriage drawn by dragons. Tillya Tepe, Tomb IV. Second quarter of the first century A.D. Gold, turquoise, carnelian. Diam. 5.5 cm; H. 1.1 cm. National Museum of Afghanistan 04.40.383.

art traveling along the Silk Road, resulting in a synthesis and reinterpretation of Hellenistic, Indian, Chinese, and nomadic traditions.

The "Golden Hoard of Bactria" was presented to the Kabul Museum and displayed in 1980 and 1991 before disappearing from view. Thought to have been lost or stolen or melted down during years of civil war and turmoil, in 2004 the treasure was dramatically revealed to be intact, hidden away in a vault of Kabul's Central Bank in

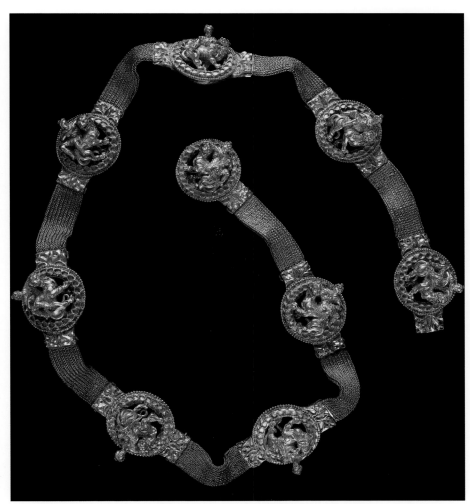

Belt. Tillya Tepe. Tomb IV. Second quarter of the first century A.D. Gold. 97.5 x 2.0 cm.
National Museum of Afghanistan. 04.40.384.

the presidential palace. A wide selection of the most representative objects from Tillya Tepe shown in the present exhibition is on view for the first time outside of Afghanistan.

Typical of nomadic burials, the graves at Tillya Tepe were dug into an earthen mound. In the Eurasian steppes funeral mounds were man-made constructions of overwhelming size, erected with a huge amount of the sod of grazing lands. In Tillya Tepe, however, the nomads reused an existing "hill," which was actually the earth-covered remains of a fortified mud-brick temple of earlier antiquity. The most important person, the chieftain in tomb IV, was interred at the highest point in the center of the mound, and the female burials were arranged roughly in a circle around him. The deceased were interred in lidless coffins that were wrapped with burial shrouds and placed in simple trenches covered by timber planks and earth.

No evidence survives to suggest how the people buried at Tillya Tepe died. Perhaps they were victims of sickness or the harsh Afghan environment. It is also possible that the women were sacrificed upon the death of the chieftain. According to Herodotus' description of the burial practices of Scythian nomads, a man did not go alone into the hereafter, but was accompanied by members of his household. Archaeological evidence from nomadic graves scattered from Ukraine to Siberia complements this account, attesting to impressive burials filled with gold adornments, weapons, symbols of high status, and provisions, servants, grooms, and horses to accompany the deceased into the eternal pastures.

Omar Sultan, Former Deputy Minister of Culture, Afghanistan
Fred Hiebert, National Geographic Archaeology Fellow

Carved marble enclosure around the tomb of Muhammed Zahir al-Din Babur, first Moghul emperor (1483-1530) in the Bagh-e Babur.

AGA KHAN
DEVELOPMENT NETWORK

THE MOGHUL EMPEROR'S PARADISE GARDEN[1]

In 2002 the Aga Khan Development Network[2] (AKDN) began the rehabilitation of the terraced and walled garden—a project designed to conserve and restore Afghanistan's cultural heritage while stimulating local economic development and improving the quality of life for people living in surrounding neighborhoods. Known as the Bagh-e Babur, or the Babur Gardens, this project involved the restoration of walls and the Queen's Palace, the re-laying of water channels, the reconstruction of a caravanserai, which will offer space for a visitor's center, shops and offices, and the replanting of trees favored by the Moghuls. The project also includes a range of community upgrading activities, improving water and sanitation facilities for 10,000 inhabitants of the surrounding residential area.

Bagh-e Babur has a long history closely intertwined with the history of Kabul itself. In 1528 A.D., Babur, the great-grandson of Tamerlane and founder of the Mogul empire, gave instructions for a "paradise garden" to be built. It is believed that Bagh-e Babur is just that garden. This is one of several gardens that Babur had laid out for recreation and pleasure during his life and chose as his last resting place. In 1638 the Emperor Shahjahan erected a marble screen around the group of tombs and built a mosque on the terrace below with the following dedication:

> *Only this mosque of beauty, this temple of nobility, constructed for the prayer of saints and the epiphany of cherubs, was fit to stand in so venerable a sanctuary as this highway of archangels, this theatre of heaven, the light garden of the god forgiven angel king whose rest is in the garden of heaven, Zahiruddin Muhammad Babur the Conqueror.*

Accounts from that time describe a channel of water running from below the mosque along the line of an avenue, with small reservoirs at each terrace and larger pools at intervals. In true Moghul tradition, this gave the site the character of a mausoleum.

Visitors to the site during the 19th century recorded that it had fallen into disrepair. But by the 1880s new development included construction of a central pavilion and Queen's Palace. Nadir Shah (1930-1933) transformed the garden into a public recreation area with fountains as the focus for a flower garden; later a public swimming pool was added.

The garden's location, close to the frontlines between fighting factions occupying Kabul in 1992, turned it into a "no-man's land." The pavilion and Queen's Palace were destroyed, the mosque damaged. Most trees were killed and, in spite of landmines, Bagh-e Babur became merely a convenient source of firewood.

Bagh-e Babur represents a site of major historic significance and also a public space for picnics, swimming and recreation. As early as 2003 a Kabul guidebook remarked, "…these six hectares of walled gardens are going to be one of the most beautiful spots in the city.[3]" Today, the pleasure gardens of Babur are, indeed, a gem—respecting the memory of Afghanistan's past and creating a place of exquisite beauty and peace for all Afghans.

[1]Largely extracted from "Babur's Garden Rehabilitation Framework," Kabul, January 2004.
[2]Read more about the Aga Khan Development Network on page 11.
[3]Medley, Dominic and Jude Barrand, "Kabul: the Brandt Mini Guide," Brandt Travel Guides Ltd., 2003.

The tomb of Muhammad Zahir al-Din Babur, first Moghul emperor (1483-1530), in the Bagh-e Babur.

ENABLING AFGHANS TO TRANSFORM EXTREME POVERTY TO CHOICE AND OPPORTUNITY: AGA KHAN DEVELOPMENT NETWORK (ADKN)

We would like to reiterate our long-term commitment to this region, of which Afghanistan and we are an integral part of its peoples. The Development Network is already scaling up its efforts, in collaboration and with the support of the international community, to enable Afghans to transform their existence from extreme poverty to choice and opportunity within a context that safeguards, for each of them, their right to their own identities, and to preserve and practice their faiths and traditions.

HIS HIGHNESS THE AGA KHAN'

At the conference on the reconstruction of Afghanistan, held in Tokyo in 2002, His Highness the Aga Khan made an initial pledge of $75 million to Afghanistan's reconstruction. To date, AKDN's assistance to Afghanistan has exceeded His Highness' original pledge by 80 percent. With the support of its donors and partners, nearly $750 million has been channeled through the AKDN for Afghanistan's reconstruction. Among other things, this investment has helped to produce large-scale rural development, health, education and civil society programs; the provision of a range of microfinance services; the safeguarding of historic landscapes and neighborhoods in Kabul and Herat; a rapidly growing mobile phone network; and the renovation of a five-star hotel in Kabul.

In his statement at the Tokyo conference, His Highness identified three priorities for national recovery: the creation of a "safety belt" in Central Asia through selective investments in areas within the wider region that remain volatile and fertile grounds for permanent instability; the repatriation of refugees and reintegration of former combatants in a manner that fully recognizes and respects the rights, cultures and traditions of the country's ethnic communities; and the establishment of competent, stable, transparent and accountable institutions, which emerge from, and respond to, the needs of the majority of the population, and through which the processes of building confidence, strengthening democracy and fostering development can be channeled.

HUMANITARIAN ASSISTANCE

Focus Humanitarian Assistance, an AKDN affiliate, started emergency and relief work in northeast Afghanistan in 1995, before AKDN's main development programs began. Rugged terrain and the absence of roads meant that humanitarian aid often had to be transported on inflatable boats across the Pyanj River from Tajikistan. At its peak in 2001, Focus delivered more than 20,000 metric tons of emergency food and non-food aid to 500,000 beneficiaries in the country. Food aid was later complemented by agricultural support to farmers, and grants, transport, reception services, vocational training and shelter provision to returning refugees. High-energy rations and milk were distributed to schoolchildren, and tens of thousands of children were immunized.

Local communities were involved in the construction of more than 1,600 km of irrigation channels and 700 km of roads through food-for-work initiatives. Schools, clinics and other community infrastructure were also rehabilitated through similar programs. This humanitarian assistance paved the way for AKDN's long-term development programs in Afghanistan. Today, Focus continues to be involved in emergency response, disaster mitigation and shelter provision in the country.

SOCIAL DEVELOPMENT

In 2002, AKDN's rural development program responded to food shortages in Afghanistan by distributing quality seeds and fertilizers aimed at improving agricultural yields and productivity. Shortly after, AKDN began working with local communities to build infrastructure projects, including water supply schemes, latrines, irrigation channels, micro-hydroelectric plants, roads, bridges, schools and health centers. Such projects are part of a comprehensive rural development program aimed at enabling people to improve their quality of life. This program, including community development, natural resource management and enterprise development, is mainly implemented through community development councils organized under the Afghan Government's National Solidarity Program[2]. AKDN currently assists more than 1,200 community councils in seven provinces of northern and central Afghanistan.

AKDN has established health centers and medical services in northeast and central Afghanistan to assist the Afghan Ministry of Public Health in its delivery of basic health and hospital services. AKDN manages the flagship French Medical Institute for Children in Kabul and the Bamiyan Provincial Hospital, both among the best hospitals in the country. AKDN staff work in about 30 health centers and clinics and in some 200 health posts across northeastern and central provinces.

Working through the Aga Khan University's School of Nursing (Karachi), AKDN has revised Afghanistan's nursing curriculum. Today, all of the country's pre-service nurses are trained using this curriculum. To improve the skills of existing and future health professionals, AKDN conducts refresher training for doctors, nurses and midwives; trains community midwives in two schools in Badakhshan and Bamiyan; and assists in the management of the Government's Institute for Health Sciences in Kabul, the country's main center for the training of nurses.

1.5 kilometers of traditional walling surround the Bagh-e Babur, its mosque and tombs.

Since 2002, AKDN's Rural Micro-credit Program has disbursed more than 90,000 loans, totaling more than $71 million. With nearly 30,000 active clients, the program now operates in more than 50 rural districts across 12 provinces to create income-generating businesses and to encourage entrepreneurship.

FIRST MICROFINANCEBANK OF AFGHANISTAN

In 2004, AKDN launched the First MicroFinanceBank (FMFB) of Afghanistan to operate primarily in urban areas. The first bank of its kind under the country's new regulatory structure, FMFB provides microfinance to small businesses, helping Afghans to create productive and sustainable sources of income. It is the largest microfinance provider in Afghanistan, serving some 38,000 borrowers and savers in towns and cities in eight provinces. Since 2002, it has disbursed more than 60,000 loans, totaling $100 million.

ECONOMIC DEVELOPMENT

AKDN aims to create replicable models of success and encourage other investors to follow suit by making strategic large-scale investments in Afghanistan's economic development. Investment decisions are based on whether a particular investment will improve the quality of life of those affected by it, and not simply on bottom-line profitability. Any profits are then reinvested in other development initiatives.

In 2003, AKDN and its partners launched Roshan, which has become Afghanistan's largest mobile GSM provider. In 2003 there were less than 50,000 working fixed and mobile telephone lines in the country, but Roshan has now invested more than $380 million in Afghanistan and its network coverage includes over 180 cities and towns, with over a million subscribers. Roshan directly employs more than 900 people, making it one of the largest private sector employers in the country. Indirectly, the company provides employment for nearly 20,000 people through distributors, contractors and suppliers.

AKDN activities in education include the construction and rehabilitation of schools, the construction of facilities for two government teacher training colleges, provision of adult literacy classes and in-service teacher training, the distribution of learning aids, and tutorial assistance and extra-curricular programs in English and information technology. The Network supports the Afghan Ministry of Education's national education strategy, paying special attention to female pupils and teachers. More than 80,000 pupils and 3,000 teachers benefit from AKDN activities to provide better access to quality education.

RURAL MICRO-CREDIT PROGRAM

AKDN has pioneered the provision of innovative and flexible microfinance products in Afghanistan, which play an important role in driving economic development in rural areas. One aim is to discourage the cultivation and trafficking of opium and heroin. Microfinance has eased the burden on indebted farmers, in some cases allowing them to buy back land sold to drug traffickers.

The Kabul Serena Hotel was inaugurated in 2005, the first five-star hotel to open in Afghanistan in more than 35 years. The hotel, representing a $38 million commitment, was built at the request of the Afghan government to provide accommodation of an international standard for diplomats, investors and other travelers visiting the country. The hotel aims to aid the revival and development of central Kabul, and to help revive the crucial hospitality and tourism industries in Afghanistan. It directly employs nearly 400 people and emphasizes the sourcing of materials from local producers, craftsmen and artists.

Through investments in Habib Bank, AKDN is making financial services available to Afghanistan's entrepreneurs and burgeoning private sector. The Habib Bank has been able to draw on its experience in 30 countries to help update Afghanistan's banking laws and regulations and to build capacity in the industry.

CULTURAL DEVELOPMENT

The goal of AKDN's cultural development activities is to conserve and restore Afghanistan's cultural heritage, while stimulating local economic development and improving the quality of life of people living in surrounding neighborhoods. The following projects are in addition to AKDN's work restoring Bagh-e Babur.

AKDN has restored an imposing 19th century mausoleum in central Kabul over the grave of Timur Shah, the king who made Kabul the Afghan capital. The surrounding open space has been reclaimed and landscaped to create a green park in the heart of the city.

Since 2003, war-damaged quarters of the old city of Kabul have been the focus of an AKDN program to conserve key historic buildings, including houses, mosques, shrines and public facilities. Upgrading works have also improved living conditions for some 15,000 residents of the old city in the neighborhoods of Asheqan wa Arefan, Chindawol and Kuche Kharabat.

In Herat, in western Afghanistan, documentation, conservation and upgrading work has also been carried out since 2005 in surviving historic sections of the old city. Two historic cisterns have been restored, along with an adjoining covered silk bazaar and a mosque. Five houses of particular architectural merit have also been repaired and conserved, while grants and other assistance have been provided to more than 70 householders to repair their traditional houses. In addition, restoration work has been undertaken on an important Timurid shrine complex in Gozargah, northeast of the city.

In another initiative to preserve and develop Afghanistan's cultural heritage, AKDN has established two schools of classical Afghan music in Kabul and Herat. The disruptions of the war have threatened the disappearance of the country's classical music tradition. Under the Ustad-Shagird training scheme begun in 2003, master musicians teach students, selected on merit, to preserve and pass on this musical tradition. Instruments taught include the rubab, dilruba, sarinda, dutar and sitar.

[1]From a statement delivered on behalf of His Highness the Aga Khan at the International Conference on Reconstruction Assistance to Afghanistan, Tokyo, Japan, January 20, 2002.

[2]AKDN is a facilitating partner of the Government's National Solidarity Progam (NSP). Under the NSP, AKDN assists villages to establish village-based Community Development Councils, elect an accountable and transparent Council leadership, formulate village development plans, and prioritize village needs. A 2004 World Bank-commissioned external evaluation of AKDN's community development approach found that it is both innovative and effective in forming credible, legitimate and self-reliant community institutions and is making a significant contribution to democratic governance and civil society in the country.

Building on its work with Community Development Councils, AKDN is engaged in a number of other activities to enhance rural livelihoods including business development services, vocational training, adult literacy classes and training in watershed management. Since 2007, AKDN has been working with more than 1,200 Community Development Councils in the country.

Gul Ahmad playing his flute in the Bagh-e Babur.

Dancing in the Bagh-e Babur.

A family picnicking in the Bagh-e Babur near the terraced fountains (right).

AFGHAN
RED CRESCENT SOCIETY

ARCS: ALWAYS THERE

The Afghan Red Crescent Society, or ARCS, is simply always there when and where help is needed. Through disaster relief, healthcare and social welfare programs, it plays a critical role in Afghanistan's growing ability to care for itself. By promoting humanitarian values to all it serves and by developing an extensive volunteer youth network throughout the country, ARCS is also helping Afghanistan define itself as a nation made of many tribes—rather than multiple tribes trying to pass for a nation.

Disaster relief is ARCS's most urgent and obvious work. In Afghanistan, disaster relief has two critical elements: disaster management and disaster preparedness.

- In 2008 alone, ARCS addressed the needs of 10,000 winter-affected and spring flood-impacted families. In these cases, relief took the form of food, housing and medical support. In one case, for example, on a day when 300 families lost their homes to flooding in the morning, Fatima Gailani was able to tell the Afghan nation by 8:00 p.m. that all affected individuals were already in temporary housing— the result of a disaster relief grid ARCS developed several years ago. ARCS has also made significant progress during disasters in understanding the extent of damage and casualties.

- Key to ARCS's disaster preparedness is its extensive network of trained volunteers. Through recruiting and youth clubs, ARCS has trained over 40,000 youth and volunteers in 28 provinces. Aiding them

in their work are disaster preparedness manuals that ARCS prints and distributes to communities throughout the country. ARCS's Disaster Management Department, as an auxiliary to the government of Afghanistan, has created depots for assistance materials in Afghanistan's five biggest provinces and small depots in all others.

Health, a second major ARCS initiative, touches a growing number of Afghans annually.

- Permanent health clinics—46 in 34 provinces—provide medical services to vulnerable populations.

Fatima Gailani, President of the Afghan Red Crescent Society, and her husband, Anwar-ul-Haq Ahadi, Former Minister of Finance for the Islamic Republic of Afghanistan.

- Ten mobile medical teams provide services in underserved areas and are available to support disaster relief efforts.
- ARCS has rehabilitated a 70-bed hospital in Kabul, which is now a comprehensive medical facility and includes specialized wards for treatment of Leishmaniasis and malaria. The hospital also houses dental treatment facilities and an HIV/AIDS program focusing on prevention.
- With drug addiction a growing problem in Afghanistan, ARCS is providing awareness programs and training for prevention as well as maintaining centers for the care and treatment of addicts.

ARCS also serves as a primary responder to the needs of returning refugees and those internally displaced by natural disasters and lingering results of war. Some 250,000 Afghans voluntarily repatriated in 2008 alone—most to the eastern provinces of Nangarhar, Kunar and Laghman. At the same time, ARCS, with the International Federation of Red Cross and Crescent Societies, helped support 40,000 families, or about 280,000 individuals, who left their homes this past winter due to drought, rising food prices and/or security issues. Annually, hundreds of thousands of Afghans are supported either from ARCS's available resources or from its International Red Cross and Red Crescent Movement partners.

Finally, caring for the neediest remains an important element in ARCS's social contract. Five *Marastoons*, or Social Welfare Centers, provide services to the most needy. In Kabul, Nangahar, Balkh, Herat and Kandahar provinces, *Marastoons* take care of families completely unable to care for themselves. The centers include schools, so children of afflicted families can be educated; vocational training is also available to prepare the way for self-sufficiency for clients prior to reintegration into the greater community.

Through its work, ARCS strives to reinforce humanitarian values—the value of coexistence throughout the community and the need for respect for all. ARCS's efforts to "be there" when help is needed— to help communities recover after disasters, to solve tough public health problems, to engage individuals in the care of their communities, to help integrate people on the move into a stable community—are true building blocks for a healthy, secure nation of Afghanistan.

Father of Fatima Gailani, Pir Sayed Ahmet Gailani is the spiritual leader of the Qadiria Sufi Order in Afghanistan (the Qadiria Order has a hundred million followers in the Muslim world) and the leader of the National Islamic Front of Afghanistan.

Wakhi men guide a horse over a treacherous section of trail reinforced with wood and slabs of rock on a cliff high above the Wakhan river in the Pamirs.

The Wakhan Corridor, home of the Marco Polo sheep.

THE MEGAFAUNA MAN
GEORGE SCHALLER

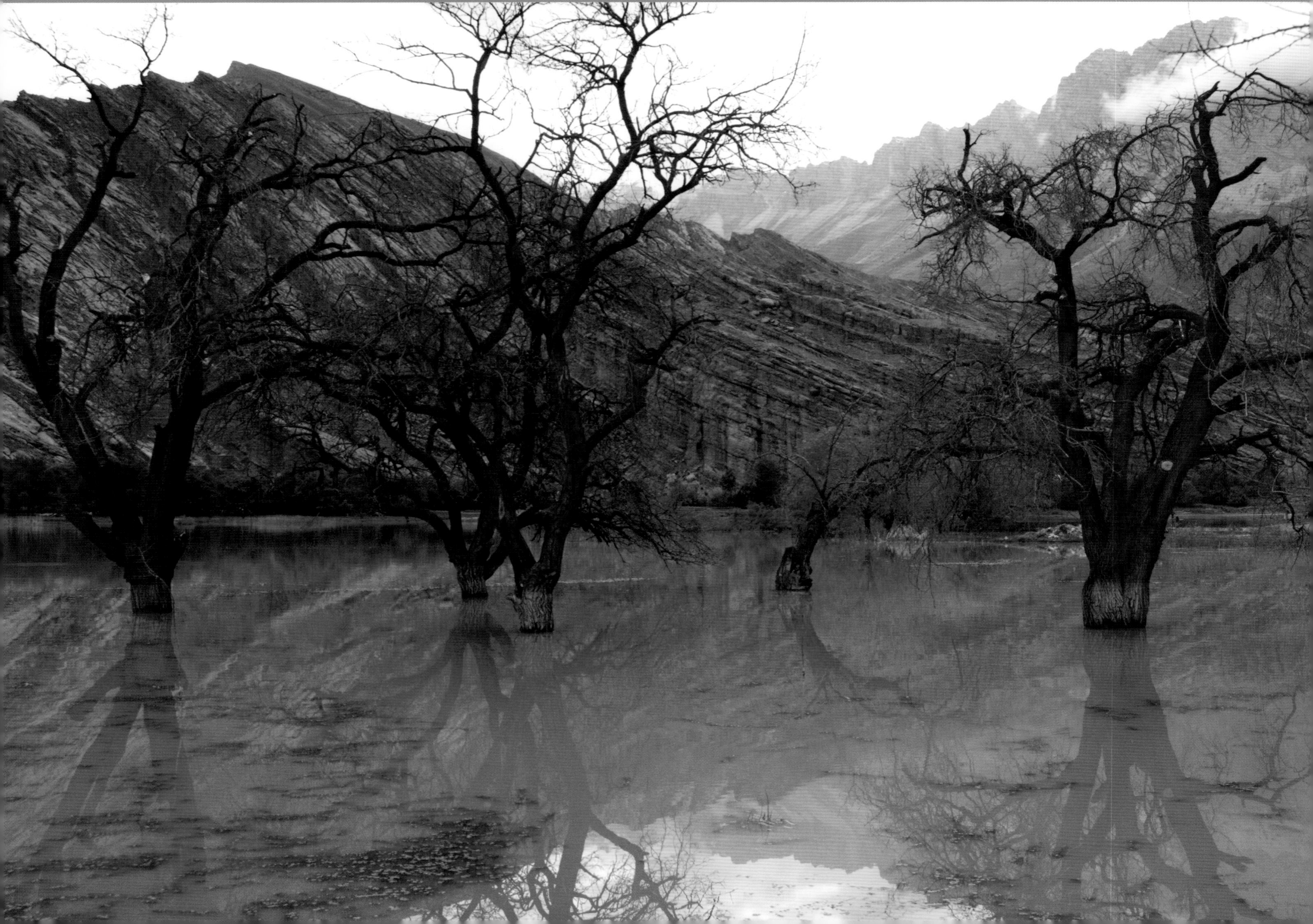

After 50 years of fighting to save the world's endangered creatures, George Schaller has it down to a science. But in Afghanistan—home to the Marco Polo sheep—the biologist must contend with murky tribal politics and rogue opium dealers.

The armed men came out of nowhere. There were a half dozen of them—ghostly silhouettes emerging from the driving snow with AK-47s slung on their shoulders. George Schaller, the world's most influential naturalist, stopped in his tracks and took stock of the group. From a distance he could make out tattered battle fatigues beneath their khaki woolen wraps; they were leading a cluster of shaggy, long-horned yaks.

"Who could this be?" he wondered aloud, his voice registering both curiosity and apprehension. Out here in the rugged Wakhan corridor of northeastern Afghanistan, there were only a few possibilities. The strangers hastening toward us were either gun-toting Islamic extremists, thieves trolling for targets of opportunity, or—we hoped—government soldiers on border patrol.

"*Salaam aleikum*!—Peace be with you!" yelled our guide, Sarfraz Khan, with an exaggerated wave meant to put the approaching men at ease. "George," he lowered his voice, "maybe you have the letter from the commander?"

Schaller nodded and reached into his rucksack for a note of safe conduct he'd received from a local warlord. With it, we could operate with a modicum of freedom and security in these forbidden lands. Without it, we faced a troubling and uncertain fate.

But before Schaller could produce the letter, Sarfraz's furrowed brow gave way to a broad, flashing smile. He had spotted an old friend in the group. "Border patrol!" Sarfraz shouted, rushing forward to greet the oncoming soldiers. Schaller and I exchanged looks of relief: We were safe.

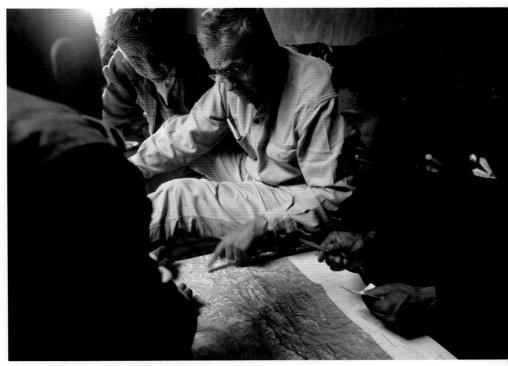

George Schaller consulting with village leaders in Sarhad, Afghanistan.

At 73, the German-born scientist stands tall and slim, with deep-set hazel eyes and a small hawkish nose. He keeps his salt-and-pepper hair neatly combed and, even out in the wild, manages a clean-shaven appearance every morning. We had been hiking up to eight hours a day at elevations above 14,000 feet for more than a week, and he never seemed to tire.

Amid embraces between the soldiers and our Afghan guides and porters, Schaller located the hand-scrawled letter and passed it to a gaunt, be-whiskered man who identified himself as the ranking officer. What were we doing out here? the soldier asked, eyeing our group of a dozen donkeys, half as many Wakhi porters and three foreigners—Schaller, photographer Beth Wald and myself. Outsiders rarely visit the Wakhan (also called Vakhan) corridor, a narrow mountainous strip that projects like a crooked finger for 190 miles between Tajikistan and Pakistan to China. "Searching for Marco Polo sheep," Schaller replied. We'd left the last road over a week earlier, heading for the Little Pamir, on the northern edge of the Hindu Kush, and then on to the Wakhan Mountains.

The officer frowned. This was no place for an unarmed research party, he said. When he arrived at his base in a few days, he'd send some soldiers to escort us to the Little Pamir. Schaller bowed and pressed his hand to his heart, a customary gesture of respect and deference, and we took our leave. It was only August, but already snow had started to blow through the mountains.

Schaller had come to this remote corner of the western Himalayas in pursuit of perhaps the most ambitious project of his 50-year career: the creation of an international peace park in a vortex of strife that stretches across parts of Afghanistan, Pakistan, China and Tajikistan. The proposed park's most celebrated inhabitants are dwindling herds of Marco Polo sheep—the world's largest and most magnificent wild sheep, which share the labyrinthine, windswept valleys of the Wakhan corridor with nomadic communities of Wakhi and Kyrgyz herders. Known for their spiraling horns that measure up to six feet long, the sheep have become a mythical trophy for international hunters and a rare source of meat for the impoverished Wakhi and Kyrgyz nomads. "The Marco Polo is a beautiful animal," Schaller asserted when we set out. "It has as much right to exist as we do."

George Schaller and his local assistant carry a skull and horns of a wolf-killed Marco Polo sheep (Ovis ammon polii) near the border with Tajikistan in the Wakhan Corridor.

A Wakhi woman milks a yak in an early fall snowstorm, while baby yaks huddle in a corral at the shepherds' camp high in the mountains of the Big Pamir.

As he has done with other so-called "charismatic megafauna" —animals such as jaguars and snow leopards, which can capture the public imagination through their startling beauty alone —Schaller intends to use the Marco Polo sheep as a symbol, a flagship species, to galvanize support for the protection of the entire habitat. "So you're fighting not just for the sheep but for the whole environment, all the plants and animals in this area," he told me. "My focus is on the sheep, because it's the most conspicuous animal here."

It's a strategy that Schaller, the vice president of science and exploration at the Wildlife Conservation Society, has employed again and again to become perhaps the greatest force for conservation in more than a century. "He is one of the finest field biologists of our time," says writer Peter Matthiessen, whose 1979 National Book Award-winning classic *The Snow Leopard* depicts Schaller as the intensely private, indefatigable "GS" during their shared trek through the Himalayas. "He pioneered the practice of turning regions of field research into wildlife parks and preserves."

Schaller's work as a biologist includes the first studies of mountain gorillas in central Africa (which later served as a field manual for Dian Fossey), lions in the Serengeti, giant pandas in China's Wolong Mountains, snow leopards in Nepal and *chiru* (antelope) in Tibet. His conservation efforts led to the protection of large stretches of the Amazon and Pantanal in Brazil, the Hindu Kush in Pakistan and upland forests in Southeast Asia, as well as Alaska's Arctic National Wildlife Refuge and Tibet's massive Chang Tang Wildlife Preserve—in total, more than 20 parks and preserves worldwide.

George Schaller measures a Marco Polo sheep skull.

George Schaller searching for Marco Polo sheep in the Pamirs.

29

For the two years leading up to this trip into the Afghan Pamir, Schaller worked on the far side of the Amu Darya River in Tajikistan, lobbying officials and tour operators to share fees from foreign trophy hunters with local herdsmen. Thirty-one years before that, he convinced Pakistan's then president Zulfikar Ali Bhutto to create Khunjerab National Park on the Wakhan Mountains' southern flank. And for the past 20 years, he has spent more time in China than he has at home in Connecticut, much of it on the highland steppes of Tibet and Xinjiang, across the Wakhan's eastern frontier, where he pushed the Chinese to establish the second largest protected area in the world, the 115,500-square-mile Chang Tang Preserve. If he could convince Kabul to get on board, support for his 20,000-square-mile International Pamir Peace Park would reach critical mass.

But Afghan officials couldn't justify sanctioning the preserve until they had reliable census data. How many Marco Polo sheep lived in the Wakhan?

What was their range? What threats did they face? No one had attempted a thorough study here for 30 years. That was why Schaller had come to Afghanistan. Over the next two months, he planned to survey some 500 miles of the Wakhan region—on foot.

If the mission seemed to border on the absurd—searching for an elusive animal in a country beset by armed conflict and on the verge of its first democratic elections—Schaller was not the least bit deterred. "If you waited for the world to be quiet," he said, "you'd end up staying at home."

A bomb had rocked the provincial capital of Fayzabad the night before Schaller, Wald and I arrived there in mid-August of 2004. We immediately hired a pair of decrepit vans and drove down a washed-out road to Sarhadd, a Wakhi village of stone huts set beneath the towering Hindu Kush. There we picked up guides and pack animals and followed an ancient caravan route into the mountains. This part of Afghanistan was George Schaller's

A group of yurts that make up a winter camp for Kyrgyz nomads at dawn in the Little Pamir region of the Wakhan Corridor.

Nomadic Kyrgyz women in traditional dress.

Buzkashi is a traditional Afghan game played on horseback and a wild one that has been played since the time of Genghis Khan. Buzkashi is played on a large, flat field with a chalk circle six feet in circumference at one end, and at about 75 yards at the opposite end, a small post. Three teams of riders attempt to grab a headless goat from the ground while riding at a full gallop. The goal of a rider is to get it clear from the other players, take it around the small pole, bring it back to the other end and pitch the goat into the circle. It is a sport where men ride their horses with guns strapped on and much yelling and grunting, while whipping their horses and each other in pursuit of the headless goat. With a rifle strapped on his back and armed with a bullhorn, a former warlord is usually chosen to judge these exhilarating games. The onlookers take care to stay out of the way of this raging horde, who are hurling and racing around in the extreme excitement. The victorious side is rewarded by roasting and eating the headless goat whose meat has become very tender by the pulling and pushing.

kind of place—rugged, wild, lost in time, where a herd of lumbering yaks could suddenly emerge from the vast emptiness and vanish into it again.

"I think I was misplaced by 150 years," he told me, with a reference to the era of the great scientist-explorers, such as Charles Darwin, Alexander von Humboldt and Alfred Russel Wallace. "It's far more satisfying to me to be in a remote area, traveling slowly on foot or in a caravan. You look around, you see things, smell things."

A week after leaving the road in Sarhadd, we arrived in the broad central valley of the Little Pamir and, on its northern edge, a Kyrgyz encampment. A wedding was in progress, and the celebration resembled a medieval carnival: Boys led prancing horses through the crowd and girls cupped their hands to their mouths, whispering secrets. Children snatched at banknotes tossed into the breeze by the hosts of the feast. Out on the dusty steppe, horsemen jostled over a stuffed goat hide in a game of buzkashi, Afghanistan's free-for-all version of polo.

Schaller waited discreetly off to the side. A pep talk on conservation might have seemed a bit ill-timed at a wedding party. But with so many of the Pamirs' inhabitants gathered in one place, he couldn't afford to let the moment slip away. He suspected that the Kyrgyz, migratory herders who keep sheep, goats and yaks, were hunting Marco Polo sheep for food.

As the feast wound down and the bride and groom disappeared into the nuptial yurt, Schaller stepped forward to address the men. Their high cheekbones and Siberian-style fur hats suggested a distant time of Mongol hordes and omnipotent khans.

"We come here because we've heard about the legendary generosity of the Kyrgyz people," Schaller began. "Last year I had the hospitality of the Kyrgyz across the border in Tajikistan." He paused to allow Sarfraz, an ethnic Wakhi from Pakistan, to translate his words into Dari, the lingua franca of the Wakhan's distinct ethnicities. "Many foreign hunters are coming to Tajikistan. They spend $25,000 to shoot a Marco Polo sheep. But local communities get nothing." A volley of disgruntled murmurs arose from the crowd.

"Someday soon, foreign hunters may come here to hunt Marco Polo sheep," he said. "If that happens, the Kyrgyz people must benefit." The men nodded approval. "Foreigners will spend big money to hunt, but only if there are big Marco Polo sheep with big horns." He let that sink in before making his final pitch. "That means the Kyrgyz people must protect the sheep so they can grow big and you can make money from them." The meeting concluded with a hearty round of applause.

Though Schaller is no fan of trophy hunting, he is a pragmatist. If controlled hunting and tourism can bring income to the struggling Kyrgyz, it might provide them incentive to protect Marco Polo sheep from a slow slide toward extinction. "Conservation depends on the goodwill of the locals," he said. "You've got to get them involved, so they have a stake in the outcome."

Wakhi women and children pack for a journey from high mountain pastures of the Big Pamir to their lower village along the Wakhan River.

A week after the Kyrgyz wedding celebration, in the pitch-dark of the pre-dawn, I was awakened by a cheery voice outside my tent. "Scott, I'm leaving in 10 minutes!" Schaller called. I looked at the blue glow of my watch face: 4:30 a.m. When I emerged from my tent a few minutes later, the biologist had already eaten his breakfast of tea and *chapati* and was on his way up the valley for the day's survey. A brilliant sliver of moon dangled above the dark ridge and Jupiter shone like a luminescent boulder in the sky.

Two hours later I caught up to Schaller at the entrance to a narrow canyon. It was the kind of austere, post-apocalyptic landscape I had grown used to over the past three weeks—jagged cliffs, barren slopes, a cobalt blue sky overhead. The sun was just clearing the mountaintops, melting the ice crust off the rocks in a nearby stream. I was panting and nearly doubled over. "At least you're getting to see what old-fashioned natural history is all about," he said.

A young Hazara boy swings on a rope while other children look on.

George Schaller consults with a local commander and village leader.

But Schaller's impatience is borne of more than just a passion for collecting data. After years in the field, he has developed a near-cosmic connection with the landscapes he protects, and he feels most himself when out in the wilderness. "Most men enjoy adventure, they want to conquer something, and in the mountains a biologist can become an explorer in the physical realm as well as the intellectual one," he wrote in *Mountain Monarchs*, his 1977 study of Himalayan sheep and goats. "Research among the ranges affords the purest pleasure I know, one which goes beyond the collecting of facts to one that becomes a quest to appraise our values and look for our place in eternity."

I t was typical of Schaller to be the first to break camp in the chill of early morning and to head out on his own across the desert steppe. "I don't like people on my heels," he said one day when I asked if I could join him. "It makes me feel rushed, and I begin to miss things." But sometimes Schaller's penchant for solitude was ill-advised, like the morning he slung his backpack onto his shoulders and vanished into the desert steppe without a word.

Several hours later, when he failed to appear and our caravan continued to lumber toward China, Wald and I scaled a nearby slope for a vantage point. The great expanse of the Wakhan spread before us motionless, save dappled shadows thrown from the clouds that drifted overhead. In the distance, snow fell in diaphanous curtains. Wald and I were stumped: A man in his 70s was out there alone, the temperature had plunged severely, and a rescue attempt amounted to a needle-in-a-haystack proposition. Fortunately, however, after scouting for most of the day, we found Schaller atop a dusty rise just before sunset. He seemed shaken.

A few hours earlier, he told us, he'd been surprised by three "disreputable looking" men who emerged from a deep gully. As they came into view, Schaller noticed they had no cargo—a suspicious way to travel in such a far-flung place. Forgoing the customary Muslim greetings, the group asked

For more than a half century Schaller's career has been defined by a single quality: impatience—an impatience to get into the field to collect data, an impatience to prove himself through his work, and an impatience to save the world's most imperiled species and landscapes. It is a characteristic that has not softened in the 30 years since he traveled the Himalayas with Matthiessen: "[Schaller] will not really be at ease until he reaches the land of the blue sheep and the snow leopard," Matthiessen wrote in *The Snow Leopard*.

Schaller if he was alone and motioned toward his pockets and the binoculars strung around his neck. Schaller assessed the situation: He was at least a few miles away from the caravan. If something should happen, no one would hear his calls for help. His only way out, he decided, was a quick retreat. As the men inched closer, Schaller replied that, in fact, he was traveling with a "very big group" and, before they had a chance to respond, he scrambled away across a steep talus slide.

As Schaller told us the story, he seemed, perhaps for the first time since we'd entered the wilderness, unsure of himself.

Later that night, as we rested by the fire after dinner, the same trio of men turned up in our camp and wedged themselves in among the group. Schaller discreetly pointed them out, and Sarfraz nodded gravely. "They sell *afim*," Sarfraz whispered. "Opium dealers." The night proceeded without incident, but still Schaller seethed with anger. "I had good reason to be suspicious," he said. "These people are stealing the future of the Kyrgyz people."

"George, look," whispered Mohammed Saqid, one of our guides, pointing toward a line of dots moving across a large snowfield high above us. "Marco Polo!"

After four weeks on the trail, we had reached the peaks marking the border of China at the far end of the Little Pamir. Along the way, we'd passed through several Kyrgyz camps scattered throughout the valley, each consisting of a half dozen large felt yurts. When we arrived at a settlement, Schaller would endear himself to the children, handing out candy and blowing up balloons to squeals of delight. Only then would he ask the adults where we might find Marco Polo sheep. The answers were usually vague—deliberately so, Schaller suspected. We'd seen a few small herds from a distance, but as soon as they caught a whiff of us, they would bound away across slides of black shale. To Schaller that meant the animals were probably under continuous fire from the Kyrgyz herders, a fact they would not be keen to share with nosy strangers.

But now some 25 males were scattered in the snow just above us like dull brown rocks. As he scribbled notes, Schaller passed me his binoculars for a look. It was the first time I'd seen Marco Polo sheep from close enough to make out their flared horns silhouetted black against the snow. Some faced up the slope; others had turned down. They seemed paralyzed with indecision—afraid to move into deeper snow on the mountain crest, but equally fearful of us. "Well, they're not the smartest animals in the world," Schaller said with a chuckle. They were magnificent creatures, some the size of donkeys, but after watching their confused dance for a few more minutes Schaller suggested we head back toward camp, some three hours away on foot.

Over the previous several weeks, our meals had been drab affairs—rice or noodles flavored with onion and Tabasco and prepared by Saqid over the dung fire. But a few days after sighting the sheep, we returned to camp to find a pot full of meat, a gift from a shepherd encamped in a stone hovel down the slope. Saqid mixed the meat in with tomato paste and rice, and we devoured the slow-simmered stew, all the while pondering its provenance. Was it yak? Ibex? It was far more tasty and tender than any of the lamb we'd been offered. Only the next morning did we learn the truth: We'd had a dinner befitting Marco Polo himself.

"I would have eaten it anyway," Schaller was quick to say. "It had already been killed, no point to it going to waste." What about having one shot to order? I asked. It was meant as a joke, but Schaller didn't laugh. "Up here, I wouldn't have even a hare shot to order."

By the end of September we had explored 13 valleys in the Little Pamir, recording 549 Marco Polo sheep, about half of the estimated population in the Afghan Pamir.

The national election had gone off peacefully and Schaller had briefed officials in Kabul about his findings in the Wakhan region. The next step: to bring together representatives from all four countries to discuss the peace

George Schaller and his wildlife survey team ride yaks and walk through snow as they cross into the Shikargah Valley, Big Pamir, Wakhan Corridor.

park concept, a process Schaller began this fall and expects to finish by early 2007.

When we parted ways at Dubai International Airport, I was eager to get home to see my family. But Schaller was going in the opposite direction, boarding a plane for Urumqi, China, to reconnect with acquaintances and promote the park. Later he'd stop in Tajikistan for further talks, risking a Thanksgiving away from home.

As Schaller ambled away across the shimmering tarmac, I thought back to a morning early in the trek, when I asked him how long he could maintain this breakneck pace.

"I don't know," he replied. "I think I'll keep on walking until I just fall apart."

Scott Wallace, Adventure Magazine, December 2006/January 2007.

A collection of mud huts that make up a winder camp for Kyrgyz nomads.

REGROWING THE ORCHARD OF THE EAST

GLOBAL PARTNERSHIP FOR AFGHANISTAN (GPFA)

Children helping to plant hybrid poplars that begin as sticks.

Hybrid poplar nursery—immediate gratification: sprouts in two weeks.

Planting poplars at Kapisa University.

The nursery is protected 24 hours a day by the villagers.

Shura and GPFA, including Suzanne Thompson, seal the deal to plant orchards, nursery and poplars.

Dana Freyer examining poplars four years old. At three months, these trees are five feet tall.

Panjshir extensionist with farmers.

39

When Gul Mullah returned from exile to his farm in Afghanistan's Guldara district in 2002, he was greeted by a war-ravaged landscape, devoid of life. "Not one green tree remained standing on my land," he recalls. The Taliban would not only cut the fruit trees but would also uproot them so they would not put out new shoots. After struggling to revive his farm without success, he met Mohammad Hashim, a GPFA extension worker. Today, thanks to 50 fruit tree saplings, tools and fertilizer from GPFA—and Mohammad Hashim's careful training—Gul Mullah has a thriving orchard.

In 2002, Dana and Bruce Freyer; Professor M. Ishaq Nadiri, a leading Afghan-American economist; and Mohammad Anwarzai, an Afghan-American

diplomat, formed the Global Partnership for Afghanistan (GPFA), a New York-based 501(c)(3) not-for-profit organization. Their goal: to help rural Afghans rehabilitate and replant their fruit and nut orchards, vineyards, croplands and forests. Their work began with Mr. Freyer transporting a bundle of 450 cuttings of special fast-growing hybrid poplars to Afghanistan where, with the agreement of local communities, GPFA started a number of demonstration projects in five Guldara District villages in the Shomali Valley.

Since 2004, GPFA has planted 6.1 million trees. Its programs reach more than 400 villages in 11 provinces. More than 10,000 families are now building sustainable businesses with revenues that often rival or even exceed income from poppy cultivation. From its original idea of restoring orchards, GPFA's staff has developed a comprehensive, integrated program that embraces the entire business of farming—from planting stock to tending plants to marketing crops. As Mohamed Nazir, a GPFA teacher-farmer and partner, put it, "[We are] investing in two different varieties: our students and our saplings!"

Today, GPFA's programs provide farmers with:

- New models for agro-forestry, forestry-farms (woodlots), orchards, and nurseries
- Material support including improved plant stock varieties, planting materials and fertilizers
- Enterprise development

When Rabia and her family returned home to their village in Farza, Kabul Province, the village was in ruins, her house destroyed. Part of her land was washed away by floods and the rest lacked water. "I simply sat down and cried," she says. Today, after meeting two GPFA women staff members, Sister Rabia has 8,000 newly planted poplars on her two acres—a loan of fast-growing poplars and supplies such as fertilizer that she could not buy for herself. With training from GPFA, she has learned to tend her trees and shares her experiences with other female farmers. Her trees provide both short- (through vegetable intercropping) and long-term income for her family as well as urgently needed wood supplies for the country. When the trees mature in six years they can generate as much as $60,000 when harvested as timber.

- Orchard management and post-harvest training
- Underground fruit storage facilities that generate improved incomes
- Technical tools and support for planning, planting, irrigation and pest control
- Water management

Belqis, Dana Freyer and other female staff at GPFA Tree House in Guldara.

41

Farmers harvest poplars to sell in local market.

Sorting the apple harvest in Guldara.

Each harvest season, Khalid—an apple grower in Gardez, Paktia Province—used to load a tarp with freshly picked apples and sell them to a trader at the farm gate. In 2007 GPFA began training Khalid and other farmers to improve their production as well as measure, grade and crate their fruit to achieve higher value for their crops. GPFA staffers demonstrated how to use tools such as "penetrometers" to determine fruit firmness, "refractometers" to measure sugar levels and "sizing rings" to sort produce to market specifications. Later, they helped Khalid deliver the crated fruit to his new cold-storage unit where it would be safely preserved until markets were less glutted with recently harvested produce. By

pacing their sales, Khalid and other participating farmers now earn an average of 153 percent more than they did without storage facilities and GPFA's technologies and training.

- Access to demonstration farms and nurseries
- Farmer learning groups—farmer field schools, study tours and opportunities for participation in agricultural fairs and exhibitions
- Opportunities to interact with government, NGOs and academic institutions

The Tree House is a farm-forestry and horticulture Center of Excellence for agriculture training and enterprise development created by GPFA to develop the knowledge, skills and power of Afghans to expand the number and productivity of their farm forestry and horticulture enterprises. Through demonstration projects, training workshops and partnerships with experts and other institutions, the Tree House supports the development of quality planting stock, productive orchard and woodlot enterprises, producer associations, fruit storage facilities, low-cost irrigation, business skills, and market and credit access. These initiatives will provide more opportunities for farmer education and develop new agricultural professionals who will expand GPFA's existing programs and extend them throughout Afghanistan.

MARKET SUPPORT

GPFA works with farmers to form and register producer cooperatives. These provide their members with access to quality plant materials, financial services and technical support from the Afghan government, financial institutions and international donors.

A key element in advancing GPFA's programs is its close work with local communities, including Shura Councils, provincial and district authorities, and local women and farmer groups—to identify lead farmers, secure cooperation among farmers and ensure local contributions to program funding. Additionally, from its inception, GPFA has worked to ensure that rural Afghan women are able to translate their hard work in agriculture into improved income and food supplies for their families.

GPFA's work, while extremely beneficial to recipients, is not a gift handed out "gratis" by foreigners who then disappear. Many of the farmers who work with GPFA receive a loan of "in kind" plant materials, tools and fertilizers. These loans are repaid to GPFA in plant materials—poplar cuttings—which can then be loaned to other farmers. As noted by one GPFA-supported farmer, "We do not want handouts. We are a proud people and we will work hard to enable others to benefit."

Hashim (l) and Zalmay (r) were two of GPFA's first extensionists hired in 2004. They are joined by Directors Dave Hardman, Dana Freyer (Co-Chair), Suzanne Thompson and Executive Director Roger Hardister.

GPFA's work continues to expand and even grow and evolve. Today, planned projects include raising turkeys in "sleighs" for weeding in fruit tree orchards and woodlots, training women to become beekeepers, providing training for food processing to increase markets for fruits and vegetables, and making fuel briquettes from sawdust, waste paper and agricultural waste. Tomorrow, more inventive projects will follow.

"We are able to support our family and, for once in our lives, feel that we might one day be able to escape the poverty into which we were born," commented Mohamed Amin, one of GPFA's clients.

GPFA Panjshir extensionists visit women's nurseries, orchards and woodlots.

Khalid uses the roof of the underground storage unit as a shop for daily local sales.

Rabia of Guldara's son with turkey chick.

Water holding and filtering: a simple water basin can make the difference for family farmers; this is a demonstration at the Guldara Tree House. GPFA is the only NGO with a full-time water engineer.

Khalid at Baladeh Village in underground storage with stored apples in plastic crates. Underground storage is a new addition for GPFA.

Vegetable production is a key source of food and income.

Finished briquettes made of sawdust and farm waste used for firewood.

Gul Mullah with GPFA staff checking apples for quality.

Rabia of Guldara with turkey chicks.

Turkey sleigh—weed remover and egg machine.

HRH The Prince of Wales and Rory Stewart, Chief Executive of the Turquoise Mountain Foundation at an exhibition of Turquoise Mountain calligraphy, 'Ink from Ashes: Contemporary Calligraphy from Afghanistan' held at the Beit Al Qur'an Museum in Bahrain, 2007 under the auspices of The Crown Prince of Bahrain, H.H. Shaikh Salman bin Hamad al Khalifa.

MOVING MOUNTAINS

TURQUOISE MOUNTAIN FOUNDATION

The river bank in Kabul, looking south towards the Pul-e-Khishti mosque.

MOVING MOUNTAINS BY RORY STEWART

At the beginning of 2006 I found myself sitting in the front room of a tailoring shop in Kabul containing a frayed pink Bokhara carpet, a safe, a feather duster, six glasses and a Thermos® of green tea. A laminated brochure on the safe promised that I would conserve a section of the medieval city, improve living conditions, restore ancient buildings and create an academy for traditional crafts. I was listed as the chief executive of the Turquoise Mountain Foundation. There was, however, no other employee and I was not quite sure what I was doing.

Kaka (Uncle) Khalil, who often liaises between the Turquoise Mountain Foundation and the community, with builders using traditional techniques to renovate Kabul's old town center.

My life to date had been more institutional: a brief period as an infantry officer in the Black Watch and then service with the Foreign Office in Indonesia, the Balkans and as the coalition deputy governor of two provinces in southern Iraq. The only two years that I had spent outside government were from 2000 to 2002, when I took unpaid leave to walk from Turkey to Bangladesh. I had fallen in love with Afghanistan on that journey and written a book about it. When I returned in 2003 to work for the coalition in Iraq I often dreamt, while dodging mortars or emails from Washington, of moving back to a mud fortress in the Afghan mountains.

Beginning reconstruction of a damaged building.

A young woman practices traditional Persian calligraphy at the Higher Education Institute for Arts and Architecture, run by the Turquoise Mountain Foundation in Kabul, Afghanistan. The Institute is working to preserve traditional Afghan arts and crafts, to train masters in the arts and to provide sustainable livelihoods for a new generation of craftsmen and-women.

In Iraq I had been given $10 million a month to spend, delivered in vacuum-sealed packets. Every day Iraqis had demanded to know what we had done for them.

"We have restored 240 schools."

"Apart from that, what have you done?"

"All the clinics and hospitals."

"Apart from that…"

I had become used to crowds carrying banners that said DEATH TO THE DEPUTY GOVERNOR. In 2004 the Prince of Wales had written to me suggesting that I establish a carpentry school to train street children and find them jobs. It was the only project I did that really appealed to Iraqi imaginations. Suddenly, we had the mayor and the police chief competing to give speeches to the students and all the Arab television stations filming the school.

The following year the Prince had suggested that I go to Afghanistan to establish a school to train Afghans in traditional crafts. I thought I could combine his interest in craft training with my own desire to save a poor community in Kabul. The Prince had raised seed money for the first six months of operations. Thereafter, I would largely be on my own. My first act had been to rent the room in the tailoring shop and buy the Thermos and feather duster. Now I needed to start work.

The area I hoped to save was called Murad Khane and the man whom I had first met there was called Kaka (Uncle) Khalil. I called on him the day after my arrival. He was wearing an old dark *shalwar kameez*, muddy white gym shoes and a tweed jacket and, because he was a pigeon-master, his hands were scarred by beak marks and by the sharp thread with which he pinioned his birds' wings. Khalil was from the Qizilbash Shia minority, which had been persecuted for centuries, but like most of his neighbors he was a house-owner. All but one of the houses in the district had been passed down, father to son, for more than 100 years. This was the northern edge of the old city; the houses were built of mud brick and their courtyard walls were paneled in carved cedar wood. It was impossible to tell how many centuries people had lived in Murad Khane but Kabul was around before the visit of Alexander the Great.

We followed some children chasing a dog through the wasteland that formed the center of Murad Khane. Two old men squatted in the open to relieve themselves. Nearby, three cooks were peeling onions. I watched a woman in a burqa clamber over a heap of rubbish into her courtyard because the garbage had submerged her entrance. Four acres of Murad Khane were covered in rubbish. There was no electricity, no water, no sewerage. One in

Kaka (Uncle) Khalil with his grandson.

HRH The Prince of Wales hosts President Karzai of Afghanistan and Rory Stewart, Chief Executive of the Turquoise Mountain Foundation, at a dinner at Balmoral, on October 24, 2007.

five children died before they were five; most of the population could not read or write and life expectancy was about 40. Around the edge of the central landfill site ran a narrow bazaar, a couple of mosques, some bath-houses and about 60 mud-brick courtyard houses, crammed between the river and shabby six-story 1970s shopping arcades.

In the bazaar I was introduced to Abdul-Hadi, one of the greatest carpenters in Afghanistan. He was 76 years old and had been selling fruit in the market for 15 years. War, material costs, declining quality and lack of contact with the outside world had all combined to destroy the market for Afghan woodwork. He had no students to whom he could pass on his skills. I explained to Khalil that my dream was to build a craft school in the center of Murad Khane and use it as a catalyst to regenerate the neighborhood. He suggested that I talk to the government and try to get international support.

It was now four years since the US-led invasion. The coalition was angry at the corruption, the heroin production, the violence in rural areas and the lack of economic growth and governmental control. They had decided to send more troops. Three thousand British soldiers were deploying to Helmand to replace 200 American soldiers. Soon, there would be more than 7,000. Meanwhile, the Taliban were re-emerging. It was already too dangerous to travel on the main road to the south. Kidnapping was increasing, bombs were beginning to go off in Kabul itself. The international community had prepared a $20 billion aid package. The military wanted it to go to the unstable areas of the south and east, the European Community wanted programs only in "gender, rural development and governance," and the Afghan government demanded that all funds be placed in the central budget of the Ministry of Finance. Kabul was in ruins and its population had ballooned from a million to more than five million in four years, but no one wanted to support projects such as ours.

Officials from seven Afghan ministries, eight foreign embassies and four charities told me that my plans were unwise and possibly illegal. It was illegal to demolish a building in the old city; it was also illegal to rebuild there. Only charities could export tax-free traditional crafts, but charities were not permitted an export license. The best craftsmen were semi-literate descendants of traditional craft families, but vocational qualifications could be given only to people who had graduated in Persian literature from high school. There was demand abroad for carved cedar and replicas of Afghan jewelry but the Interior Ministry banned the purchase of cedar and the Culture Ministry banned replicas.

A senior Pashtun lawyer confided that the real problem with Murad Khane was the inhabitants: "dirty, illiterate, superstitious Shia criminals, who would be better pushed out." He called them foreigners because "they only moved to Kabul in the early 18th century." The new mayor had also been the mayor of Kabul in the 1970s. He had spent 15 years in Canada but had not learned

A local shoemaker.

English. One of his first initiatives was to try to stop the women's hour at the municipal swimming pool on the grounds that women could not swim. When I mentioned Murad Khane he pointed to a map behind his desk, inscribed in Cyrillic: MASTER PLAN FOR KABUL 1976. This 30-year-old scheme, drawn up by Soviet and East German planners, remained his dream for the old city. He wanted to demolish the ancient streets and courtyard mansions and replace them with concrete blocks. The next official I met was equally determined to flatten the historic site. His resolve was apparently strengthened by understandings with property developers eager to launder their new, often heroin-derived wealth through the construction of skyscrapers.

But Kaka Khalil and the people of Murad Khane still seemed to share my belief that traditional Afghan art and architecture were beautiful, worthy of international admiration and could create jobs. I was determined to continue, even if the project seemed contrary to public policy, private interest and municipal regulations. The only way to do so was to rely on the community, make rapid improvements and dare the government to demolish what we were rebuilding.

Many charities are founded with feasibility studies and seminars, strategy papers and grant proposals. Ours really began with a wrestler. Aziz had won the Afghan national wrestling championship in 1963, gaining a broken nose, cauliflower ears, damaged knees and the title "*Pahlawan*" or "wrestler". When I was not making much progress with the government, Khalil suggested I should talk to Wrestler Aziz. "I am the sub-district chief, the keeper of the shrine." Aziz roared on our first encounter. "I defend this area with my arms. I will make your project work. I challenge anyone to say I have ever taken a bribe." He paused and added in a stage whisper, "But I am a bandit."

Turquoise Mountain laborers clearing rubbish—the charity has removed 15,000 trucks of garbage since 2006.

Karim Khan, a specialist well-digger.

I had seen a 200-year-old mud-brick mansion, where three goats browsed a courtyard littered with crates of bananas. The wooden shutters were carved with Moghul stars and floral arabesques, framed with delicate latticework. The wood was unpainted and the plaster patterns lightly washed with lime. I explained that I wanted to rent the mansion and to restore it as our craft school. Aziz told me instead that I should rent two other houses. "I will place you—the foreigner—at each corner, so the government will not send in the bulldozers. If you take the center, the government will demolish the edges." The owner of the mansion would not rent to me without agreement from the wrestler, so I had to follow the wrestler's plan.

Next, I recruited staff. Even an uneducated Afghan who had attended a development training course and could speak passable English could earn $1,000 a month in Kabul. I could not afford those salaries. My first employee, also called Aziz, had worked as a salesman in a Pakistani carpet shop and in the "informal export sector" during the Taliban period, which seemed to involve carrying semi-precious stones across mountain passes. But an old friend had employed him as a driver and said that he had once risked his life to save her from kidnapping. Within a week I had added an Afghan woman, a young radio operator from the north, a 50-year-old white-bearded engineer, a one-legged horseman, a high school literature teacher, a woodworker and a physically disabled academic administrator. Thus, respectively, I had appointed my logistics manager, office administrator, finance director, chief engineer, guard, calligraphy master, woodwork

master and office manager. One of them explained that he was working for me because "other charities tell us we live in the wrong kind of houses, have the wrong breed of sheep, are unhealthy and uneducated; your project says traditional Afghan art and architecture is beautiful, worth preserving, will find admirers around the world and can generate incomes." Another confessed he just wanted a job. None had had senior jobs in an international organization; none spoke fluent English; the majority had not completed a high school education and I suspect they would not have been employed in any formal recruitment process. But I believed I could trust them.

Each employee built his or her own team. Within three weeks we had 40 staff and could no longer fit in the tailoring shop. An English businessman called David suggested that I could occupy and restore a 19th-century fortress, set above two acres of gardens. The owner now lived in Delhi, and David and his friends lived in the only occupied wing. We replaced ceilings, installed lavatories and repaired the underfloor heating system of the 19th-century bath-house so that we could bathe in the winter. In the garden we set up the first campus of our Institute of Afghan Arts to train craftsmen, find them jobs and sell their products. This was a temporary home, while we were restoring the two houses recommended by the wrestler.

The early staff came from different social classes and from ethnic groups that had recently been at war. Each favored his or her own: the manager from the persecuted Hazara minority hired a Hazara cook and translator, while Panshiri Tajiks came to dominate the driving pool. My personal relations with each, stretching back from my time walking across Afghanistan or through mutual friends, made it almost impossible for me to fire anyone. I had to spend a great deal of time at weddings, lending money, trying to help their relatives and paying medical bills from my own pocket. But it proved a wonderful team: Each was bound to me by some form of personal loyalty. Their eight separate origins meant that they kept an often jealous eye on each other, ensuring that as the organization grew it could never be dominated by a single cabal.

I had reservations about appointing my landlord the tailor's brother, Engineer Hidayat, to oversee restoration work, not only because he had little formal education or knowledge of architectural conservation but also because he came from a different ethnic group and a different sect of Islam from that of the community of Murad Khane. But when he walked over the rutted mud lanes of Murad Khane and met Pahlawan Azuz, he seized him by the biceps and began a mock reenactment of a wrestling match, laced with jokes and elaborate compliments. It was he who negotiated with the wrestler and who convinced me to follow the wrestler's housing plans. We were rewarded with a petition signed by the 50 most senior members of the community, asking us to work in the area. Henceforth, community support

Hashim and his wife, Haleema, both work for Turquoise Mountain—he as a guard at the clinic and school, she as a cleaner.

was our greatest defense against the municipality and the mayor, international policy shifts and greedy developers.

We decided it would be strategic to begin by shifting rubbish. The engineer conjured up a workforce and began. At this point the municipality director, wearing a lilac suit, appeared with police and a document ordering us to stop. Here then was the first test of our model. The police advanced with Kalashnikovs; the laborers fell back; I rummaged for dog-eared registration documents and the municipality director wrote in bold strokes on a clipboard. Behind me, I sensed a gathering crowd. An old man, whom I had not met before, stepped forward and shouted, "How dare you stop these men? I remember when you last cleared the garbage: I was 10 years old and it was 1947." The wrestler shook the hands of the now-smiling police. The engineer put his arm around the lilac-clad director's shoulders and walked him out of Murad Khane. The next day we received a letter from the municipality authorizing us to proceed.

Foreigners had told me that Afghans were slow and inefficient. That was not my experience. Over the next 18 months, the engineer cleared more than 15,000 trucks of rubbish, dropping the street level by over seven feet and creating near-total employment. Then he leveled the streets, dug drainage and wells and laid paving, and began emergency repairs on 50 houses, making them watertight, propping walls, installing lavatories. This was not expensive work since the materials were recycled mud—all the cost was in the seed-funding money raised by the Prince of Wales.

Afghan shoppers began to come back into the area and the drug peddlers, who had long made Murad Khane one of their central markets, moved elsewhere, perhaps because clean, well-lit and populated streets were not a fitting environment for their customers. But the engineer's real genius was political, in defusing the conflicts over jobs for relatives, wages and which properties should be repaired first. He dealt with things in his own style,

An antique door carved in traditional Afghan style opens into offices at the Higher Education Institute for Arts and Architecture, located in a restored fort and run by the Turquoise Mountain Foundation in Kabul, Afghanistan. The Institute is working to preserve traditional Afghan arts and crafts, to train masters in the arts and to provide sustainable livelihoods for a new generation of craftsmen and-women.

grabbing an angry mullah by the beard after we had accidentally brought down the mosque wall. Astonishingly, the mullah laughed and forgave us.

Meanwhile, in order to cope with demands, our lack of funding and the shortage of professionals, I brought in more than 100 international volunteers, who came for a few months at a time over a period of two years. A 22-year-old Dari-speaking American and a Dutch ceramicist in his seventies worked with a curator from the Tate and a Cuban urban planner. Many lived three to a room and we all ate at a common table. Sometimes we were awakened by gunfire; a volunteer was walking 50 yards from a bomb that scattered body parts across the pavement; gunmen broke into a hotel and shot men in a locker room that many of us used. But we were able to travel by yak in the High Pamirs, ski in the Hindu Kush and listen to old men hold forth in tea houses in the old city.

Where we had no expertise we had to make things up. I had started with a few prejudices: In the absence of conservation architects on our team, I wanted the repairs to buildings to be visible but not too obvious. But that was hardly a coherent conservation philosophy. I thought the high temperatures in electric kilns eliminated all that was intriguing in the low-fired pots, but that didn't help us win contracts from Trust House Forte, which wanted less fragile glazes. I didn't think we should pay too much for international volunteers, but what about providing life insurance? Should the financial year start in January or April? Should we have a substantial document detailing our plans for urban regeneration and who should lead it: an architect? A planner? A property developer? Me?

It was clear that we needed to work quickly to prove to the government that the arts and crafts were worth saving and to the community that we were serious, competent and helpful to them. Our initiatives multiplied, responding to sudden crises or the shifting expertise of our volunteers or the community's demands. Within a year we produced a traffic plan for Murad Khane, largely to placate the ministry; took an exhibition of calligraphy to

a museum in Bahrain; built different designs of self-composting lavatories (one under a Nubian vault); and fitted earth buildings with new types of mud brick, solar panels and elaborately carved calligraphic doors. We created factory management systems around new carpentry equipment; launched IT and business courses for students; developed partnerships with Pakistani art schools; opened a rural museum for potters; and sold an Afghan carved suite to the Connaught in London. Anna, our extraordinary young American development director, who had been working with Coventry Cathedral, recorded the recipes of the old city and designed a restaurant in a historic building that would provide employment and draw Afghan visitors back to the old city with good, affordable food. We wanted to start with Afghan tourists, since the security situation would not attract foreigners.

Some of the best ideas came from the community itself—such as the primary school, which we opened last year. Education is bad in Afghanistan; perhaps a quarter of teachers are illiterate and as recently as 2001 girls were not permitted to attend. There was no school and a great deal of domestic violence and drug abuse in some of the poor homes in Murad Khane, and a school would provide children not only with education but also with a safe haven during the day. But we were overstretched and I was reluctant to launch something new. We argued and then we compromised: The community provided the land and the building while we focused on the teaching.

Within an hour of opening the doors we had 160 boys and girls, most of whom had never been to school before. Their smiles alone made me feel our project was worthwhile. Yet it was no easier than anything else in Afghanistan. The school would have remained second-rate if we had not hired better teachers, negotiated with the ministry of education, built new classrooms and introduced local history and art classes, city tours, adult literacy classes and extra mathematics. And much of this depended on foreign staff. The curriculum was reformed and the teachers were trained, for example, by the head of science from an inner-city school in Boston, Massachusetts.

The Institute for Traditional Afghan Arts began as an apprentice workshop for carpenters, calligraphers and potters with people huddled on rough benches, watching Master Abdul Hadi. A year later, there was a full timetable for the students including IT, English, business studies, Islamic art history and design. Our new business development section, whose aim was to generate income to sustain the institute into the future, launched catalogues and websites, won commissions from embassies, represented us at international trade fairs, sold coasters in Canada and a wooden library to Japan. The fashion chain Monsoon gave us money to train women in embroidery to sell in its stores. We began to sell Turquoise Mountain products through our website, turquoisemountain. org. We planted trees to make our timber source sustainable. We built a girls' school near the potters' community of Istalif (in addition to the primary school) for a fraction of the cost of a concrete building. At the start of the second year we had 650 applicants for 33 places.

It was only after a year's work and once we had shown visible results that the relevant Afghan ministries began to support us. A new minister of education recognized the degree certificates from our school and registered us as a national higher education institute. Two decrees were issued to register the area as a protected historical site. Our architects trained engineers from the Ministry of Urban Development and they in turn worked with us on land-use plans. Flattering profiles appeared. We were often on the Afghan evening news.

I was the only person aware that we were dangerously short of cash. I needed to raise thousands of dollars a day. I was able to support myself with income from my book sales, and I began to lend more of my own money to try to keep things going. Many had trusted us: donating land for our schools, working long hours, enrolling to learn complex skills in traditional crafts and architecture. But we had to slow the building projects, which meant laying people off at the onset of winter. I began to wonder what might be raised by selling our minivan or carpets.

By November 2006 I was only two weeks from having to give everyone a month's notice and shut the charity down. I woke at three in the morning and felt very afraid. No one was used to supporting a brand-new organization that was operating on this scale. Most donors required two years of audited accounts. As I walked to work, I was greeted by people—the gate guard who had lost his leg to a landmine; the receptionist who needed a heart operation; and the driver who had been the first to leave his job to join us—and when they thanked me, I felt like a fraud. An objective examination of the costs and probabilities suggested that we should close. I continued through stubbornness, not reason. I flew back to Britain and left behind the conversations and the crises that I had loved in the old courtyards of Kabul for a life of fundraising. I made it a rule to return every fortnight, but I was on almost 300 flights over the next two years.

In countries I had never visited I waited for meetings that never happened. Once, when I made it past a secretary in a Gulf state. I was accused of terrorist financing and shown the door. Some of the wealthy would support us only if we changed what we were doing: to advocacy for women or schools for the blind. If by luck they would support something we were doing, they could change their mind and suggest something that we were not. One boasted to me that after an exhaustive analysis of proposals he had ignored us and instead allocated hundreds of thousands of dollars to an Afghan woman who was running thousands of girls' schools. I knew these schools did not exist.

I was hopeful about our chances with foundations created by young dot-com leaders and dedicated to "social entrepreneurs". They should not have been bound by the paperwork of government aid bureaucracies; it was their own money and they should have been able to take risks. But they wanted synergies and income streams and compared us on cost-per-unit metrics. They did not want to be distracted from their "core mission".

Ahmed Shah, a carpenter.

But we didn't just do one core activity. We believed, for example, that to regenerate the bazaar we had to develop attractive sites for visitors; we had to train craftsmen to manufacture products to sell, teach the shopkeepers to read and write and count, give incomes to women, provide shelter, water and electricity. Our strength was our local knowledge: We had been in every house, employed someone from every family, worked alongside them, negotiated, shaped their aspirations and were shaped in turn. But there was no universal model: What worked for us might not work elsewhere.

The only way to convey our work is to get donors to visit because it is almost impossible to imagine the environment of the old city or grasp how our many different activities come together without being on the ground. One of our best supporters was an 84-year-old American woman who immediately on arrival called on senior ministers and generals and forced them to act, establishing an orphanage and bringing equipment to eliminate water-borne diseases. She clambered up stairs, over dangerous gaps in the roof, trudged through mud, interrogated our female students, watched the customers buy the products that provided the income to sustain the project and listened to the community itself. But few people dared to come.

In the end we were saved by private generosity. An Afghan night-club owner crossed a street in Washington, DC, to give me $1,000 because he had heard about us from his family in Kabul; a Swedish woman cycled up to our office to give us $50; our English volunteer did a skip-a-thon with an Afghan friend in Dorset. And the Prince of Wales was in touch weekly, writing to people on our behalf, arranging dinners and meetings, advocating Afghan government legislation and providing advice. It had been his idea in the first place, and it couldn't have happened without his support.

Our largest donors gave from their private accounts because their foundation bureaucracies were too restricted to be able to support us. Some had heard of us, others gave randomly with no prior contact. A lady talked to me about Afghanistan for 20 minutes over lunch in California, and later

The primary school was opened last year.

A young man incises a ceramic vase with designs in the Istalif style, at the Higher Education Institute for Arts and Architecture.

sent $1 million. Then she visited us and sent another million. The Canadian government became our first and most generous public donor. Finally, after three years and $12 million from donors, the Afghan government is now putting its own money behind us.

Last week, I stood in the central square of Murad Khane for the spring kite festival. For once I could move without sinking into the mud because the drainage and stone-paving has worked. We had grown in two years from one to 350 employees. I noticed that the carving on the windows of the upper gallery of the great mansion needed to be redone: The Nubian vault had been removed from the lavatory of the jewelry school because of a rumor we were building a pagan temple. There was a new community donation box outside the clinic that we had established for women who could not leave the area and did not want to see a male doctor. People had put in $30, which would cover prescriptions for the next two months. Three streets had agreed to take over the cost of rubbish clearance from us with each household contributing 30 cents a month; one had not. I noted that the students at the primary school had new uniforms.

The structures of government bureaucracies and philanthropic foundations often seem to exist to stop this kind of project. If it succeeds, it will not be a neat lesson in "social entrepreneurship", in management or a new model for international development. And it seems surreally distanced from the ambitions and priorities of my former colleagues in the Army or the Foreign Office.

A young man turns a ceramic vase on a wheel in a pottery studio that produces ceramics in the Istalif style at the Higher Education Institute for Arts and Architecture run by the Turquoise Mountain Foundation.

Rather, it is a story of sudden expressions of faith, acts of grand generosity and amateur flair. Ours was a local project in a mud city spun by an aging wrestler, teased by volunteers, tugged by a grey-bearded engineer, deconstructed in conversations around a table at mealtimes.

After three years in Afghanistan, I am now dividing my time between Kabul and teaching human rights at Harvard. My hope is that I will continue to steer the project until it is completed and that I will be able to return in 30 years to admire the old city's arts and architecture, and encounter a community whose lives are more just, prosperous and humane. But I cannot guarantee we will succeed. I have never had a more satisfying job. But I am not sure whether I would have the energy to do something like this again.

A young man sands a stool in a wood workshop that produces traditional wood carving and furniture at the Higher Education Institute for Arts and Architecture run by the Turquoise Mountain Foundation.

Creating ceramic tiles in the pottery studio at the Higher Education Institute for Arts and Architecture run by the Turquoise Mountain Foundation.

BAND-E-AMIR, AFGHANISTAN'S FIRST NATIONAL PARK, WAITS FOR TOURISTS

AFGHANISTAN'S FIRST NATIONAL PARK WAITS FOR TOURISTS

BAND-E-AMIR

BAND-E-AMIR, AFGHANISTAN—It's got the soaring mesas of Canyon de Chelly and Monument Valley, the contrasts of oranges and reds found in the Grand Canyon, and the snow-dolloped peaks of the Rockies—all in one place.

That's how Dennis, a tourist from Colorado, tries to put the beauty of Band-e-Amir in context, as he helps his German friend Lukas (they decline to give last names) pitch their tent by one of the area's famed travertine lakes.

"I've never seen any other lake of that stunning blue," Lukas says.

On June 18, 2009 Band-e-Amir will be officially inaugurated as Afghanistan's first national park. International organizations, the Afghan government and local villagers are all hoping that the designation will inspire more tourists to come to this war-ravaged nation.

The idea may sound quixotic, given the surge in Taliban violence and U.S. troop deployments here. But the park lies in the safest region of the country, in the Baba Mountains of central Afghanistan—a mixed blessing, since foreign donors have focused their help on hot spots first.

The park's fruition has also been hampered by problems that hinder other Afghan development projects, including slow government decision-making, tensions between jet-setting coordinators and rural locals, and disappearing money. And, as with other projects, this one seems to be getting in gear just as security is slipping.

"Last year was a particularly discouraging year," says Andre Mann, manager of The Great Game Travel Company in Kabul. "We've decided to give it another year and see what happens. We hope [August] elections stabilize things so that our business can grow."

Band-e-Amir, at 3,000 meters altitude, is a spectacular set of five lakes. Each lake, enclosed in high walls of limestone, pours its waters into the next, lower lake. Foreign tourists have pitched a tent along the shore of one of Band-e-Amir's lakes as water spills over its travertine walls.

The potential is much bigger: Crowds thronged here in the peaceful 1960s and '70s.

"We are working to set up the infrastructure to make this sustainable, so it doesn't end up like [overdeveloped] Thailand," says Mr. Mann. "In the '70s it was heading in that direction. The war spared it that, and now we are trying to do it right."

Locals have fonder memories—especially of the money tourists brought. Dennis and Lukas's driver, Ezat Ullah, gets $50 a day to bring visitors here. Other Western tourists here recently, Jerome Mathieu and Berengere Travard, say they spent $80 a day on a hotel and meals.

"Tourism is one of the only industries that quickly brings money to everyone," says Muqim Jamshady, head of Afghan Logistics & Tours.

WHERE HAS THE MONEY GONE?

Residents of the 13 villages around the park are hoping the national park will bring those quick dollars, but that hasn't happened. That's because preservation efforts have proceeded much faster than tourism development.

Motorcyclists ride up to the shores of the lake. Among the new protections that have been put in place, drivers can no longer drive cars up to this shoreline. Uniformed park officials scolded one driver who disobeyed the restrictions.

At its busiest in 2007, his company booked some 300 foreigners on tours of Afghanistan. Last year, the number slipped to 150, and this year he estimates he will only get 80. The other tour operator, Afghan Logistics & Tours, saw a similar falloff from roughly 75 tourists a year to 50 or 60.

Exactly how many tourists visit Band-e-Amir is unknown, with the governor of Bamiyan Province saying 500 last year and aid agencies saying it was thousands. The discrepancy might relate to who is counted as a tourist—many Afghans visit the site, as well as expatriates like Dennis and Lukas, who work in Kabul. The one guesthouse in the park hosts 500 to 800 guests each year.

The views have improved: Shops no longer encroach on the lake, a fuel-leaking motorboat is now banned, and "fishing" with grenades has been quashed. But the new restrictions—which also apply to hunting, grazing and adding cultivation to nearby fields—have cut into local livelihoods.

Residents are suspicious about where the park fees collected from visitors go. A portion is supposed to help fund local community projects.

"They have not paid a penny. It's collected, but no one knows where it goes," says Muhammad Hussein Azimi, who runs the local guesthouse.

Until recently, the shore of this lake had more than a dozen shops and kebab stands. Now campers in Band-e-Amir can enjoy a wilderness waterfront, thanks to new national park restrictions that forced the demolition of encroaching businesses. The park's protection committee agreed to set up a new area for vendors away from the lake, but few shopkeepers have reopened, saying the stalls are now too far from the tourists.

The money is safe in a bank account, says Bamiyan Governor Habiba Sarabi. It cannot be distributed until the Ministry of Finance in Kabul signs off on the revenue-sharing plan. She blames this and the "slow process" of getting the park up and running on the "very centralized" government system. Just getting rid of the polluting motorboat involved a two-year battle between an Afghan vice president and the governor.

A NATIONAL PARK IN NAME ONLY

Much work has been done by the Wildlife Conservation Society (WCS) using U.S. Agency for International Development funds to preserve the land, survey the wildlife and manage a broad committee to create the park. But locals have seen little action on the ground. One person from each of the villages received tour-guide training last year, but they don't seem to know what to do next—or even where to meet tourists. One obvious place would be the welcome center, built two years ago by WCS, but rangers say it's used by officials more than by tourists.

"Honestly, it's a national park in name only," says acting park representative Sayed Muhammad Husseini Dartmond. "Even this building you are sitting in, if [aid groups] paid for it, it's not to help us do more: It's just for them to come here for themselves and stay overnight."

The station is no longer used for overnight stays. "We realized it was inappropriate," says Chris Shank, a WCS program manager. The vision is that the station will be a hub for tourists, he says, and there has been "a lag time, no question," in tourist development.

Natural beauty leads to tourists, which leads to income for locals, says Dr. Shank. But, he adds, "We've been very clear right from the beginning that there are no guarantees."

The good news is that New Zealand has dedicated money to tourism projects here, and the road linking Kabul to Bamiyan and Band-e-Amir is finally being fixed, widened and paved. Frustration over the road's neglect erupted last year in a protest.

But even with a good road, news of violence in other parts of Afghanistan may scare visitors away from Bamiyan, where international forces have yet to fire a bullet in eight years. "If we had stability here, there are rivers to be rafted, so many peaks to hike," Mann says. "But you've got to have peace."

MORE THAN BAND-E-AMIR[1]

Band-e-Amir is a long way from its halcyon days of the 1970s when some 60,000 tourists visited the area. It's not even up to where it was in 2005 when tourism hit some 30,000,[2] Then it dried up. Now, with recognition as a national park, work beginning on paving the road into the area and growing interest in cultural- and eco-tourism, hope is on the rise that the tourists—international and Afghan—will return.

Just outside the Band-e-Amir park is The Silk Road Hotel, a gem nestled among green fields with a view to the cliffs honeycombed with caves and the caverns that once held the great Buddhas. It's a top-of-the-line establishment featuring authentic Japanese food, electricity 24/7 and pristine rooms with wireless Internet. Other guesthouses and hotels are being built, but for now, Hiromi Yasui's is premier. For the time being, most guests are still ex-pats working in Kabul—the room price is high because of high costs—but the rewards of clean air and peaceful, breathtaking surroundings are a strong draw.

For the local population, The Silk Road Hotel offers new employment: jobs. In spite of local custom that regarded working in a hotel as half a step away from prostitution, women applied for jobs out of desperation. Today they see things differently. As Yasui noted, "Most of the ladies had no food at the beginning because their men didn't have a job. Now most of them have land, are saving money and hope to build a house."[3]

The Silk Road Hotel is a glimmer of what many hope will be Bamiyan Province's future. For the area around Band-e-Amir they see economic development in the form of tourism as the way to prosperity. Bamiyan, however, has a difficult and harsh environment (The Silk Road Hotel, for example, is closed during the winter months). Its undeniable asset is its scenery, its world heritage sites and, of course, the cascading lakes of Band-e-Amir. But, as Amir Foladi, head of Bamiyan's Ecotourism Program, stated, "We have

unique historical sites that can attract many tourists to Bamiyan, but the weak element is services and information."[4]

Progress in developing Bamiyan has been slower than anyone had wanted, partly because Bamiyan is a relatively peaceful area of Afghanistan, placing it low on the development priority list. But that's changing. USAID, working with the Wildlife Conservation Society, Ecodit and the Aga Khan Development Network, are working with enterprising entrepreneurs who are building shops, restaurants and more hotels—this time in accordance with the park's environmental management plan. In addition, New Zealand has recently given $1.2 million to help Bamiyan officials and residents develop a strategy to build tourism. Their task is not trivial. It involves funding inns, training staff, setting up tour guide services and even advocating for paving access roads.

While tourism development in the 1970s was on a path to turn Band-e-Amir and surrounding Bamiyan Province into an overdeveloped tourist destination, perhaps the deliberation of its development this time will ensure preservation of its beauty and provide a unique opportunity for eco-tourism at its best.

By Ben Arnoldy. reproduced with permission from the July 24, 2009 issue of The Christian Science Monitor (www.CSMonitor.com) ©2009 The Christian Science Monitor.

[1] Our thanks to the following news organizations for their reporting on Band-e-Amir: EurasiaNet, Reuters.

[2] Graham-Harrison, Emma, "Next Hot Tourist Destination: Afghanistan?" Reuters, May 14, 2009.

[3] Graham-Harrison, "Bringing Japanese Hospitality to an Afghan Valley," Reuters, May 14, 2009.

[4] Ibid.

MEDICINE

NEW SMILES IN AFGHANISTAN BY BRIAN F. MULLANEY

SMILE TRAIN

A young boy and his father traveled 800 kilometers just to get surgery for a cleft palate—that's like traveling from Ohio to New York on foot. It took them three weeks.

I have just returned from Afghanistan and I thought you might like to hear how donations are helping children in this very poor, war-ravaged country.

Months ago, when our partners invited us, they told us it was safe. Of course, one week before our trip, a suicide bomber in Kabul killed 35 police recruits, part of a new Taliban offensive aimed at bringing the war to the capital. We almost canceled. But a celebration had been planned. Patient home visits had been arranged. It seemed the staff of our partner hospital was counting on us. So off we went.

Flying into Kabul was, I must admit, a little spooky. Looking down from the airplane the terrain was bleak, barren and lifeless. Rocks, rubble and dust. Our airplane felt more like a time machine bringing us back to the Stone Age.

Mother holding child with newly repaired cleft.

What looked godforsaken from the air looked even worse from the ground. Afghanistan has been at war for years—and it looks it. Thirty years of bombs, bullets, betrayals, executions, rebels, insurgencies, beheadings, broken promises, honor killings, forced marriages, tribal warfare, occupation, religious extremism, invasions, etc. The drive to the hospital from the airport was one I will not soon forget.

Every child we met was different and yet they all told the same story. They were all extremely poor. Most had to borrow money to make the trip. Some sold off family possessions. For many it was the first time they ever left their villages. Virtually all the parents were illiterate and uneducated, but somehow each one was smart enough to know that this might be their only chance to ever help their child. Their only hope to save their child from a lifetime of heartache and suffering.

We met a 17-year-old boy and his smiling dad two days after surgery. I asked the dad how he felt when he first saw his newborn son. "I was so ashamed," he told us. "I decided to kill him." Now this actually happens quite often in many countries. We have met hundreds of children who were thrown away hours after they were born because of their clefts. But I've never heard anyone actually say these words. I asked why he never killed his son. "I never found the time," he told us with his arm around his son.

We met a remarkable young man who'd been born with a massive cleft that ran down the entire middle of his face. We wondered how he managed to survive 22 years. His picture at left on page 72, is AFTER he had already received two surgeries. He is scheduled for several more. He kept trying to thank us by putting his hand over his heart and bowing his head. He can't speak. It was heartbreaking.

We met a schoolteacher, a very polite, soft-spoken man who tried to tell us how much this surgery meant to him and the future of his son. He started to cry as he thanked us, and told us in his broken English how important it was for his son, his only son, to have a chance to go to school and to marry and to have a life. This surgery saved his son's life, he told us.

We met a remarkable Afghan surgeon named Dr. Hashimi. As often is the case, the key to a successful Smile Train program is a local, dynamic, determined leader like Dr. Hashimi. He used to perform only a small number of cleft surgeries because so few parents could afford it. Now with our support, he can provide free cleft surgery for thousands of children who would otherwise never receive it. One of the reasons we went to Kabul was to thank and recognize Dr. Hashimi for performing 250 cleft surgeries in just the first eight months of our program. He and his very capable staff are off to a very good start. He is excited about just how many children he can help and so are we.

"There are so many children who need this surgery," Dr. Hashimi told us, shaking his head. "So many years of war have created a very large backlog." We didn't have the heart to tell him just how big a backlog. Our data shows there are more than 25,000 children in Afghanistan with unrepaired clefts.

Young boy with newly repaired cleft.

Dr. Said Aolfat Hashimi, an Afghan surgeon who performs more than 20 cleft surgeries a month with the Smile Train program.

With two surgeries complete, two more will let this boy learn to talk.

A man now proud of his 17-year-old son with a repaired cleft.

A mother waiting for her child to receive surgery to repair a complicated cleft.

We asked how many surgeries he could do in a year. Maybe 800, maybe 1,000, he told us. "I will do the very best I can," he told us. We assured him that whatever the number was, we would give him all the support he needed. We encouraged him to get those TV commercials back on the air and promised to help him build an additional O.R. if needed.

We told him how the Smile Train has never turned away any child who asked for help and that whether there were 2,000 or 20,000 kids in Afghanistan, we would stick with him till we helped each and every one. This made him smile. "That's very good," he laughed, nodding his head. "We will need your help. Because for every child I send home after surgery to a village, five more will come when they learn about this program. We are going to be very busy for a very long time."

After we had a short ceremony at the hospital celebrating the 250 surgeries, thanking the staff and giving Dr. Hashimi a plaque to thank him, we raced to the airport to catch our plane back to civilization and the 21st century. As we drove away from the hospital, I thought of all the remarkable doctors and nurses we were leaving behind in this truly godforsaken place. I thought of what a special guy Dr. Hashimi is. He could easily be in the U.K. or the U.S. with his family safe and sound, making many hundreds of thousands of dollars a year doing cosmetic surgery and playing golf every Wednesday. He and his colleagues are true modern-day Good Samaritans. I meet a lot of surgeons in my job—I feel pretty lucky to have met Dr. Hashimi.

A SNAPSHOT OF KABUL WITH HOPE

Crumbling cemeteries with broken headstones and crooked graves. Bombed-out buildings. Burnt-out trucks and cars. Bullet holes everywhere. Rotting garbage. A dead donkey. A dirty, smelly stream trickling through the center of town where a vibrant river once ran. A city that looks like it is on life support.

The one nice thing we saw were HUNDREDS of girls in school uniforms coming home from school, laughing, smiling, wearing backpacks just like ordinary teenage girls. Little symbols of hope amidst so much destruction and desperation.

The average life span in Afghanistan is just 43 years. (In the U.S. it is 79 years.) The annual per capita expenditure on healthcare is $13.50. ($6,096 in the U.S.) One out of every three Afghan children is an orphan. One out of five children die before they reach their fifth birthday. (Some parents don't give their children names until after their fifth birthday.) Eighty percent of marriages are arranged and 57 percent of the brides are under the age of 16. Four out of five women are illiterate. They face the highest maternal and infant mortality rates in the world. Annual income per capita is $231.18 ($36,276 in the U.S.).

SmileTrain doctors, Dr. Gran Zawan, Dr. Keith Rose and Dr. Said Aolfat Hashimi.

As if living on 63 cents a day is not bad enough, the Taliban are doing everything they can to make life even worse. They're killing as often and as many as they can—foreigners and Afghans. Burning down schools. They beheaded a schoolteacher in front of his wife and eight children because he had the audacity to teach girls. The week we were in Kabul, the Taliban sent a six-year-old boy on a suicide mission. Luckily soldiers spotted the oversized jacket and disarmed him.

I could go on and on about all the things that are going wrong in this poor country, but instead, I want to tell you about something that is going right. Right smack in the middle of Kabul stands an oasis of hope: our partner hospital.

This small 60-bed hospital is run by a heroic staff of Afghans and ex-pats who've come from all over the world to help the people of Afghanistan. It is a nonprofit hospital supported by donors from America and around the world. It has had a very big impact in a very short time. In addition to the life-saving work this hospital does with OB/GYN and orthopedic surgery, it is now a Smile Train partner and offers free cleft surgeries.

Just a few free TV commercials aired over a couple of days brought hundreds of children with clefts and their parents from all over Afghanistan to this hospital begging for help.

I apologize for the length of this letter and I thank you for reading it. I hope that somehow I have conveyed a few very important things that you should know.

First of all, the Smile Train uses contributions for work in the poorest countries on earth where the value of every dollar is 1,000 times greater than it is here in the U.S.

Secondly, we don't just send your money around the world—we send ourselves. My colleagues and I have traveled to Bangladesh, India, Indonesia, China, Nigeria, Kenya, Malawi, Ethiopia, Mozambique, Brazil and Mexico to make sure your donations are being spent on helping children and that our programs are being run as best they can.

Finally, and most importantly, every Smile Train contribution helps children no one else will help, changing lives with a simple surgery that takes as little as 45 minutes and costs as little as $250.

Since Brian Mullaney was in Afghanistan two and a half years ago, the airport road to Kabul has been landscaped and lined with trees and the city is significantly cleaner with new buildings going up everywhere.

Brian Mullaney with young Smile Train patient.

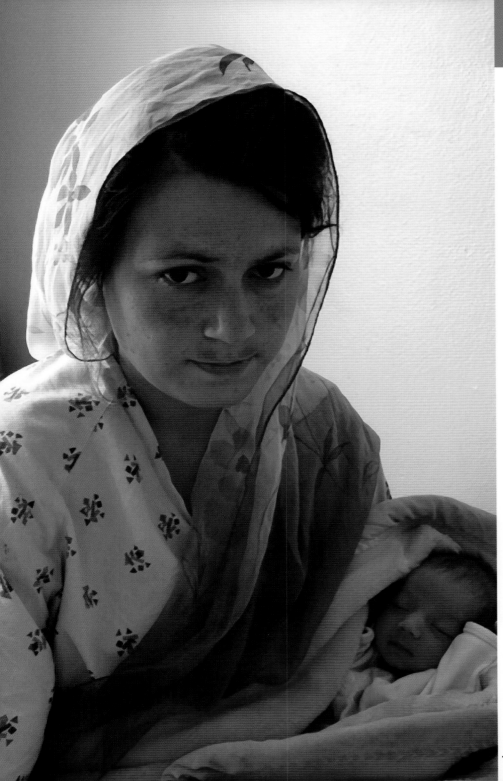

TRAINING FEMALE PHYSICIANS TO COMBAT MATERNAL MORTALITY
CURE INTERNATIONAL

Marzia has suffered greatly from past pregnancy problems. During her most recent pregnancy, she was desperate to find a facility that could help her safely deliver her baby. Then she heard about CURE's hospital and its excellent doctors. She was able to get prenatal care there and delivered a healthy baby girl. Now she has dreams her girl will grow up to be a doctor just like the ones at the CURE hospital!

With a nationwide maternal mortality rate of 1,600 maternal deaths per 100,000 live births, Afghanistan ranks next to last in the world. Unlike its neighbors, Afghanistan has not been part of the dramatic improvements in maternal health that have occurred during the past several decades…

• Every 30 minutes a woman dies giving birth; it is estimated that over 80 percent of these deaths could be prevented.[1]

• More than 70 percent of women do not receive medical care during pregnancy; 40 percent have no access to emergency obstetric care.[2]

• An infant whose mother dies giving birth is up to four times more likely to die before its first birthday than other infants.[3]

• Females comprise just 21 percent of the health workforce.[4]

Despite more than seven years of international concern for the lives and rights of Afghan women, much remains to be done. Afghan women still face enormous obstacles to receiving an adequate education and to accessing healthcare, while maternal mortality rates are essentially the same.

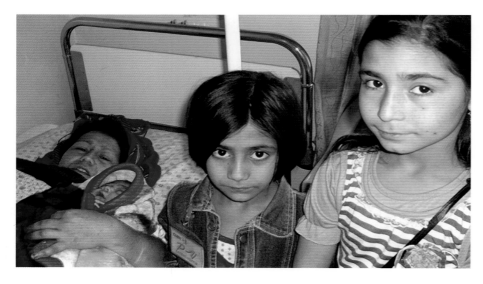

Since the inception of this landmark program, CURE and the MoPH have celebrated the graduation of 15 fellows. Several have assumed key leadership positions within Afghanistan's healthcare system. Three lead the CURE OB/GYN Fellowship Program, one has assumed a senior post within the MoPH, one is currently on staff as senior OB/GYN faculty at Kabul Medical University, and others work as OB/GYN clinicians and trainers in various hospitals throughout Afghanistan. A fourth cohort of female physicians recently began their fellowship training at CURE.

One of the most encouraging results of the CURE OB/GYN Fellowship Program is that it has served as a catalyst for the development of additional training programs in maternal health. It has led to new programs that train government employees in OB/GYN and NICU care on monthly visits from other hospitals. More than a dozen doctors, nurses and midwives receive specialized training at CURE every month.

The CURE International Hospital in Kabul is a 90-bed facility with services in family medicine, obstetrics and gynecology, general surgery, internal medicine, pediatrics, orthopedics, anesthesia and pathology. CURE integrates the specialty care of the hospital with community-based primary care provided at its Family Health Center located in a village near the hospital.

Since 2005, CURE International has served over 250,000 patients in Afghanistan, the majority of whom are female. CURE has performed more than 10,000 surgeries and helped women deliver 10,000 babies in its facilities in Afghanistan. The CURE International Hospital functions under the guidance of the MoPH and is a registered nonprofit organization. CURE employs more than 300 Afghans, nearly a third of whom are female.

To reverse the harmful trends in maternal health, CURE International is supporting the Afghan Ministry of Public Health (MoPH) by training female doctors to meet the critical maternal healthcare needs of the population.

CURE INTERNATIONAL OB/GYN FELLOWSHIP PROGRAM

Preparing the next generation of Afghan OB/GYN doctors to meet the maternal health challenges in Afghanistan is an essential component of the effort to reduce maternal mortality.

The CURE International OB/GYN Fellowship Training Program for female physicians is the only program of its kind in Afghanistan. This 18-month intensive fellowship is offered to Afghan physicians who are specialists within the national system and teaches evidence-based medicine. The program is designed to upgrade knowledge and skills to first-world levels and to prepare Afghan specialists to teach and work in provincial hospitals within the MoPH system. It is estimated that the impact of training five OB/GYN fellows will benefit as many as 200,000 Afghan women during the fellows' future medical career.

[1] UNICEF and the U.S. Center for Disease Control (2002). Maternal Mortality in Afghanistan: Magnitude, Causes, Risk Factors and Preventability. Summary Findings.
[2] Ibid.
[3] Ibid.
[4] WHO/EMRO (2006 July). Report of the Health System Review Mission—Afghanistan (p.6).

HEALTH AND CONFLICT RESOLUTION IN RURAL AREAS
SANAYEE DEVELOPMENT ORGANIZATION

Basic Package of Health Services (BPHS) is one of Sanayee Development Organization's (SDO) most successful programs. Initiated in 2003 and implemented in four districts of Ghazni Province, BPHS has resulted in SDO operating 16 health facilities, including five Comprehensive Health Centers, one Critical Health Center, seven Basic Health Centers and one Sub-Center. Under the Community Based Health Care (CBHC) component of this program, SDO also established 225 health posts at the village level. Each SDO facility is staffed, based on the BPHS guidelines and supplied with essential drugs, equipment and all necessary items needed for the smooth running of the facility.

Support of community is very important in implementation of the BPHS. Each facility and post is supported by a health Shura comprised of committed influential men and women in the community. There is a strong referral system between the facilities so a patient who cannot be managed at one level can be referred to another for proper diagnosis and treatment.

Abdul Jabaar, one of our villagers, had missed a number of prayers in the local mosque. Daulat Khan, a community health worker, said Abdul had come into the post complaining about aches all over his body. He was given painkillers. The following day Daulat Khan and I went to see Abdul at his house. From bed, Abdul told us he had been feeling terrible. He complained about pain all over his body, fever and cough. He also said he was short of breath while walking and could no longer work on his farm. His condition was worsening and the medication wasn't helping. This time, Daulat recommended that Abdul see a doctor in the nearby health clinic. There he was examined by a doctor who found, with tests, that Abdul had tuberculosis. Sharing this information with Abdul, the

doctor stressed that Abdul must complete proper treatment. Otherwise, his family members and others around him could be infected. The doctor gave him a treatment card, reiterated that he must follow the full course of treatment and, at the same time, must rest, work less, eat healthy food and avoid sharing his kitchen utensils, towel, mattress, pillow, etc. with others. The doctor also arranged to have the post near his house dispense his medication and treatment. As part of support for TB patients, Abdul also received a fixed amount of wheat, cooking oil and other food supplies. After almost three months of treatment, carefully following the doctor's directions, Abdul Jabaar fully recovered.

Community-Based Peace Building, another important Sanayee program in various provinces, involves peaceful conflict resolution. The story below is one of the hundreds of cases resolved peacefully with the intervention of SDO. With this community-based program, SDO aims to strengthen social structures for constructive transformation of conflicts through addressing the root causes of conflict in order to promote stability, justice, goodwill and cooperation among community members. At the same time, SDO's peace-building program prepares the way for development work.

Ahmad Ali, a local youth in Hafto Ulya village, hit and injured Shahla, a middle-aged woman from the same village, while recklessly speeding through town on his motorcycle. Soon after the accident, Shahla's family reacted violently by beating Ahmad Ali. His family, equally unable to tolerate the situation, began insulting and abusing Shahla's family members. The conflict had now escalated, involving many more people and becoming more serious. Unable to listen to one another, the two families turned to district authorities, where the district administrator decided to refer the case to the nearby Faizabad Village Peace Shura. Both parties were invited to the community peace room built by SDO.

Using conflict resolution learned from SDO's community-based peace-building program, Haji Abdul Rahman also invited a number of elders from the disputing parties' village. Next, he encouraged each party to narrate what exactly happened during and after the accident. After listening attentively to both parties, he applied a number of mediation and negotiation tools to bring the conflicting

parties closer together. He also referenced the Holy Quran and sayings of the prophet Mohammad (SAW) regarding peace and peaceful co-existence. Ultimately, the parties came to a solution: Ahmad Ali agreed to pay for treatment of Shahla's injuries and committed to ride his motorcycle more responsibly. At the same time, Shahla's family members apologized for their violence and promised to avoid any violent acts in the future. As a matter of goodwill, one of the elders from Ahmed Ali's family brought grapes from his garden and invited everyone to eat. Later, a number of women from his family visited Shahla and presented her with fruit and fresh bread.

Sanayee's Community-Based Peace-Building Has:

- Resulted in the formation of 88 Peace Shuras (69 men's, 11 women's and eight mixed).
- Trained over 2,000 women and men, including teachers, elders, key informants, community leaders and youth, in conflict resolution and peace-building concepts.
- Sponsored nearly 5,000 peace-building and conflict resolution workshops.
- Promoted peace and non-violence through local TV, radio, papers, mosques, schools and other community gatherings.
- Peacefully settled 7,000 conflicts over resources (land, water, heritage, trees, etc.) and family relationships.
- Constructed and equipped 25 peace rooms where communities can gather to address their issues and conflicts.
- Established three libraries, five computer training courses and two literacy courses for women.
- Convinced elders, leaders and community representatives to ban the practice of various negative traditions, such as excessive wedding and funeral costs, violence against women and others.
- Created 28 school peace committees to promote peace among students.

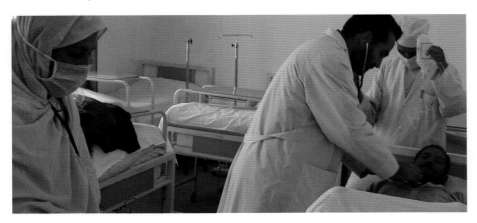

BABY AND MOTHER ARE DOING QUITE WELL!
INTERNATIONAL MEDICAL CORPS

I work as a program development officer with the International Medical Corps in Afghanistan. A major focus of our programs is women's health. This is largely because of the tragic irony facing expectant mothers in Afghanistan—every 28 minutes, a woman dies while giving life.

Living in isolated villages scattered throughout some of the most unforgivable terrain in the world, 81 percent of Afghanistan's women deliver their babies at home without skilled birth attendants. As a result, 1,600 mothers die for every 100,000 live births, making Afghanistan second only to Sierra Leone for the highest number of maternal deaths in the world. This rate is 123 times higher than that of the United States.

However, mothers are not the only ones whose lives are lost because of the many complications that can arise in delivery. Newborn deaths also result, mostly from causes that are easily preventable. In the worst cases, both the mother and the baby die, but thanks in part to the International Medical Corps' work, one woman's story had a happy ending.

I was doing a regular monitoring visit of the International Medical Corps' programs at Rabia Balkhi Hospital (RBH) in Kabul, Afghanistan's largest full-service women's hospital where we created the first in-service OB/GYN residency curriculum and the first hospital-level nursing curriculum. Thanks to funding from the U.S. government, this International Medical Corps program provides improved healthcare to more than 27,000 women and 13,000 children every year.

I was fortunate enough to witness what this program did for two of the tens of thousands of lives it saves every year—28-year-old Ameera and her baby girl.

When Ameera came to Rabia Balkhi she had been in labor at home for more than 24 hours. It may be hard to imagine giving birth in your home, let alone waiting a full day to go to the hospital, but Ameera faced a common pressure in Afghanistan—to have a natural birth. That not only eliminates the possibility for an epidural, but also for a cesarean section, something that many people, including Ameera's mother-in-law, see as a *ballah*, or a curse.

Ameera was under particular pressure to deliver vaginally because she had delivered her first baby—a 7.7-pound baby girl—through a cesarean section. When she went into labor with her second child, she did not tell anyone in the family for nearly eight hours, until the pain was too great. Her mother-in-law, not wanting a cesarean section to happen again, encouraged her to be strong and deliver at home. But when the baby had not been delivered after 24 hours, they went to Rabia Balkhi for medical assistance.

When we admitted Ameera to the hospital, her condition was fair. While her vitals were stable, the baby was stuck. Because they had waited so long to seek medical care, the baby was too far down to be delivered via a cesarean section. Ameera was so weak that, despite the hospital staff's encouragement to push, she simply couldn't muster the strength. The International Medical Corps' midwife trainer administered an IV and oxygen to give Ameera the strength she and the baby needed. The baby's heart rate started to drop.

As I watched our midwife trainer, the doctors, nurses and midwives, I realized the options were limited. Pushing the baby back into the uterus for a cesarean section could result in brain damage and a dangerous infection for the mother and the baby. And because the baby was showing signs of distress, she needed to be delivered immediately.

Although no longer used in modern obstetric settings, the only option at RBH that morning was to use forceps, which can bruise a baby's delicate nerves and skin if they are not used perfectly. Ameera's scar from her cesarean section made the forceps even more risky. One wrong move could mean a ruptured cervix or, even worse, a fistula, a severe gynecological tear that can be completely debilitating and lead to incontinence. The doctors had no other choice but to make it work.

We all held our breaths—Ameera, the health staff and me—as the doctor carefully inserted the forceps around the baby's head. Ameera pushed and we pushed with her until we were all blue in the face. And then, out came a beautiful, healthy baby girl.

Ameera was triumphant, while we, the International Medical Corps team with her, could not stop shaking. We were all overjoyed—Ameera for her new baby and the International Medical Corps team for having saved two lives that could have easily slipped through our fingers to become yet another statistic of maternal and child mortality in Afghanistan.

While both Ameera and her baby are alive and healthy, the work in Afghanistan is far from over. Thousands of women all over Afghanistan aren't this lucky—but after watching this birth, I know it doesn't have to be that way. If we keep pushing the importance of women's health, not only in Afghanistan but all over the world, Ameera's case will become the norm instead of the exception.

INTERNATIONAL MEDICAL CORPS AFGHANISTAN

The International Medical Corps was established in 1984 by volunteer doctors and nurses to address the critical need for medical care in war-torn Afghanistan during the Soviet occupation. Twenty-five years later, the International Medical Corps is still in Afghanistan, delivering services that improve the health and livelihoods of nearly one million people. From women and children to internally displaced persons and refugees, the International Medical Corps supports Afghanistan's most vulnerable people

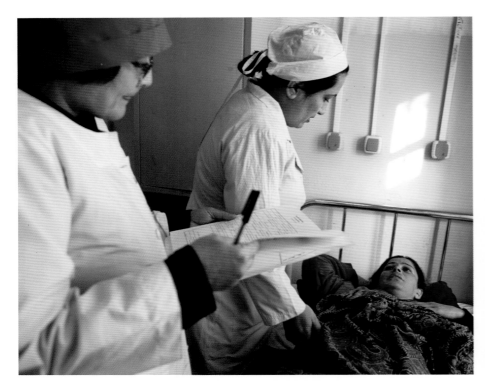

with a broad range of interventions that include healthcare, dental care, maternal and child healthcare, women's livelihoods, agricultural support and infrastructure rebuilding. True to its mission not only to provide relief but enable self-reliance, the International Medical Corps incorporates education and training into all of its programs so that the Afghan people can continue these programs and lead their own development long into the future.

RABIA BALKHI HOSPITAL FOR WOMEN

The International Medical Corps also created the first in-service OB/GYN residency curriculum at Rabia Balkhi in support of a larger program for Afghan OB/GYNs. Every year, more than 27,000 women and 13,000 children benefit from the International Medical Corps' work to improve care at Rabia Balkhi.

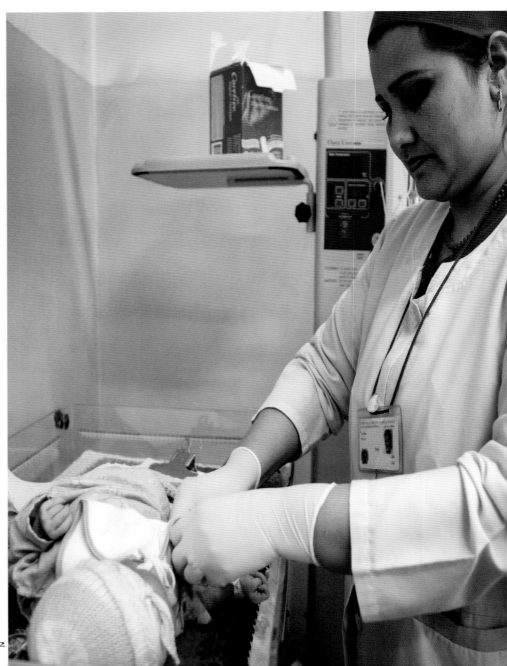

THE WORST SHAME FOR WOMEN: A SILENT EPIDEMIC

COLONEL GARY DAVIS, CLINICAL ADVISOR TO GENERAL YAFTALI, SURGEON GENERAL OF THE AFGHAN NATIONAL ARMY

In some remote provinces of Afghanistan, fewer than 15 percent of women are attended by a skilled healthcare provider during the process of childbirth. Coupled with the fact that many Afghan women marry and deliver children at an early age, obstructed labor is common. Obstructed labor results when the maternal pelvis is too small to enable delivery of the baby. Without medical assistance, the labor can last for days and result in the death of the baby and the mother. Many of the mothers who survive develop obstetric fistula, a tear or opening between the woman's vagina and bladder or rectum, through which urine and/or feces continually leaks. The social and hygienic problems in resource-poor regions lacking in clean water and sanitation facilities are enormous. These young women often find themselves living in shame and isolation, abandoned by their husbands and excluded by their families and the community. These women are generally uneducated and are unable to earn money, thus falling deeper into poverty and despair.

Afghanistan is emerging from over 20 years of warfare and social dis-order, and despite the devastating impact on the lives of young women, care for obstetric fistula has been neglected. It has remained the "silent epidemic" because it affects the most marginalized members of Afghan society, the poor, young and often illiterate girls and women living in remote regions of the country.

Colonel Gary Davis, previously Surgeon General for the United States Army in Afghanistan.

Recently, American physicians and nurses have helped organize national and international efforts to prevent and treat obstetric fistula in all regions of Afghanistan. Afghan women are finally receiving the political, educational and financial support necessary to develop a network to reduce the incidence and provide early

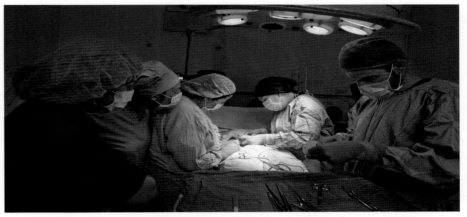

Dr. Davis reports that these Afghan women surgeons are, three years later, as capable as any U.S. doctor.

treatment for obstetric fistula. The program strives to prevent fistula through health promotion and awareness and the development of high-quality basic and comprehensive maternal healthcare, available to all Afghan women. Secondly, the program strives to ensure that all women living with fistulas have access to skilled professionals capable of repairing both simple and complex fistula. For the past four years, Afghan physicians have worked closely with American doctors and nurses, enabling them to master the surgical skills necessary to effectively repair simple and complex obstetric fistula. More importantly, by working together, they have come to fully understand the teamwork and medical and psychosocial support required to return these women to fully productive and active lives. This program has produced a number of highly trained young Afghan physicians with world-class surgical skills, capable of treating even the most complex obstetric fistula. They are in turn teaching others in Afghanistan and improving the health and prosperity of the people of Afghanistan. They are indeed the future of Afghanistan and its brightest hope.

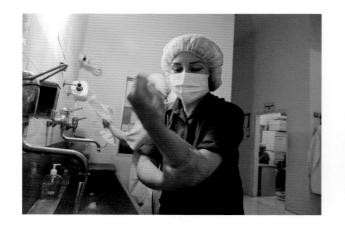
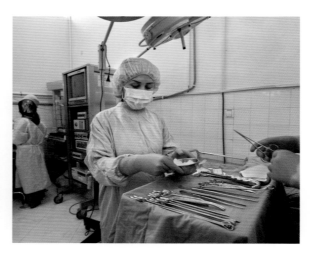
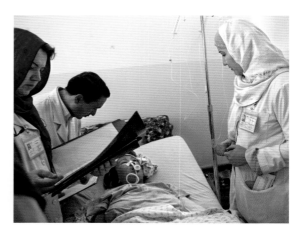
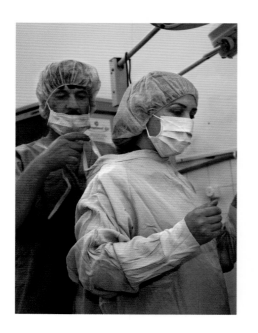
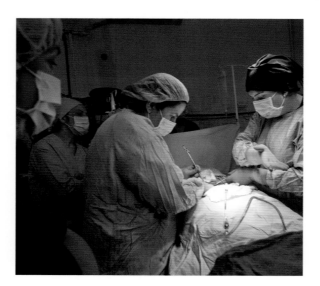
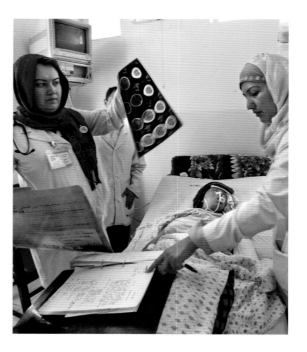

WOMEN AS WELL AS MEN IN THE NEW NATIONAL MILITARY ACADEMY

COLONEL GARY DAVIS, CLINICAL ADVISOR TO GENERAL YAFTALI, SURGEON GENERAL OF THE AFGHAN ARMY

Medical professionals in Afghanistan must be capable of providing healthcare during peacetime and during times of conflict—as conflict remains a periodic and unpredictable challenge to the delivery of healthcare throughout the country.

The varied skills necessary to meet the challenges of this diverse environment are not addressed by any civilian medical school curriculum. To meet these requirements, the Afghan Armed Forces Academy of Medical Services was established in 2008. In addition to the requisite clinical skills, a unique military curriculum was developed, designed to teach critical competencies essential to the development of leaders capable of succeeding in an environment marked by technological advancements, information overload and uncertainty. In peacetime, Afghan military medical officers must possess skills necessary to operate the country's healthcare system. During periods of conflict, they must be capable of organizing and managing healthcare delivery in austere and often hazardous conditions.

The first medical school class at the Armed Forces Academy of Medical Services of the National Military Academy of Afghanistan. The women are the first ever admitted to the Military Academy.

In 2008, the inaugural class of 36 students was picked from over 600 applicants from all provinces in Afghanistan. Each applicant met the challenging scholastic and physical requirements for admission to the National Military Academy of Afghanistan. Nine outstanding young women met all selection requirements and became the first female cadets ever admitted to the National Military Academy of

General Yaftali, Surgeon General of the Afghan National Army.

Afghanistan. The 36 students have begun seven years of intense medical and leadership training provided by both Afghan and American instructors and mentors. On graduation, they will have the degree of Doctor of Medicine and a commission in the Afghan National Army or Afghan National Police Force. The training these students receive will enable them to provide the leadership necessary to move the Afghan healthcare system forward.

THE SHOT BRIGADE

LENA L. SOTO, U.S.A.F.

Many of these children, well actually almost all, were so skinny they had to have all their immunizations in the leg. Many of their arms were smaller than a 50-cent piece! I don't think any of them had bathed over the winter so it took at least two alcohol swabs to get a "clean spot." This area had very few people who had been immunized before, so many were terrified. We tried to make sure all the children got a little bag of candy and a small toy. This at least made things a little better. My partner and I gave shots from 12 noon to 5:30 p.m. without a break. It was the first time I ever got blisters on my knees.

This is one of the reasons I asked to stay another six months, to make a difference in the people's lives.

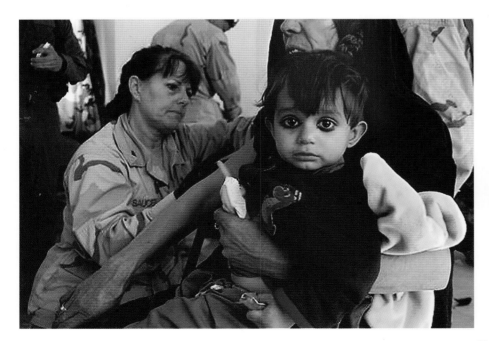

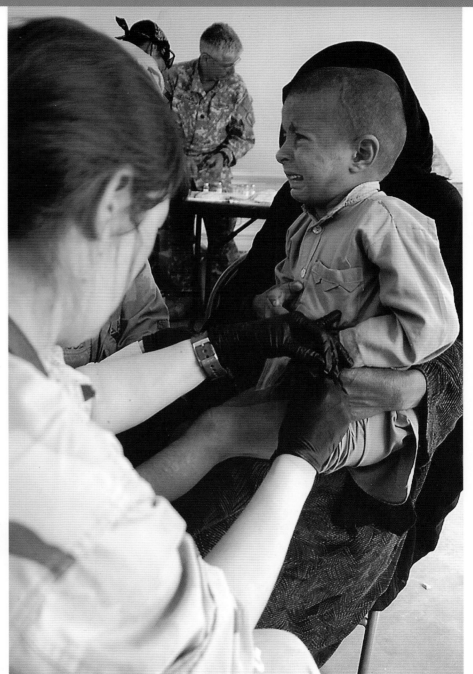

GOODBYE POLIO

In 1998, 350,000 Afghans had polio. By June of 2008, there were only six reported cases—thanks to vaccinations. In mid-2008, *Toronto Star* columnist Rosie DiManno reported on a conversation she had had with Dr. Abdul Nazar Ahmadi in Kunduz about the status of polio in Afghanistan[1]. The story at that time was:

It was actually the Mujahedeen, back in the late 1980s, which first began advocating and enabling polio vaccination for children in the regions they held. In 1988, there were 350,000 documented cases of polio in Afghanistan; by 2006, under programs established by the central government through the auspices of the UN and the WHO, that number had been slashed to 1,956.

But Afghanistan remains one of four countries where crippling polio is still endemic. There was a huge outbreak in 1997 and again in 2006. Six cases have been found so far this year, though none in the north, where eradication has been declared complete.

"For every single case, that means up to a thousand have been exposed to the virus and have it in their system," says Ahmadi, who is in charge of the regional polio office. "It's like the iceberg phenomenon. We only see the tip of it."

Of the six cases this year, two are in Helmand, the rest in Herat, Kandahar and Farah. "With the security situation in the south, accessibility for vaccination is very difficult," says Ahmadi.

"We need to vaccinate them at least three times over three years to completely control the disease. But in some conflict areas, the Taliban have shot at our volunteers or they have intimidated tribal elders so we can't go into villages."

A Taliban spokesperson has denied this, insisting volunteers have been guaranteed secure access to immunize children. They lie.

Still, some 7.3 million Afghan children under the age of five have been vaccinated this year.

Some things improve with time. On May 23, 2009, Afghanistan launched a three-day "National Immunization Days" campaign with a goal of immunizing almost 7.7 million children under five years of age and stopping circulation of wild polio virus inside Afghanistan and importation of the virus from neighboring countries.

A stunning effort, the three-day campaign involved a significant awareness campaign by the Ministry of Public Health and the participation of nearly 5,500 Ministry of Public Health staff and volunteers to cover all villages in all 34 provinces of the country.

[1]DiManno, Rosie, "Finally, a Hopeful Story Emerges from Afghanistan," Toronto Star, June 3, 2008. Reprinted with permission—Torstar Syndication Services.

ERADICATING LEISHMANIASIS AND MALARIA
THE LEISHMANIASIS AND MALARIA TREATMENT CENTER

The Leishmaniasis and Malaria Treatment Center, located in the Afghan Red Crescent Society's hospital in Kabul, is run under the supervision of Dr. Najibullah Safi. These two diseases, both carried by insects and both rampant in various parts of Afghanistan, are targeted for extinction through Dr. Safi's Center.

Leishmaniasis is the third most important vector-borne (insect-carried) disease globally and is responsible for an estimated 57,000 deaths annually.[1] The vast majority of leishmaniasis cases in Afghanistan are of the cutaneous form, which causes sores on the skin that can take months, if not years, to heal and often leave ugly scars. There is also a visceral form of the disease that causes high fever, weight loss and an enlarged spleen and liver. Leishmaniasis is transmitted by sand flies.

Prevalence of the disease in Kabul has been variously estimated to be between 2.7 percent and 12 percent of the population while a recent survey in the north of Afghanistan found leishmaniasis lesion prevalence as high as 24 percent in some districts. The majority of cutaneous lesions occur on the head and upper arms. They're rarely fatal but cause severe stigmatization and social and familial exclusion. Cases of visceral leishmaniasis are also periodically reported, although presumably there are many cases that go unreported due to poor knowledge of the disease among both the population and healthcare providers as well as the lack of reporting mechanisms.

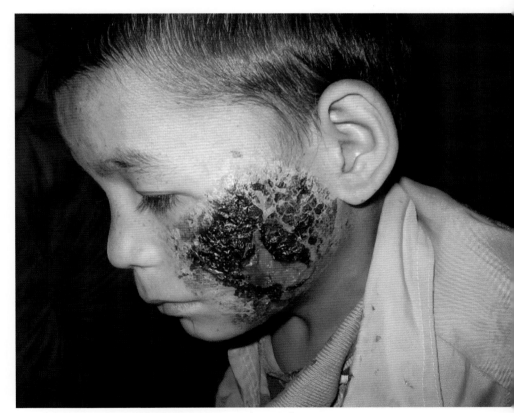

Boy with leishmaniasis beginning treatment with Dr. Safi.

Efforts to control the epidemic both in Kabul and in the north are proving to be a considerable challenge. While there are no vaccines or drugs that can prevent infection, personal protection methods have proved effective—covering skin and using insect repellent on exposed skin, using insecticide-treated clothing and sheets—but expanding control of the sand flies and effective treatment remain major challenges. Nevertheless, efforts are now underway to expand the use of insecticide-treated nets in Kabul. Additionally, an intensive public health awareness campaign has been undertaken.

Until recently, the only available treatment for leishmaniasis has been drugs. But these can provoke serious side effects, they are expensive and, because they involve a painful course of injections, there tends to be poor compliance with treatment. Recently, the Center has been involved with a trial of thermotherapy, where localized heat is applied to the lesion. This seems to be proving effective, and a final detailed report will be available shortly.

Malaria is one of the major public health problems in Afghanistan. According to the World Health Organization, Afghanistan has the second highest burden of malaria in WHO's Eastern Mediterranean Region and the fourth worldwide outside of Africa. Approximately 14 million Afghans live in malaria endemic provinces and are exposed to high risk of the disease.

Because malaria is so widespread, it places an unacceptable burden on the health and economic development of Afghanistan. The government, through the Ministry of Public Health (MoPH), is firmly committed to the control of the disease. In this regard, the MoPH has endorsed the Global and Regional Roll Back Malaria strategies and the Millennium Development Goals—the largest international effort in 50 years to eradicate malaria. Afghanistan has developed a National Malaria Strategic Plan which covers the 2008-2013 period. The estimated cost of the plan was calculated at 55 million euros. Program implementation is expected to begin August 1, 2009. Key elements of the plan include:

- Expanding the network of laboratory services to rural areas, which will improve access to early diagnosis (already 30 laboratories have been established in three impacted provinces to date).

- Improving distribution of free long-lasting insecticide-treated bed nets (in the last two years some 1.3 million nets have been distributed)

- Increasing awareness to promote behavioral change (even before the program's August implementation date, some 600,000 notebooks, posters and brochures have been distributed through schoolchildren).

Notably, the plan expands services to women, and special attention is given to targeting program interventions in known risk areas and the vulnerable populations of pregnant women, children under five years of age and populations in remote rural areas often underserved by existing public sector health facilities. Particular emphasis will be placed on increasing access to the key affected populations of refugees returning from neighboring countries (returnees), internationally displaced populations and nomads.

Dr. Najibullah Safi, Leishmaniasis and Malaria Treatment Center.

[1]World Health Organization, 2004.

TREATING BURN PATIENTS
THE GROSSMAN BURN FOUNDATION

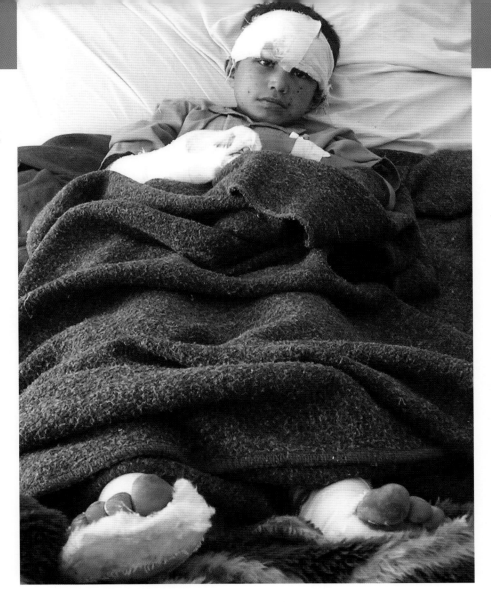

The Grossman Burn Foundation (GBF), under the leadership of Foundation Chairperson Rebecca Gray Grossman, Dr. Peter Grossman and Executive Director Stacy Tilliss, is renowned for assisting needy families around the world in the areas of healthcare, safety and education.

The GBF mission is to expand medical opportunities in developing countries by providing world-class quality medical care to those who suffer from debilitating injuries, burns and congenital deformities that have left them physically impaired.

The GBF is equally committed to addressing critical situations in the United States and various countries around the world such as Afghanistan and Indonesia where the health status of local villagers—particularly Afghan women—ranks among the worst in the world. Dr. Peter Grossman is a member of the U.S.-Afghan Women's Council—a public-private partnership established by Presidents Bush and Karzai to mobilize public and private resources to empower Afghan women and children. Dr. Grossman specifically leads the healthcare efforts of the Council.

International Burn Center: In 2008, the Grossman Burn Foundation formed a strategic partnership with Direct Relief International to open a burn treatment facility in Kabul. The launching of this first, highly specialized, nonprofit Reconstructive Surgery and Burn Center in Kabul is a beacon of hope to those who suffer from debilitating injuries, burns and congenital deformities that have left them physically handicapped, including cleft cases and women in need of obstetric fistula reconstruction.

While it is possible to fly patients from impoverished countries and treat them in the U.S., the cost of doing that is exceptionally high. It makes eco-nomic sense to treat them in their own country. More importantly, consistent with USAID's mission to support sustainable development in impoverished countries, the opening of a Reconstructive Surgery and Burn Center in Kabul contributes to the development of a critical hospital infrastructure for the betterment of Afghans' lives. Furthermore, this highly specialized center makes emergency medical treatment available for American soldiers awaiting transport back to the United States.

TEACHING BURN PREVENTION
TRIWEST HEALTHCARE ALLIANCE

President and CEO of TriWest Healthcare Alliance, David McIntyre, visited Kabul and other parts of Afghanistan following the fall of the Taliban. As CEO of the military's private-sector healthcare provider from the Western Region of the United States, he spends time visiting bases, meeting with senior military leadership and reviewing the status of healthcare for our men and women in uniform. After a visit to Kabul in 2006, Mr. McIntyre was overwhelmed by the number of children (patients in our military hospitals) he saw that had been severely burned. He wondered about the cause of the burns and why there were so many victims. He felt that if the problem could be identified, TriWest might be able to lend a hand.

Upon returning to the United States, he met with Dr. Peter Saleh, a health attaché in the Office of the Secretary of Defense, to discuss the problem. Dr. Saleh had explained that often in developing countries children are the ones that end up lighting kerosene lamps, stacking wood-burning stoves, or exposed to butane and cooking oil. Because of their size and unsteadiness—often reaching up to light lamps, losing their balance around fires and/or spilling flammable liquid—circumstances lead to unthinkable disasters. Dr. Saleh further mentioned that the problem had become so bad in Herat (along with self-immolation patients) that the Department of Defense funded a burn treatment center there. However, the cost of critical care and curative services is so prohibitively high for Afghanistan and the Ministry of Public Health, it seemed that the most effective remedy might be more preventative measures. Mr. McIntyre recalled that in the 1970s in the United States there was a need to educate Americans about the dangers of children's pajamas, which were often flammable. After a successful awareness

and prevention campaign was implemented throughout the country, the problem became virtually nonexistent. On the spot, it was decided that a comprehensive awareness and education program would likely be useful in Afghanistan to help mitigate this horrible problem.

Dr. Saleh immediately engaged Dr. Amin Fatimie, the Minister of Health in Afghanistan, in consultations. Dr. Fatimie agreed and approved an implementation plan. Over the next 10 months Dr. Saleh worked out a Memorandum of Understanding (MOU) between the Ministries of Health, Education and Women's Affairs to

Girls in a health education class learn about burn prevention.

recipients included community leaders and volunteers, schoolchildren and burn victims themselves. All 3.7 million district trainees took burn prevention messages directly to households in their respective communities, dramatically broadening the program's indirect household impact in the three provinces, effectively reaching isolated rural households and homes that do not typically have access to radios or televisions.

In addition to community and household-level training, mass marketing of burn prevention messages created national awareness of this health crisis, reinforced program activities at the community level and delivered basic educational messages. Radio and television public service announcements (PSAs) were broadcast throughout the program year on a national level. In the fourth quarter alone there were 10 television and 50 radio PSAs aired. Billboards and banners were posted throughout the provinces at major traffic intersections and important community centers. Over 300,000 posters were distributed at clinics, hospitals, maternity wards and community centers in the three target provinces. In addition, over 19,000 villages held street-by-street campaigns where burn prevention messages were broadcast over mobile loudspeakers and flyers were distributed at community centers with speeches by program trainers. In 2008-2009, the program expanded to the provinces of Parwan, Laghman and Logar.

devise a coordinated approach that would allow for education in schools, health clinics and women's centers. Because of the high illiteracy rate, the plan would also involve posters, radio and TV commercials throughout the country. Dr. Saleh reported back to Mr. McIntyre and $1 million in funding was secured from TriWest Healthcare Alliance to begin the program.

After the MOU was in place, Dr. Saleh turned to the U.S.-Afghan Women's Council, of which he is a member, to implement the program. SOZO International, a 501(c)(3) nonprofit, was charged with carrying out the four-year nationwide program. Following its first year of funding, SOZO reported that in the three target provinces of Kabul, Nangarhar and Herat, over five million Afghans directly received burn prevention training through district level training, school training and patient education. These training

MORE ABOUT MEDICINE

Wakhan Corridor: Doctor. In 2007, Dr. Alex Duncan, along with his wife and four children, found themselves living in a classic one-room Wakhan house (one room, one stove for cooking, no furniture) but pleased with their contribution to humanity. Dr. Duncan was improving healthcare—sometimes with medicine, but often with advice. Cookstoves with no chimneys encourage respiratory disease. Babies especially need their mother's milk the first four days of life (contrary to traditional lore). Marrying a first cousin can be a cause of birth defects. Though the work is hard, living conditions more akin to the 15th than the 21st century, and the location is isolated, the family is happy because they're able to tangibly contribute to changing the world—one small step at a time.

Taloqan: Midwives. The *dayees*—traditional birth attendants—are being replaced by trained midwives. No more will superstitions be the guide to baby deliveries. In a USAID-funded program, villagers select young women for training; the trainees agree to go back to their villages after 18 months of training where they will work for at least five years. Hopes are high that the expanded presence of female medical help will encourage women to get trained help for their deliveries. As the training progresses, clinics are being built.

Islamabad: Polio Elimination. In February 2009 officials from Afghanistan and Pakistan spent two days developing joint strategies to stop cross-border transmission of polio. Insecurity in the border areas is the major barrier to immunizing every eligible child with polio vaccine. Leaders are reaching out to religious leaders and tribal elders to win program support and negotiate access. Plans were developed to improve existing vaccination posts where they exist at border crossings and a needs assessment was planned to determine where new posts are needed.

Building a yurt—the Wakhan's traditional one-room house.

WOMEN AND CHILDREN

"NO ONE CAN STOP WOMEN FROM ADVANCING IN AFGHANISTAN"

— HABIBA SARABI,
GOVERNOR OF BAMIYAN PROVINCE

THE U.S.-AFGHAN WOMEN'S COUNCIL

The U.S.-Afghan Women's Council (USAWC or Council) is a public-private partnership that was established by President George W. Bush and President Hamid Karzai in 2002 and is designed to mobilize public and private sector resources to empower Afghan women. Specifically, the Council seeks to identify concrete actions to benefit women to enable them to undertake leadership roles in Afghanistan. To this end, the Council focuses on four key areas: economic empowerment, education literacy, political leadership and legal awareness, and access to healthcare. In 2006, the Council added a special children's initiative called Ayenda, ("Future" in Dari). From 2002-2008, the State Department's Under Secretary for Democracy and Global Affairs, the Afghan Minister of Foreign Affairs and the Afghan Minister of Women's Affairs co-chaired the Council.

Mrs. Laura Bush and Habiba Sarabi, Governor of Bamiyan province—the only female governor in Afghanistan—at the construction site of the Ayenda Learning Center in Bamiyan, 2008.

USAWC members represent a wide range of government, business and other leaders bringing critical guidance and knowledge to issues affecting Afghan women.

In December 2006, Mrs. Laura Bush, Honorary Chair of USAWC, announced the United States government's intention to transition to Georgetown University in 2009 as a way of continuing and enhancing the important work of the Council in the years to come. At Georgetown University, the Council works under the direction of Dr. Phyllis Magrab, Director of the Center for Child and Human Development and United Nations Educational, Scientific and Cultural Organization (UNESCO) Chair. Dr. Magrab also leads a consortium of Georgetown's other academic stakeholders, including the School of Foreign Service, the Mortara Center for International Studies and the Office of the President to assist with this initiative. Dr. John DeGioia, President of Georgetown University, is the U.S. co-chair of the Council. The Afghan counterparts remain the same.

Dr. Phyllis Magrab, Vice Chair of the U.S.-Afghan Women's Council, Georgetown University.

PROJECT PARTNERS:

Education/Literacy Programs

International School of Kabul (ISK). The ISK opened in September 2005 and is designed to provide Afghan and international students, grades K-12, with a first-rate education through U.S.-style curricula to help prepare them for higher education and leadership roles. The school is at maximum capacity and graduated its first class of students in 2008.

US military nurse visiting villagers to give vaccines.

Additionally, the director of the ISK, Bryon Greene, launched a separate initiative called the Silk Road Solutions (SRS) in 2006 in response to a request from the families of the ISK to offer adult English language courses to the parents of ISK students. In 2007 the program began and soon co-workers of ISK parents and other family members, as well as people in the local community, began requesting access to the program. Currently there are about 200 students enrolled at SRS. In addition to parents of ISK students, the program is also training employees of NGOs, the Ministry of Rural Rehabilitation and members of the Combined Security Transition Command—Afghanistan.

Afghan Teacher Education Project (ATEP). In cooperation with the State Department's Bureau of Educational and Cultural Affairs, USAWC supported the pilot phase of ATEP at the University of Nebraska to provide training for Afghan women teachers grades K-12.

Belquis Dawood, 22, a senior at AUAf pursuing her business degree.

The American University of Afghanistan (AUAf). The American University of Afghanistan is the country's only independent, private, not-for-profit, non-sectarian, coeducational institution of higher learning. It was founded by leading Afghan personalities who knew the strengths of higher education on the American model and valued the decisive contribution it can make to the reconstruction and development of Afghanistan. AUAf opened its doors in 2006 and, with the support of the United States government and private donations, has reached an enrollment of over 300 students and offers more than 60 courses taught by some 30 permanent instructors with internationally recognized degrees.

AUAf is addressing critical shortages in Afghanistan's supply of skilled labor in sectors not yet well-served by existing higher education institutions. The university provides an English language undergraduate curriculum in business management, information technology and public administration with more degrees planned for the near future.

This university answers to a need and an obligation: Afghanistan is the poorest country in the world, outside of sub-Saharan Africa. Its position on the international Human Development Index is near the bottom and declining. Thirty years of war, foreign invasion, internecine strife, displacement of populations, and all kinds of turmoil and violence have ravaged the country. Through all the troubles the people of Afghanistan have shown remarkable fortitude, resilience and courage. They now deserve to flourish and to find their rightful place in the community of nations.

Below is a personal story of one of the students:

Belquis Dawood, 22, is now a senior at the American University of Afghanistan in Kabul. Belquis is a member of the first class to enroll at the University. She is pursuing her business degree and is expected to graduate in 2010. During a trip to the United States, which was funded by the Laura Bush Afghan Women's Leaders Fund, Belquis

Tim McBride, Shamim Jawad and Paula Dobriansky in front of the Ayenda Orphanage

stated, "I love going to AUAf. The teachers are great, the business curriculum is challenging, and I have a lot of friends." When asked what she wanted to do upon graduation, she proudly stated that she wants to open her own business, possibly get an MBA, and one day she wants to run for President of Afghanistan.

The Friends of AUAf Scholarship Program/Sunshine Lady Foundation.

The Friends of AUAf have raised approximately $550,000 for scholarships for deserving young Afghan students—especially women. Additionally, the Sunshine Lady Foundation has made a generous donation to educate 10 students over the next four years.

Women's Teacher Training Institute (WTTI). Established in September 2004 and part of Afghanistan's National Literacy Center, this train-the-trainer program, which begins with master trainers in Kabul and reaches out to rural provinces across Afghanistan, provides teachers and students with an innovative program that combines literacy and math courses with practical life skills training.

PROGRAMS FOR CHILDREN

Ayenda Foundation. Ayenda Foundation, a U.S. nonprofit organization, was founded in March 2006 by Shamim Jawad and co-founder Timothy McBride as a special program of the U.S.-Afghan Women's Council. The mission of Ayenda (which means "future" in Dari) is to implement projects that enhance and improve the education, health, shelter and safety of Afghan children, especially girls. Ayenda committed to help the children of Afghanistan grow into intelligent and courageous leaders of the future. Children constitute one-third of Afghanistan's population. Child malnutrition and mortality remain pervasive due to both abject poverty and the destruction of social institutions. There are hundreds of thousands of orphans and one million children who suffer from post-traumatic stress syndrome. Access to basic healthcare and education is still limited. However, with the help of our generous supporters Ayenda Foundation is starting to change this. This year Ayenda was able to open its first school in the Bamiyan Province.

Shamim Jawad, wife of Afghanistan's ambassador to the U.S. with Ayenda children.

On March 25, 2009, the Ayenda Foundation inaugurated the Ayenda Learning Center, a new school in the historic and picturesque province of Bamiyan. The Ayenda Learning Center, which sits in the shadow of the Great Buddha statues that were destroyed by the Taliban in 2001, will provide 300 children with a modern learning facility and enhanced vocational training opportunities, unavailable in this impoverished province. Standing two stories tall and housing 24 rooms, the Center is a safe and nurturing place for the children of Bamiyan. The cost-effective construction of the Learning Center was managed free of charge by the Bayat Foundation and funded through private donations by generous U.S. individuals and corporations.

Shamim Jawad, Founder of the Ayenda Foundation, who has received the Liberty Award from Dialog on Diversity for advocating women's rights and social welfare for women and children in Afghanistan, indicated during the opening ceremony, "The beautiful children of this historic valley that once was a center of science and spirituality along the Silk Road are receiving the care and attention that they deserve from their friends and supporters in Afghanistan and the United States. As we open this school on the first day of spring, let's hope that the new year and many years to come bring peace, prosperity and further opportunities for education to the sons and daughters of Bamiyan and Afghanistan."

The students of the Ayenda Learning Center expressed their enthusiasm about their new school. Zarafia, 9, is one of the 300 kids that will benefit from the Center. She says, "Life was very hard under the Taliban rule. My father was killed when I was just one year old. My whole family had to work just to survive. Today, things are much better and I really like going to school and learning." Since the Taliban left, she says, "I can do anything that the boys can do." She aspires to be a doctor one day. The Ayenda Foundation is delighted to assist in giving these children hope for the future, as well as helping Afghanistan achieve stability.

The Ayenda Foundation has implemented and supported a number of other significant projects based on critical needs, potential for high impact, efficiency and visibility, among other factors, for Afghan children such as:

The Aschiana Foundation. Ayenda has granted $10,000 to help with the daily operation of the Aschiana Center in Kabul. The grant will not only enhance Aschiana's effort to help the 60,000 street children of Kabul lead more productive lives, but also to sustain basic programs, such as daily meals.

The Mir-Bacha-Kot School Soccer Field. Ayenda joined forces with Roots of Peace, a nonprofit organization, to provide children in Mir-Bacha-Kot village with a mine-free soccer field, equipment and uniforms.

Women Poverty Reduction Program. Ayenda Foundation funded the Women Poverty Reduction Program through the Afghan Women's Business Federation Organization. About 135 children and their families received food and school supplies through this program.

American University of Afghanistan. Ayenda has granted scholarships for two girls from the provinces to receive education at the American University of Afghanistan. A higher education for the young generation of Afghans, especially girls, is the key to unlocking a safe and prosperous future not only for girls, but also for the country as a whole.

The Afghan Songbook Project. Please go to page 256 for information about the Afghan Songbook Project.

The Grossman Burn Foundation (GBF). Please go to page 91 for information about the Grossman Burn Foundation.

POLITICAL LEADERSHIP/LEGAL TRAINING AND AWARENESS PROGRAMS

Women's Resource Centers (WRC). A total of 17 WRCs have been completed in Afghanistan (one built, in part, by Time Warner and one newly renovated by Afghan Women Leaders CONNECT). The centers provide opportunities for women to gain literacy and computer skills, constitutional/human rights awareness classes, and entrepreneurial and business training.

Capacity Building Project/Afghan Ministry of Labor. Working with The Asia Foundation, the Department of Labor has launched a program designed to increase knowledge and awareness of the new labor code and internationally recognized core labor standards (including anti-discrimination practices) among judges, workers and employers.

The Woodrow Wilson Center and RAND Corporation. Together, these organizations researched and published a comprehensive study entitled "Best Practices: Progressive Family Laws in Muslim Countries" that depicts family laws in 12 Muslim nations.

Afghan Women Leaders CONNECT. CONNECT supports Afghan-led women NGOs, legal aid clinics and other legal institutions that provide training in Afghan civil law/civil procedure codes and international conventions on civil rights.

ENTREPRENEURSHIP/MICROFINANCE PROGRAMS

ARZU. Please go to page 105 for information about ARZU's programs.

The New Hudson Foundation (NHF). Please go to page 122 for information about The New Hudson Foundation's work.

Daimler Chrysler. In 2003-2004, Daimler Chrysler teamed with the Foundation for International Community Assistance (FINCA) and opened seven community banks in Herat Province, providing critical support to women with access to micro-credit loans.

Sunshine Lady Foundation. Please go to page 107 for information about the Sunshine Lady Foundation.

Project Artemis/The Global School of Management at Thunderbird University. Please go to page 115 for information about Project Artemis.

Institute for Economic Empowerment of Women (IEEW). Please go to page 110 for information about IEEW's programs.

PBS/Afghanistan Unveiled. After providing internships and camera equipment to the five camerawomen of the movie *Afghanistan Unveiled*, PBS purchased the rights to the film in 2005 and broadcast it in over 200 affiliates. Later, the film was nominated for an Emmy in the "News and Documentary" category.

HEALTHCARE PROGRAMS

TriWest Healthcare Alliance. Please go to page 92 for information about TriWest Healthcare Alliance.

Future Generations. Please go to page 118 for information about Future Generations.

Grand Rapids Middle School, MI. In 2006, Grand Rapids Middle School raised funds to provide resources to a women's shelter in Kabul for health-care supplies, blankets and counseling.

The Abbott Fund. The Abbott Fund has partnered with Direct Relief International and the Afghan Institute for Learning (AIL) to help reverse the country's high maternal mortality rate and increase the survival and overall health of infants and children by supporting Afghan women through the training of female midwives. To date, the Abbott Fund has given more than $444,000 in grants to AIL and assisted in coordinating $3.7 million in product donations from Abbott. In 2009, additional support will help AIL expand their patient base and ensure quality patient care and services across all three of their clinics (two in Herat, one in Kabul).

Afghan Family Health Book. In 2004, the Department of Health and Human Service, in cooperation with LEAPFROG Enterprises, Inc., launched the Afghan Family Health Book. This "talking book" provides useful and practical information about health practices and hygiene, focusing on health promotion and disease prevention. The books were distributed via hospitals, clinics and women's centers in Afghanistan. Please go to page 154 for information about the Afghan Family Health Book.

REACH Program/Midwifery Training. In 2003, USAWC contributed several million dollars for the pilot phase of USAID's Rural Education and Community Health Care Initiative (REACH), which provides accelerated health literacy training for women and girls to become midwives and community health workers throughout Afghanistan.

Working with the Abbott Fund are Kate Firestone, former board member of Direct Relief International, with Beth Pitton-August, Director of Corporate and Foundation Relations.

ARZU's signature "Hope" rug.

ARZU EVOLVES A UNIQUE SOCIAL BUSINESS TO IMPACT AFGHANISTAN'S ARTISAN COMMUNITIES

ARZU RUGS

ARZU, which means "hope" in Dari, has become an innovative model of social entrepreneurship that empowers Afghan women weavers, their families and their communities. ARZU supports economic sustainability in order to break the cycle of poverty through female gender equality, access to education, healthcare, improved living conditions and the development of vital community improvements from clean water to multi-purpose facilities and community gardens.

ARZU's holistic approach establishes a foundation of stability upon which highly skilled women weavers earn a fair labor wage in order to support their families, refine their artistry, and invest in their future and that of their children. Their prospects shift for the better on a daily basis. Their lives positively change long term. Why?

ARZU epitomizes Connie Duckworth's steadfast belief in the power of women and reflects her own experience working in highly successful, best-of-class, competitive business environments. With ARZU, Ms. Duckworth has created a company where "…the road to equality in every field springs from the practical reality of economic independence."

ARZU is a novel, yet replicable model that ultimately relies, not on public support or private charity, but on its ability to become self-sustaining through the innovative marketing of high-quality artisan products. ARZU connects Afghans' artisan talent with the growing global movement of conscious consumers. It is the ideal union of inventive design and solid business "next practices."

From humble beginnings as a single project engaging only 30 women weavers, ARZU has transformed itself into an example of the virtual enterprise of tomorrow. June 2009 marked the fifth anniversary of ARZU's start-up of in-country operations funded by seed capital from USAID. Today, ARZU's multi-ethnic, all-Afghan team of 32, based in Kabul,

Connie K. Duckworth, Founder and Chief Executive Officer of ARZU Rugs.

Bamiyan and Andkhoi, interfaces daily with a U.S. team located in Chicago, New York, Boston, Sarasota and Asheville, North Carolina. Thanks to modern technology, from the Internet to cell communications, ARZU develops and implements an extensive array of social benefit programs while producing and distributing beautifully designed rugs. All projects are developed at the grassroots level, in cooperation with village Shuras, with respect for cultural sensitivities and with an eye to local capacity building.

ARZU's unique Social Contract promotes life changes. It requires that all children under the age of 15 attend school and that all women in each household attend education classes teaching literacy, basic numeracy and units on health, hygiene, nutrition and human rights. ARZU's women weavers comply at an impressive rate of 90 percent. ARZU focuses on maternal-fetal

health, transporting pregnant women and their newborns to clinics in four-wheel-drive vehicles; sets up emergency mobile phone systems for each village; and develops curriculum for the training of community health workers and deputy midwifes. These efforts have led to a reduction in infancy and maternal mortality rates in every ARZU community. In a country with the second highest maternal mortality rate, no women in ARZU's program have died during childbirth.

To date, ARZU has created more than 600 private-sector jobs, 85 percent of which are filled by previously destitute women, who support more than 2,000 family members in 11 rural villages. The ripple effect from ARZU's many programs positively impacts the lives of some 100,000 Afghans.

Over the past five years, ARZU has developed direct and Internet distribution channels, retail collaborations and contract custom sales in the U.S. and internationally. ARZU is now exploring concepts of lean manufacturing, quality control and environmentally sustainable practices—new to Afghanistan's traditional rug manufacturing capability.

In 2009, the "Common Threads" contemporary rug collection launched through an exciting collaboration with Designtex, the world's largest supplier of commercial textiles. This effort won two of the most prestigious awards, "Innovation" and "Editor's Choice," at NeoCon, the commercial design industry's premier international contract tradeshow.

Since inception, ARZU has received international grants, awards and recognition, not only for design innovation, but also for global social entrepreneurship. Looking to the future, ARZU plans to extend its core values by evolving into STUDIO HOPE World Design. This new umbrella organization will leverage the knowledge gained in Afghanistan to replicate the success of ARZU's social business model—the creation of other artisan design and décor products linked to economic sustainability—for other impoverished populations of women around the world. It is our intent to honor, empower, connect and sustain the hope inspired by the bravery and artisan talent of so many women in Afghanistan.

A BUFFETT—ALWAYS A CAREGIVER—
ACTING TO MAKE CHANGE
THE SUNSHINE LADY FOUNDATION

Like most Americans, Doris Buffett had no real understanding of the lives of women in Afghanistan until she was introduced in 2005 to Dr. Tahira Homayun, president of the board of the Organization for Advancement of Afghan Women (OAAW),[1] by Caroline Firestone at a luncheon in New York City. At the time of their meeting, Dr. Homayun was in need of capstone funding for staffing in order to open the Moshwani Clinic, an outpatient clinic 35 miles north of Kabul. It would serve 14,000 people from nine villages in the town of Kalakan. Dr. Homayun told Mrs. Buffett about a woman she had met whose five-month-old baby froze to death in her arms as she fled over the mountains from Afghanistan to Pakistan. In spite of this tragedy, this courageous woman returned home to Afghanistan after the retreat of the Taliban. Guided by her belief that what one accepts, one condones, Mrs. Buffett realized that she could not ignore the plight of women in Afghanistan. She directed her foundation, the Sunshine Lady Foundation (SLF), to make the donation required to staff the Moshwani Clinic, and she committed herself to reading everything she could get her hands on about the condition of women in Afghanistan.

The Sunshine Lady Foundation's mission is to provide educational opportunities to disadvantaged populations, with a primary focus on battered women. Since 1998, through the Women's Independence Scholarship Program, the SLF has offered college degree opportunities to women all across America who have left an abusive relationship and who pursue an education that will offer them and their children financial independence and lives free from violence. Over 1,000 women have graduated through this program. Opening up the SLF mission to Afghan women was a natural transition for Mrs. Buffett.

Nina Richardson (in blue jacket at left), who showed her documentary on Afghan women at a luncheon to support Afghan women, with Afghan attendees and, left to right, Caroline Firestone, Doris Buffett and hostess Molly Kellogg.

The investment in the Moshwani Clinic was followed by a significant donation to the social-business NGO startup, ARZU, Inc.[2] While ARZU, a rug manufacturing business, was purported to be an "investment in hope," Mrs. Buffett's investment was made based on ARZU's practical business model and the passion and dedication of its founder, Connie Duckworth—much more immediately reliable, Mrs. Buffett realized, than hope. The full amount of the SLF investment was restricted to use in the neglected, underserved province of Bamiyan for a capital project specifically to benefit women (such as a bath house or medical clinic), for staffing and supplies for the rug production business, and for weavers' bonuses.

The local Shura leaders for Internally Displaced Persons.

This investment was quickly followed by a donation to Future Generations[3] for two very specific purposes vetted on the ground by Mrs. Caroline Firestone. First, in collaboration with other funding, money was used to purchase three parcels of land. Additionally, it was used to purchase a building previously rented by the local Shura and for the construction of two other community buildings. These buildings, equipped with solar energy, are now used for Shura meetings and as community learning centers. The second purpose for these funds was to support the training of two women from the Kabul Shura as midwives at the International Mercy Corps training center in Paghman.

Having become more knowledgeable about "how things really are" in Afghanistan, Mrs. Buffett became increasingly proactive in looking for "on the ground" opportunities to provide financial assistance to the dedicated and competent people actually doing the work. She was fortunate to meet Fahima Vorgetts from Women for Afghan Women[4] (WAW), an organization of Afghan and non-Afghan women from the New York City area who are committed to ensuring the human rights of Afghan women. WAW raises funds for reconstruction, particularly for schools and health facilities. Learning of the critical need for washing and reusing gauze in burn clinics, the SLF, through WAW and Fahima, donated funds to purchase supplies and other equipment needed for hospital burn units in Herat, Khost, Gardez and Kabul. The SLF also supported WAW's work by funding the completion of construction of two schools for girls in Saleh Abad and in Neysan—which together serve 2,000 girls—the expansion of a clinic in Mir Bacha Kot and the development of the Family Guidance Center in Kabul, which, in addition to serving as a counseling center for families, also operates as a much-needed shelter for abused women and as transitional housing for women who are released from prison. When the Guidance Center project was begun in early 2007, there were only four functioning "safe houses" for women in all of Afghanistan. A fundamental premise of the WAW program is that women do not have to jettison their culture—or their religious beliefs—in order to take charge of their lives. The WAW Guidance Center offers counseling to men, the perpetrators of violence, as well as to the women and children who are their victims. This use of funds was particularly satisfying to the Sunshine Lady Foundation board.

Also compatible with the mission of the Sunshine Lady Foundation is its ongoing investment in the Initiative to Educate Afghan Women (IEAW), founded by Paula Nirschel, to offer education to some of Afghanistan's highly motivated young women. When Mrs. Buffett learned, in the summer of 2007, that IEAW had 17 women in Afghanistan who had been approved for placement in some of the finest East Coast colleges in the U.S., but who were unable to enroll due to lack of IEAW funding, she pledged the full amount of supplemental funding needed to support them for all four years. Mrs. Buffett has become the stateside guardian for two IEAW students now attending Mary Washington University in Fredericksburg, VA, where Mrs. Buffett lives. This relationship brings comfort and security to the girls and joy to their American "grandmother."

New IEAW students just arrived from Afghanistan.

Paula Nirschel (in blue jacket), founder and facilitator of IEAW, with current class of IEAW students—the younger already in American dress—a group of college-educated women destined for leadership positions in Afghanistan.

The young women of IEAW have promised to return to Afghanistan after their graduation to further reconstruction efforts in their country and to improve the place of women in their society. The Sunshine Lady Foundation also provides scholarship funding for 10 students—nine women and one man—for four years at the American University of Afghanistan in Kabul.

Departing from donations made specifically to advance the education and well-being of Afghan women, the Sunshine Lady Foundation has made investments in two other NGOs working on the ground in Afghanistan. First was a timely investment in Turquoise Mountain Foundation[5] made in the fall of 2007 at the personal request of Rory Stewart at a time when Turquoise Mountain was faced with severe financial distress. The Turquoise Mountain urban regeneration project in the Murad Khane historic district of Kabul successfully captures the imagination of the Afghan aficionado, the yearning of the historic preservationist and the businessman's appreciation of a plan for self sufficiency and deliverables that makes sense.

Less well known but equally inspiring is the work of the Marigold Fund,[6] an organization functioning primarily in the northern province of Takhar with a mission simply to help Afghans rebuild their country while establishing substantial friendship and understanding between Afghans and Westerners. Through the daily work at "ground zero" of field director Gary Moorehead (the only full-time employee of the Marigold Fund), a vital bridge in Taka Timuz was reconstructed, a midwife training program was launched in Takhar and the construction of a regional tuberculosis clinic was undertaken. This clinic will serve as the central outpatient clinic, office and distribution center for coordinating TB treatment in all of Takhar Province. The completion of the construction project before winter 2009 sets in has been made possible by a grant from the Sunshine Lady Foundation.

Doris Buffett believes that Abigail Adams' 1776 warning, "If particular care and attention are not paid to the ladies, we are determined to foment a rebellion, and will not hold ourselves bound by any laws in which we have no voice or representation," is as applicable to the rebuilding of Afghanistan as it was to the founding of America.

At every turn, Mrs. Buffett has been humbled by the bravery, intelligence and determination of every Afghan woman she has met.

[1]Read more about OAAW on page 153.
[2]Read more about ARZU on page 105.
[3]Read more about Future Generations on page 118.
[4]Read more about WAW on page 125.
[5]Read more about Turquoise Mountain on page 46.
[6]Read more about the Marigold Fund on page 204.

PEACE THROUGH BUSINESS®
INSTITUTE FOR ECONOMIC EMPOWERMENT OF WOMEN

- A country that is economically sound has more educated people.
- A country that is economically sound isn't willing to allow others to come in and take over.
- A country that is economically sound has the resources to educate and defend themselves from terrorists and tyranny.
- A country that is economically sound has a greater capacity for peace.

It is widely acknowledged that societies that are economically stable have a much greater capacity for peace. The case for such a bold statement can be found through evidence in the relationship between democracies and their Gross Domestic Product (GDP):

- Democracies are generally stable above $6,000 GDP per capita.
- Democracies are generally vulnerable to coups and civil wars between $3,000 and $6,000 GDP per capita.
- Democracies are likely to fail below $3,000 GDP per capita.

Just to demonstrate the challenge and put this into perspective, Afghanistan's per capita GDP is $1,000 and Rwanda's GDP per capita is $900, according to the CIA's World Factbook. So when analyzing the economic stability of these countries and their capacity for peace, both of these countries are considered "likely to fail."

But the women in these countries are not going to let that happen!

Small business has been the backbone of economic stability, and Terry Neese, Founder and CEO of the Institute for Economic Empowerment of Women (IEEW), believes that women are the key to the development and stability of business in emerging economies. The year 2007 marked the start of Peace Through Business®, a program that helps women entrepreneurs develop the skills they need to start and grow their businesses. That year, the Institute launched the maiden voyage of the program to Afghanistan, where nine Afghan women business owners graduated from an intensive, six-week course. These women spent four weeks in class at Northwood University (Midland, Michigan), where they studied business education that culminated with their in-depth business plan. The incredible part of this program is the fact that their professor at Northwood is from Afghanistan and the curriculum was in Farsi and English languages. The women then spent one week in Washington, D.C., where they met with Mrs. Laura Bush, State Department officials and other government agencies.

Dr. Terry Neese, founder and CEO of IEEW, on the ground in Afghanistan with a U.S. Army security guard.

Khalida Dunya, a 2009 Peace Through Business student, hand-sews soccer and volley balls. She's a protégé of 2007 Peace Through Business student Amir Taj Sirat.

Another week was spent in mentorship with an American woman business owner to learn how to take that business education and implement it into a real-life environment.

It was a remarkable experience not only for the international students, but also for the American mentors. But did it have an effect?

> *Amir Taj Sirat is a quiet, unassuming woman who stands firm in her character. She couldn't bear the thought of children not being educated during the Taliban rule, so she privately taught in her home at great personal risk. After the fall of the Taliban, Taj started a ball manufacturing business where home-bound women could generate an income by hand-sewing soccer balls. Taj knew this was an opportunity for these women to feed their families, but she didn't know if she was profitable or how she was going to sustain her business. After attending Peace Through Business 2007®, Taj discovered*

Khalida Dunya teaches tricks of the ball trade to another Afghan woman in her shop.

Taj Sirat's women employees sew pentagon and hexagon sections together to create soccer balls.

that she was in fact profitable and grew her business to over 250 stitchers. Taj has now announced for Parliament in the 2010 election and looks for further mentorship to help her through that process.

But 2007 was just the beginning for IEEW! The next year, 2008, brought an expansion to the program to include women business owners not only from Afghanistan but also from Rwanda. The Institute now had two separate programs running two weeks apart from each other in separate cities. It was exciting to know that the program was universal!

So many women in Afghanistan are left to fend for themselves, but are not allowed to take a job that a man would want.

Zainul Arab is an unassuming beekeeper who patiently tends not only to her bees, but also cared for other women in her community. Zainul would take a hive and give it to another woman so she could start her business, then formed an association of beekeepers so they could continue to network and learn from each other. Zainul knows that by giving away bees and training others, she is helping her community to grow and be prosperous.

Dr. Terry Neese (center at back), Founder and CEO of IEEW, stands proud with the 2008 Peace Through Business® graduates.

This is one of many shops in Muzhgan Wafiq's closed market for women only. Wafeq is a 2007 graduate of Peace Through Business.

Everyone has felt the pain and tragedy that has occurred in their country, but these women have chosen to do something about it! Realizing safety concerns for women, participant Muzhgan opened a Women's Only Market in Kabul where women can safely and freely go shopping. Master carpet weaver Fawzia, another participant, created a weavers' association to train and network with other women in the art.

Pay It Forward. Each of the Peace Through Business® participants is charged with "paying forward" their education and experience through participation at the In-Country Education classes or other business and/or public policy associations. In essence, women who benefit from the program will, in turn, share their largesse with other women. It is incumbent on the recipients of the education to take what they have learned and teach it to other women entrepreneurs in their country. The Institute's goal is to train the trainers so the country's development can rapidly multiply. For

example, the Institute contracted with an Afghan alumnus to facilitate the In-Country Education program in 2009. Several Peace Through Business® students from 2007 and 2008 spent time in the classroom.

In 2009, Peace Through Business® has evolved to combine both Afghanistan and Rwanda into one program, allowing the women to interact with each other and create a truly international network. The Institute coordinated an eight-week In-Country Education course with a total of 30 women in Afghanistan. From those women, the top 15 from each country were selected to come to the United States for three weeks of intense Leadership Development Mentorship with American women business owners, as well as to attend an International Women's Economic Summit. All events were held at Northwood University in Dallas, Texas. All three weeks are designed to capture the classroom education and apply it in the real world to develop leaders for tomorrow.

What we've discovered about these women is that they are just like us. They laugh heartily, work diligently, cling to each other and love with great passion. All of these women are strong, funny, creative, adventuresome—and perfectly suited to change the world. They will do it quietly as they build their wealth and their country's democracy. For too long, women all over the world have been marginalized, with no rights, no privileges—and the Institute is in a position where we can implement real change. Through the sense of global responsibility, American women business owners are in a position to make a significant difference in the world.

The Institute could not do its work without the support of private-sector funders.

Afghan Ambassador to the United States Said Tayeb Jawad and his wife, Shamim, meet with the 2008 Peace Through Business® graduates.

THE POWER OF DREAMS
THUNDERBIRD SCHOOL OF GLOBAL MANAGEMENT

THUNDERBIRD SCHOOL OF GLOBAL MANAGEMENT

Thunderbird's Project Artemis and the Goldman Sachs 10,000 Women initiative support female entrepreneurs in Afghanistan. After 48 hours of traveling halfway around the world, a group of 14 Afghan women entrepreneurs arrived with big dreams on October 11, 2008, at Thunderbird School of Global Management in Glendale, Arizona.

"My dream is to first expand my cosmetic company and then start an all-women's television production company in Afghanistan," Fawzia said.

"My dream is that all women will be self-sufficient, self-confident and powerful so they can support themselves," Halima said.

"My dream is to care for people in Afghanistan with quality medicine that

Project Artemis alumna Rangina Hamidi with her employees in her Kandahar embroidery business.

we can get from Europe and the United States," said Nafisa, one of two doctors in the third cohort of Project Artemis.

The program, which Thunderbird launched in 2004, provides two weeks of intensive education and site visits in the United States, followed by two years of mentoring and access to resources in Afghanistan. The goal is to empower women entrepreneurs so they can help rebuild their ravaged nation through small-business enterprises that range from construction companies to boutiques and crafts shops. So far, 44 women have graduated from the program.

Ambassador Barbara Barrett, former U.S. Ambassador to Finland and Founder of Project Artemis.

"My dream is to expand my dried fruit company to be the biggest in the world and employ all female workers," said Sediqa, a 2008 participant who helped put the world's economic meltdown into perspective during one trip to an Arizona mall.

All the Afghan women had their special shopping goals in mind … face cream, baby shoes, a nice suit, gifts for the family back home or a splurge at Victoria's Secret. As the women walked past store after store, Sediqa turned to Project Artemis program director Kellie Kreiser and said, "I can see why Americans buy all the time. You are shown so many wonderful things." She swept out her arms to all the shops and displays.

"Yes," Kellie answered. "We are fortunate to have so much, and we do shop a lot."

"But now you have the economic crisis," Sediqa said.

"It's a bad time," Kellie replied.

"But not so bad," Sediqa countered. "I don't think the crisis is that bad. People still eat."

Access to basic needs such as food, clothing, shelter and healthcare isn't always certain in Afghanistan, where thousands of women have crossed back into their native land after being forced out by Taliban leaders who did not allow women to work.

In many cases, the women of Project Artemis not only have found personal business success, but also have extended those opportunities and their business knowledge to other women.

"We women have taken it upon ourselves to stitch the future of peace for our children," said Rangina Hamidi, whose business makes embroidered shawls, pillows and wall hangings. "Embroidery is the skill we have, and love and patience is what we can give to our families and our country. We will work to help rebuild this war-torn nation."

Since completing the Thunderbird program, Hamidi has grown her business to more than 500 employees, and their products are exported worldwide.

The success of Project Artemis has led to other opportunities for Thunderbird to spread its influence in Afghanistan. One of these opportunities came in 2008 when Goldman Sachs launched the 10,000 Women project, a global initiative to provide a business and management education to 10,000 women around the world.

The Goldman Sachs Group, which organized the initiative and funded it through an unprecedented $100 million commitment, included Thunderbird as one of its initial partners after watching the growth of Project Artemis. This new initiative will allow Thunderbird to extend its reach in Afghanistan by educating more women in their homeland through an alliance with the American University of Afghanistan (AUAf).[1]

Through 10,000 Women, a partnership was formed between Goldman Sachs, Thunderbird and AUAf to offer students the Goldman Sachs Business Women's Training Program in Afghanistan.

This program will help train about 460 women over five years through classes in management at AUAf. The alliance also will incorporate distance learning opportunities and create a women's resource center for meetings, computer access and a safe space for networking events. Thunderbird alumni also will have opportunities to mentor these women and share their expertise.

"Investing in the education and economic empowerment of women in developing countries not only improves the lives of those women, but also enriches the entire community," said Thunderbird President Ángel Cabrera, Ph.D. "Our goal is to change lives and create lasting benefit. In Goldman Sachs and the American University of Afghanistan, we have partners who share this goal."

[1]Read more about AUAf on page 99.

COMMUNITIES CREATE SUSTAINABLE PEACE
FUTURE GENERATIONS

Future Generations believes that the communities within countries needing development, rather than outside actors—international aid organizations or governments—must be encouraged and allowed to determine their own needs, decide their own priorities. Only then, in partnership with outside agents, should development projects be implemented. This approach of community-driven development is implemented using a standard process called SEED-SCALE.[1] Instead of starting with a "needs assessment" that focuses on community weaknesses, this development model, used by Future Generations, relies on and promotes existing community success, encourages partnerships between stakeholders and uses community work plans and resources for project implementation instead of external assessment and budgets. Instead of seeking quantitative outcomes, SEED-SCALE seeks behavior change as a more sustainable outcome of partnership with communities.

At a time when so much development work is undertaken using the top-down project approach with limited sustainability, SEED-SCALE is being used in Afghanistan by Future Generations and a select group of NGOs and government entities—such as the Ministry of Public Health (MoPH)—to reform its existing community health program. Known as the Basic Package of Health Services (BPHS), this approach has helped Afghan communities tackle problems ranging from community-based health to literacy and education to local governance and small-scale infrastructure development to environmental rejuvenation. In addition to its own use, Future Generations is witnessing increasing adoption of SEED-SCALE as the preferred approach by others in community-related development interventions.

There is ample evidence in Afghanistan and elsewhere to show that community-driven development is a more sustainable model of promoting socioeconomic change. Take the case of Deh Khudaidad—a one-time slum community that first emerged during the anti-Soviet struggle in the 1980s located at the edge of Kabul City—and how it transformed itself using its own resources and capacities instead of waiting for NGOs and the government to fix its problems. Deh Khudaidad is a mixed ethnic community to the west of the Macrorayan housing complex, which was built during the communist government's rule in Afghanistan. Ethnically, it is a microcosm, representing all of Afghanistan's diverse cultural and ethnic groupings. While the rest of Kabul was going up in flames in the early 1990s with street fighting dividing one district from another and with one neighborhood turning against the other, Deh Khudaidad stayed out of the fray. It is one clear example of how a united and cohesive community can avoid a bloodbath and refuse to perpetuate the hatred that was engulfing the rest of the city.

Mahatma Gandhi had once said that Satyagraha, the non-violence creed he used in his struggle against British colonial domination of the sub-continent, is the weapon of the strong and not the weak. Abdul Ghaffar Khan, known as the Frontier Gandhi, effectively proved that point when he succeeded in mobilizing the most fearsome warriors, the Pashtuns of the Frontier, to create a non-violent army called the *Khudai Khidmatgars* or Servants of God. The transformation was complete. The hot-tempered and violence-prone Pashtuns changed the rules of the game and resisted British rule non-violently. Satyagraha's true potential is revealed when the strong, those capable of violence, decide not to resort to violence and prefer their own suffering instead of inflicting it on others. This capacity for self-control is said to be

the most potent human energy to achieve meaningful social transformation and transform human relationships. The people of Deh Khudaidad had done just that: refusing to kill each other in the name of a religious sect or ethnic group, with neighbors watching out for neighbors, protecting their properties when some of them migrated to neighboring countries or other provinces, and keeping their locality free of violence that had engulfed the rest of Kabul.

They showed a similar capacity for collective action in addressing their community's social and economic problems. Instead of acting for self-gratification, the Deh Khudaidad community, with assistance from Future Generations, formed a local Shura, or council, and elected their representatives who held consultations and developed work plans for community-prioritized projects. With local resources they were able to implement their smaller work plans. They then sought technical and financial resources from outside the community, including government and NGOs, to implement their larger work plans. They started by addressing their chief environmental concern: the dumping of municipal waste near their homes. Working together, strengthening one another, they pressured the Kabul Municipality to end dumping waste in Deh Khudaidad.

Today, instead of receiving Kabul's rubbish, the local district municipality is collecting Deh Khudaidad's waste and taking it elsewhere for disposal. The removal of the waste dump, which was a major source of communicable diseases, dramatically improved health indicators in the community. They then worked together to approach a donor, got the necessary funds and built better latrines in order to avoid having human waste from poorly constructed latrines, known locally as *Khak Andaz*, from leaking into the streets, causing stench and polluting water sources. Water was needed for the modern latrines to function, but the donor who had given the initial funding to construct the latrines refused to provide the additional cash. The Deh Khudaidad Shura, made up of all the ethnic groups, did not give up because of the refusal of a funding request. They approached one donor after another, until the Italian development agency provided them the money to construct a deep well and purchase a generator to pump water. However, the problem was not fully resolved. When the water was pumped out, it had to be piped to every home. The Italian development agency told the Shura that it did not have more money to give. Using a project approach, the donor had decided it had done enough. The community, however, was not satisfied. Despite many requests, no donor came forward to help with additional funding. The community, instead of feeling defeated, once again came together to discuss a resolution to the problem. They relied on their own human energy and capacity for self-help to convince every household to contribute 9,000 Afghanis per household to the Shura, which contracted with a private company to construct two large reservoirs on nearby hills to which water would then be pumped from a deep well sitting at the base of the hills; then pipes were constructed and laid to each household, with a meter to regulate the use per home. The water which was brought to homes using donkeys cost 200 Afghanis per barrel. The piped water using the home-based meter reduced the cost of drinking water by 75 percent.

Today, Deh Khudaidad has clean streets, numbered homes and streets, modern latrines and clean water. This was all possible thanks to the ingenuity and resourcefulness of the Deh Khudaidad community and their belief in a better future. They did not wait for the government, donors or NGOs to come and give them "assistance." They wanted to take their own future in their own hands and to take care of their own problems by coming up with their own solutions. That, they knew, is the road to dignity, self-sufficiency and a sustainable future. Deh Khudaidad offers hope at a time of increasing hopelessness. Deh Khudaidad also changed the way we look at communities. They have demonstrated that it is not always the government, donor or NGO that truly transforms commu-

nity life. In fact, Deh Khudaidad showed us that it is the community's own approach of working together—relying on their own value systems, community solidarity, local knowledge and skills, and household and natural resources—that is the most relevant answer to today's corrupt, ineffectual and highly centralized aid system that is creating dependency and disempowering communities.

If communities feel they are treated as mutual stakeholders and have control and ownership over project activities based on their own prioritization, then they also are the strongest guarantors of the project's success. In today's insecure Afghanistan, it is not the armies or the police that protect aid projects. It is actually the communities, working in the front lines and negotiating space with insurgents, who are essentially protecting many aid projects in rural Afghanistan. They have the greatest incentive to do so. The key to success is that the system is implemented with the people actively participating in it, rather than having been imposed or designed and delivered from outside. By such application, individuals are convinced, and as their numbers aggregate, they grow into collective action. Participation increases through partnership, building from success, acting based on evidence. This, in Future Generations' view, is the way to do community-based development.

[1]SEED-SCALE is an acronym for Self Evaluation for Effective Decision-making and Systems for Communities to Adapt, Learn and Expand. See www.future.org.

PRIVATE FUNDS BOOSTING PUBLIC PROJECTS

THE NEW HUDSON FOUNDATION

PRIVATE FUNDS BOOSTING PUBLIC PROJECTS

In 2006, Caroline H. Firestone realized her passing interest in Afghanistan wasn't passing. It had grown to a passion with increasing intensity. So she created the New Hudson Foundation (NHF) with a mission to help the Afghan people, especially women and children, in the rebuilding of their country. The Foundation believes that by helping to develop a strong Afghanistan, it will also help return American troops home. Usually working in partnership with organizations "on the ground" in Afghanistan, the Foundation's work has been wide-ranging and creative, including education, agriculture, literacy and orphans. Its major projects cover three areas:

MEDICINE AND HEALTH

First, the Foundation adopted the Afghan Red Crescent Society's hospital in Kabul, a project that involved supporting its renovation, including installation of basic utilities—hot water and air conditioning—shadowless lights for its operating theater and English training and computers for all the doctors. The result: The hospital is now able to perform surgeries and is better able to care for sick patients. But more than that, the ARCS hospital now serves as a base for Afghanistan's leishmaniasis and malaria treatment projects. (Leishmaniasis[1] is a parasitical affliction that causes skin disfigurement—usually on the face. With the simple, low-cost treatment now offered at the ARCS hospital, the parasite can be stopped and its disfiguring after-effects eliminated.) In both cases, Afghanistan's goal is to reduce and ultimately eliminate these scourges. The Foundation has provided computers and staff for the program's director, Najibullah Safi, along with funding for treatments.

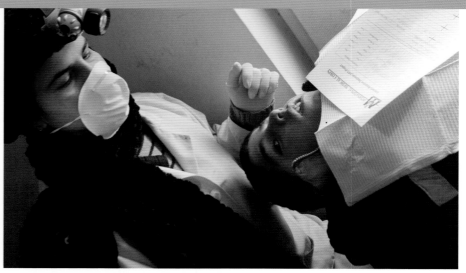

An orphan boy receives his first dental check-up and ART treatment from an IMC-trained technician.

Soon after the U.S. entered Afghanistan it was discovered that dental care was virtually non-existent in the country. In fact, there were fewer than a dozen dentists and the state of oral health was desperate. Teaming up with the International Medical Corps, the Foundation introduced Afghanistan's first community dental project. The program trains workers in Atraumatic Restorative Treatment, or ART, a technique that is both preventative and a way of treating dental decay. In just 40 days, an individual (even with minimal education) can be trained as an ART technician able to administer this treatment that involves cleaning the teeth, filling cavities (virtually painlessly and without anesthesia) with an antibiotic-laced substance that wards off further decay and training in proper dental care. Technicians are now practicing in Kabul while others are being trained to practice ART throughout the country.

STRENGTHENING COMMUNITIES

NHF has addressed community issues in a number of innovative ways:
- One thing that Afghanistan has in excess is sun. But it has lost most of its fire and fuel wood. NHF purchased sun-powered ovens to be installed in homes and commercial establishments in Bamiyan, which

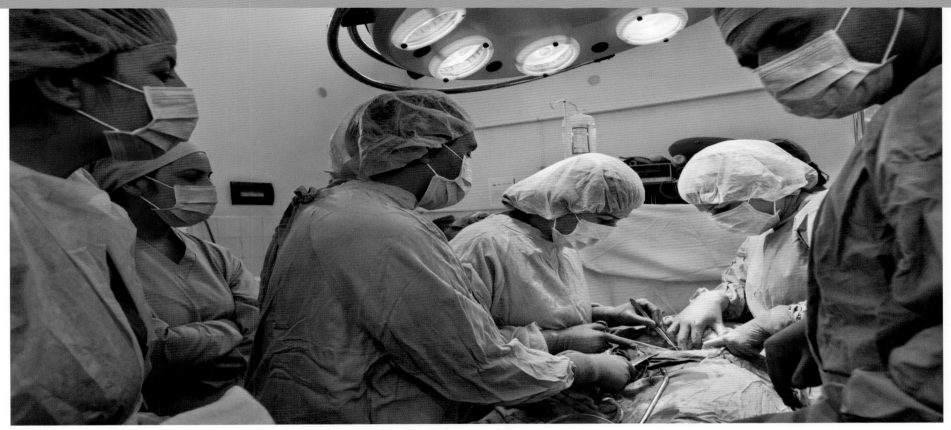

Operating safety is significantly improved with shadowless lights donated by the New Hudson Foundation.

has few trees and is at 8,000 feet. After distribution of the ovens by HOPE worldwide, the NHF paid for a trainer to introduce the ovens to families. Using solar power, these ovens have reduced or eliminated difficulties caused by still inconsistent electrical power and the high price of fuel wood.

- Along with the Sunshine Lady Foundation, NHF purchased land on the outskirts of Kabul that has been developed into three townships for internally displaced Afghans. The gift also included the construction of a municipal building for each township where its Shura can meet. The buildings are also used as a library and meeting place for other community activities.

- To support the Afghan Red Crescent in its efforts to hire and support native Afghan staff and address Kabul's notorious shortage of good-quality housing, NHF, constructed four bungalows and with ARCS, an apartment building to house ARCS employees.

- The Foundation purchased hundreds of computers for use by Afghans participating in training and capacity-building programs including BPeace's Fashion Road Trip, Columbia Teachers College advanced math training for teachers, all doctors at the ARCS hospital in Kabul, and HOPE *worldwide's* training facilities in Kabul.

SUPPORTING AMERICAN TROOPS STATIONED IN AFGHANISTAN

Perhaps the most unusual initiative of NHF has been its program to help the helpers. Remembering that thousands of U.S. troops stationed in Afghanistan are, in fact, individuals a long, long way from home, NHF has sought to make life a little more like home by supplying things from home: long-lasting razor blades that are easy to carry on far-flung missions, meat for special meals and entertainments. NHF has supplied projectors, screens and DVD players for movie viewing—along with hundreds of movies on DVD—and iPods with earphones for injured soldiers awaiting treatment. Though unusual for a foundation formed to help Afghanistan, by improving conditions for America's troops, these efforts, in fact, ease the stress of combat duty and generally reduce pressures in a still less than stable environment.

GOING FORWARD

The New Hudson Foundation is ever on the lookout for new partners and new ideas that will advance the prospect of peace for the Afghan people, improve the day-to-day quality of their lives, and eliminate the need for American troop presence.

[1]Read more about the Leishmaniasis and Malaria Center on page 89.

The new ARCS apartment building with gardens.

Din Mohammad Nazari with his sons in the garden of his ARCS bungalow.

Din Mohammad Nazari and his sons in the living room of their ARCS bungalow.

SHELTER, LEGAL AID AND HOPE FOR AFGHAN WOMEN... AND FAMILIES IN TROUBLE

WOMEN FOR AFGHAN WOMEN

We've all heard the grizzly stories about what life can be like for women in Afghanistan, where they are often seen as simple possessions of their husbands:

- A three-year-old girl is engaged to her seven-year-old cousin in an arrangement that is likely irreversible: When she is 11 or 12, they will marry and spend their lives together. "In our tribe, when they get engaged, they cannot divorce."[1]

- A father trades his daughter for nine sheep to pay off a bad debt. She becomes the wife of the lender's son.[2]

- A rape victim is punished while her attackers go free: A girl's virginity is so highly prized that if she loses it—even for violence done to her—she is deemed an adulterer and becomes unmarriageable—the worst fate in this marriage obsessed culture. A disgrace to her family's honor, she may even be executed. No one knows how many females—women or girls—are murdered each year for shaming their families in Afghanistan and in similarly patriarchal countries around the world where women can be killed with impunity.[3]

- An 11-year-old girl is sold to a 41-year-old blind cleric for $1,200—her "bride price"—used to pay off her father's debts. She is beaten repeatedly by her husband and his mother for not conceiving a child. After five years of torture and an unsuccessful suicide attempt, she runs away. She is taken to an NGO, whose lawyer sues for her divorce. The court sends her back to her husband—despite the fact that she was sold to him (illegal in Afghanistan) and a helpless child when he married her—because he agrees to sign a paper promising never to beat her again. Beatings recur as soon as she returns to her husband.[4]

Today, in 2009, important progress is being made. That last case is a good example. When she ran from home a second time, Maryam sought help from the police. Only recently, they might have taken her back to

WAW's Sunita Viswanath, co-founder of WAW, with a Kabuli client and her baby. The client had run away from home and is now married to the man of her choice. She had become pregnant out of wedlock; WAW managed to keep her out of jail.

her family or to her abusive husband. Alternatively, the police might have thrown her in the detention center since a single woman cannot be alone on the streets. The next stop would be prison. But this time, Maryam had a better result. The police took her to Women for Afghan Women's (WAW) Family Guidance Center (FGC).

This facility, which opened in Kabul in March 2007, is unique in Afghanistan. And while it shelters women and children when WAW counselors and lawyers are working on their cases or when it is dangerous for them to return home, WAW prefers keeping families together by mediating among quarreling parties to find a viable solution for everyone.

Afghan families are especially vulnerable to stress. After 30 years of almost continuous war, virtually everyone suffers some degree of post-traumatic

stress and the jarring shift from a pre-20th century culture to today's global 21st century. Continuing warfare remains an ever-present threat; when U.S. troops were transferred to fight another war, security deteriorated fast. Local Taliban regained power and other Taliban are crossing into Afghanistan to infiltrate once safe areas. Victims of a 40 percent unemployment rate, men can't feed their families; children newly introduced to the concept of marriage-for-love want the autonomy to marry their choice rather than according to parental dictates. Once optimistic about their future, Afghans today feel betrayed by the failure of foreign aid to reach places where it is most needed. As always, these pressures and frustrations wreak their heaviest toll on the lowest beings in the pecking order: females. Women may be battered, sold, handed over to other families as compensation for crimes.

WAW's FGC employs both men and women as counselors and lawyers, who serve anyone who is referred to them by the police, other NGOs or government ministries, or who comes for help under her own steam. In a family-oriented culture, Afghans find it difficult to look outside the family or village structure to resolve problems. WAW's counselors sometimes go to remarkable lengths to make help available. For example, a counselor, "under cover," might reach out to the husband of a client and suggest he get help. Counselors are able to explain the impact—the true cost—of violence on family members. The center offers more than an immediate, one-time fix. Once a resolution has been reached, unannounced follow-up home visits monitor client progress for a year. If counseling alone does not resolve intractable problems or if a woman's life is at risk, the center provides emergency shelter for her and her children. WAW lawyers defend women against charges of adultery (a crime in Afghanistan) and at court proceedings such as divorces. Though frowned upon, divorce is possible. But as WAW executive director Manizha Naderi notes, the cost to women is high: Divorced women lose their children when they end their marriage. According to a Muslim law preserved in Afghan civil law, the father gets total custody of sons when they reach seven years and daughters when they're nine.

WAW's newest Family Guidance Center in Kapisa.

• In round two of Maryam's case, the court has submitted to her husband's considerable power in Kabul and decided to hand her over to him once again. But he has agreed to a divorce if this penniless young woman pays him the equivalent of $1,600. WAW is appealing the decision and expects to win. Meanwhile, about six months ago, Maryam's stepfather sold her younger sister, age nine, to an old man. WAW has rescued this child, who is now a permanent resident of the WAW shelter and attending a private school with five other shelter children in similar circumstances.

For all the horror these stories represent, there is now important progress being made in Afghanistan on behalf of women. The pace of change may be slow and case-by-case, but it is steady. It takes time—at least a generation—and patience when the goal is to instill human rights and gender equity in a culture where tribal law generally recognizes women as mere chattel. In two years, counselors at the WAW FGC have helped some 700 families and are taking on 20 to 30 new cases a month. Because of the success of the Kabul FGC, WAW expanded it to Mazar-e-Sharif (in September 2008) and Kapisa (in February 2009). A fourth FGC, already funded, will open in Jalalabad in 2010. WAW hopes to open a fifth FGC in Kunduz the same year. The centers are funded by international foundations and governments and by individual donations.

Women for Afghan Women was founded in New York City in 2001 by Afghan and non-Afghan women. Their goal: to ensure the human rights of Afghan women then suffering under the brutal Taliban regime. WAW's other project in Afghanistan, the Afghan Women's Fund (AWF), focuses on education and village life. Since 2002, it has opened hundreds of literacy and vocational training classes throughout the country, dug wells in villages and reconstituted agricultural land destroyed by bombs or burned down by the Taliban, and started income-generating projects for destitute women. In the past three years, the AWF has raised money to build five schools for girls: two in a rural area of Herat Province, two in Logar and one in Wardak. Even in conservative areas, village elders, all of them men, beg NGOs like WAW to build schools for their daughters.

In addition to its work in Afghanistan, WAW runs a community outreach program for Afghan immigrants in New York City.

WAW's latest project is a residence for children, six to 15 years old, currently living in Kabul's women's prison where their mothers are incarcerated. The children's residence will open in late summer 2009.

[1]Tang, Alisa, "In Afghanistan, a Fiancee Aged 3," Associated Press, October 13, 2007.

[2]Tang, Alisa, "Afghan Girls Traded for Debts, Blood Feuds," USA Today, July 2007.

[3]Tang, Alisa, "Family Seeks Justice for 7-Year-Old Girl Raped by Two Men in Afghanistan," ABC News.com, August 2007.

[4]Semple, Kirk, "Afghan Women Slowly Gaining Protection," New York Times, March 3, 2009

...A LITTLE HELP FOR AFGHAN WOMEN AND GIRLS

...A LITTLE HELP

After September 11th, the Mayor of Mountain View, California, Rosemary Stasek, traveled with some of her Afghan-American constituents to Kabul to see them begin the process of re-building their home country. The need was vast and there were women and girls who seemed to be left behind by the work of large organizations. Out of a desire to reach women and girls that might be missed, ...a little help was born.

The first project involved reconstructing the women's prison, where no oth-er organizations were working at the time. Many of the women are there for offenses that would never be considered a crime in Western countries such as running away from home to avoid an arranged marriage, being a victim of rape or serving a sentence for a murder committed by a male family member. Six years later ...a little help is still active in the prison, supplying yogurt to supplement the nutrition for the 100 women and their 90 children in prison with them. School supplies are brought to the teenage girls who work to continue their education while in the juvenile detention center.

A wide variety of additional projects involve women's economic develop-ment such as food preserving training, women's health development in supporting maternity wards, women's artistic development in funding con-temporary art classes and girls' media development through equipment for a youth radio station.

As the years progressed, girls' schools came under attack from Taliban forces who oppose girls' education. Yet more sadly, girls' schools weren't

being built because local government officials often took limited funding and built only boys' schools as their priority. Once again, looking to fill a gap, …a little help began the tent project. For $250 up to 50 girls could have an enclosed place to study. In those areas where girls' schools hadn't been built yet, it was a fast, cheap way to get girls out from under trees. But even where there were lovely buildings in which to study, a class without a teacher isn't education. With the amazing dedication of volunteer science teachers from California, …a little help brought science equipment and training to girls' school science teachers in one of the most remote areas of Afghanistan.

There is a tremendous amount of need throughout Afghanistan, but it is important to make sure to not overlook those areas that are most anxious for support. The dangerously violent areas of southern and eastern Afghanistan get a large share of attention and funding from both military and government funders. Yet the northern and central regions—safe, secure areas—seem to get little or no help improv-

ing their education system. And this in an area that gives great priority to girls' education and where families take great pride in making sure their daughters attend school and have every chance to continue on to university where possible. In …a little help's most recent project, a wide range of supplies and equipment were provided to a girls' school in northern-most Badakshan Province. Badakshan was never conquered by the Taliban and they are proud of the fact that many local girls are attending Kabul University. The school had a broad range of needs from infrastructure to furniture to teaching materials. There were so many girls at the school that there weren't enough classrooms, and six classes met outside around the building. Tents created more covered teaching space. Almost 200 desks were built and repaired. A generator now provides power for a computer class. And a full library and science lab get girls ready for their university entrance exams.

There are many large organizations doing tremendous work throughout Afghanistan. …a little help has always tried to find those women and girls in areas that might not be getting the support they deserve. Even in a country where the need can seem overwhelming, a little help can sometimes mean a lot.

MAHBAKHAT, CHILD BRIDE, GETS A DIVORCE
VOICE OF WOMEN ORGANIZATION

The women's shelter in Herat looks like many others seen around the world. There are guards at the heavily fortified gatehouse and three single dormitory-style beds in every room. The building is filled with women who have sad stories of uneasy marriages. But different from most shelters is the presence of 11-year-old Mahbakhat, an orphan whose own life tale—however short—seems more sorrowful than all the rest.

"Now she finds this courage," said Suraya Pakzad, the executive director of the Voice of Women Organization, which runs the shelter, one of the first in Afghanistan. Although the shelter managers say Mahbakhat has gained a lot of weight since she arrived emaciated five months ago, she is still mousey-looking. It is difficult to fathom the slight, cross-eyed child as anything else than a schoolgirl. The youngest wife in the shelter barely speaks and stays burrowed in Ms. Pakzad's arms throughout an interview. "She's just a kid," Ms. Pakzad said.

At age nine Mahbakhat was an unhappy orphan, living with her brother and his wife. There aren't many details from this period, but the girl believed life was unbearable enough that she set herself on fire with matches and oil—a common method of suicide among Afghan girls and women. She badly burned her arms, chest and face. When asked, she shows her scars with trepidation. She doesn't like to talk about it because her brother, who is her guardian, thinks it was an accident.

After she was burned, her brother had Mahbakhat engaged to a much older man. He told her that with her scars it was unlikely anyone else would ever want to marry her.

Seven months ago, the marriage vows took place and she moved in with her 45-year-old husband. The man told Mahbakhat's brother he wouldn't have sexual relations with her until she was a few years older. But her husband broke this promise and Mahbakhat became his unwilling lover once, twice or several times a day, Ms. Pakzad said.

Mahbakhat ran away from her husband and back to her brother's house. Her brother's wife helped Mahbakhat get to the shelter—an unusual act in Afghanistan. "This is the first time I've seen a woman help a woman," Ms. Pakzad said. "Usually the abuse woman-against-woman is the worst."

Ms. Pakzad said when Mahbakhat arrived at the shelter, she had terrible infections and was in so much pain she could not sit down comfortably. She often cowered in the corner of the room and would not speak to anybody, even as the other women around her joked and worked at needlepoint.

Mahbakhat, which means "lucky moon" in Dari, now has to stay in the shelter until she can get a divorce. Otherwise the men in her family will take her back to her husband. Once the divorce goes through, she will return to the home of her brother and his wife. Her brother will be asked to sign a paper promising that Mahbakhat will not be married again until age 18.

Now, months on, Mahbakhat is beginning to smile regularly, talk a bit more and take delight in her pink painted toes and fingernails. She will travel to Kabul next week for surgery to try to fix some of the damage that has been done internally to her young body. Pakzad hopes to get her surgery for her scars as well.

It is some happiness to Pakzad, a married mother of six, who has been crusading for women's rights in Afghanistan since the Taliban days of the late 1990s. Secretly at home in Kabul she taught school classes to girls and women. "I cannot see a woman suffering," she said. "We are half of the population of the world. We are created by the same God."

Although women are not completely confined to the house as they were in those years, and Pakzad can now teach in the open, Afghanistan remains one of the most conservative countries in the world. Any woman who comes to her shelter is automatically tainted in the eyes of many.

The shelter started up because several years ago, the United Nations High Commissioner for Refugees found itself with a problem—what to do with the few single Afghan women who were among the masses being deported from Iran. Herat is about 100 kilometers from the border with Iran and there is a constant flow of Afghans being "repatriated." Single women cannot rent accommodation on their own in Afghanistan, and if they had no family to return to, they ended up in being put in jail because there was no other place for them.

By early 2006, the shelter had become a haven for women whether they were coming from Iran or not. Currently there are about 36 women and six children, even though the shelter should only be housing 25.

But the shelter itself is in a bit of danger. Ms. Pakzad has had regular funding for the past two years but that will run out in January. She is hoping one of the Western government or non-government organizations will come to her aid and provide the $10,000 it takes to maintain the shelter each month. Ultimately, she said the Afghan government should be paying for the costs. "We cannot think about sustainable projects," Pakzad said. "We are looking for a donor."

And it seems there will always be a need. Mahbakhat's case is far from being exceptional. Ms. Pakzad can't remember whether Mahbakhat is the youngest wife that has ever stayed in the shelter or not. Marriages at age nine, 10 or 11 are unusual but not unheard of, and forced marriages are still the norm in Afghanistan rather than the exception. The Women's Ministry and women's organizations say about three in five girls in Afghanistan are wed before the legal age of 16. "This situation is not common but also not rare," Ms. Pakzad said.

Kelly Cryderman, National Post, December 02, 2007
Reprinted with the express permission of CANWEST NEWS SERVICE, a CANWEST Partnership

MOTHERCARE AND CHILDCARE

TERRE DES HOMMES

Terre des hommes (Tdh) was founded in 1960 in Switzerland by Edmond Kaiser with a mission to come to the aid of children. It endeavors at all times to defend the rights of children—in times of war, natural catastrophe or in less publicized situations of distress. Tdh has been working in Afghanistan since 1995 when it began helping street children (now assisted by the CRR III, funded by the EU). Under the Taliban regime, informal schools were created for girls.

Tdh has provided Mother and Child Healthcare since the beginning in the very disadvantaged areas of Kabul and Kandahar. Tdh is also active with development activities in Takhar Province with a livelihood project funded by the Swiss Federation.

In Afghanistan women and children are especially vulnerable. Today, 40 percent of Afghanistan's population is under 15 years old. Out of 100 children, 20 do not reach their fifth birthday; 26 more will die before the age of 45. Women give birth, on average, to seven children. One mother dies every 30 minutes due to pregnancy or childbirth complications. This rate is 60 percent higher than in industrialized countries. Of those maternal deaths, some 80 percent are preventable.

The following stories illustrate how Tdh's Mother and Child Healthcare program serves the most vulnerable of Kabul and Kandahar:

Karishma, 16 years old, was introduced to Tdh activities when registering for the Home Visiting Program (HVP). She said she was a Shamshad TV employee and wanted to be a movie star. But after working with Shamshad TV for a year, she fell in love with the brother of Shukrya Barakzai, an elected member of the Afghan parliament. Though the relationship lasted only a few months, Karishma became pregnant. When her family, relatives and friends tried to work out an agreement with the baby's father, they were unsuccessful and reported the case to the police. Both Karishma and the father were imprisoned, but the father was released two months later. Since Karishma was pregnant, she was jailed in Kabul's chastisement house (Daruttadeeb). Seven months later, she was carried to the Malali Hospital and delivered a baby boy. Just four hours after delivery, she was returned to the chastisement house. When Tdh midwives met her two days later, Karishma was pale and anemic, her blood pressure was low, she had a high fever and serious signs of infection. She was neither able to nor interested in feeding her baby. Tdh midwives gave her breastfeeding counseling and other new mother education.

They also supported her psychologically. Her roommates were also encouraged to help her. Slowly, Karishma improved and she started to feed her baby regularly. Now, while she waits for a decision from the court, Tdh midwifes regularly pay her visits while she and her baby continue to improve.

Rahima was 18 years old and pregnant the first time a Tdh midwife met her in her home on an HVP visit. She was afraid for her pregnancy since her husband beat

her regularly and would not allow her to go out from her small room or to be in contact with her own family. By the Tdh midwives' second meeting, Rahima was sad and depressed. She cried, telling the midwives that she had tried to jump down a well the night before but was rescued by her family. Rahima, injured in the fall, said she did it because of the oppression by her husband. According to the working procedure of Tdh/Home Visiting Program, the midwives examined her, gave her health instruction, provided basic medicines and psychological counseling. They also gave her their phone numbers in case of emergency or any problems. Rahima did have problems—the result of a beating—and the family called for assistance. Based on a physical examination, her blood pressure was very low and she was in shock. Because the husband had no car, the midwife gave Rahima an emergency infusion and called an ambulance.

Rahima delivered her baby at the hospital, was taken home after 24 hours and received follow-up visits from Tdh midwives who continued health instruction and nutritional information. The midwives were unable to visit Rahima again for nearly a month, at which time her husband called the midwives to come for a visit. When they arrived, he was feeding his baby and told the midwives that his wife had escaped to her father's house. Tdh midwives used this opportunity to talk to him about his behavior and responsibilities. He finally agreed to go to his father-in-law's house and to ask him if Rahima could come back home. At their last visit, the Tdh midwives found Rahima at home with her husband; her physical condition was good and she was psychologically supported. The baby also gained weight. Rahima is now happy because her husband no longer treats her badly and is grateful to Tdh midwives. She's now busy transferring her experience and lessons learned to the other women in her community.

DEMANDING JUSTICE FOR RAPE VICTIMS

Ali Khan braved death threats and public scorn to out the powerful men he accuses of gang-raping his 12-year-old niece. Now he says it is up to Afghanistan's president to prove he can prosecute her assailants and their warlord protectors in the country's north, where President Hamid Karzai's government holds little sway.

Rape—a crime long hidden in Afghanistan by victims fearing a life of scorn—is getting a public airing in this conservative Islamic country. In recent weeks, several outraged families have appeared on nightly news shows, demanding justice while sharing heartbreaking stories of sexual assaults on teenage daughters.

Government officials say at least five rapes have been reported in the past four months, though they and women's rights groups say any reported statistics likely fall far short of reality. The Interior Ministry has announced a crackdown on sexual assault, one of the first times the government has acknowledged a problem long dealt with as privately as possible. On Sunday, President Hamid Karzai called for rapists to face "the country's most severe punishment."

After families appeared on TV, Karzai met with Khan and another man whose daughter was raped in Sari Pul. The president promised punishment as he "hugged my niece and said she was also his daughter and cried."

But it could prove a formidable task for Karzai, whose government has little influence outside the capital. In northern provinces like Sari Pul, warlords command private armies and well-connected criminals regularly bribe their way out of prison. "Some of them (criminals) are taken to the jails, but because they belong to the commanders, they pay money and are set free," said Parween Hakim of the Revolutionary Association of the Women of Afghanistan.

One of the men accused of attacking Khan's niece was convicted of rape a month ago and sentenced to nearly 20 years in jail. But Hakim said she has never seen an assailant serve more than six months. Still, there are signs of progress. The government fired five top police officials in Sari Pul for negligence in the two cases.

Interior Ministry spokesman Zemer Bashary said officials are taking action because the five rape reports must mean other assaults are being committed. But he calls the few public cases a hopeful sign. "Families are trusting the security forces and reporting these incidents," Bashary said.

Khan said his niece was raped when five men broke into the family home two months ago. They beat his sister and her husband and forced themselves on the girl. The father remains hospitalized. Khan says he's received death threats since going public, and his sister and niece have not left a guarded Kabul hotel room—provided as a safe house by the government—for two weeks. The girl's mother recognized two of their attackers as associates of a provincial lawmaker, Khan said. The lawmaker's son is one of those accused of involvement in the rape of Sayed Noorullah Jafery's 13-year-old daughter in Sari Pul in February. Both Khan and Jafery say they can identify the girls' attackers, but that the powerful family is shielding the men.

Calls to numbers held by Paunda Khan, the lawmaker accused of protecting the attackers, went unanswered. The head of the Sari Pul provincial council, Abdul Ghani, said Paunda Khan had done nothing to obstruct justice.

In both cases, police initially refused to take down the families' accusations—a situation the U.N.'s Special Representative for Children and Armed Conflict, Radhika Coomaraswamy, said is typical in a region where police are more likely to answer to warlords than to Kabul. "It's because of the impunity given to these warlords for such a long period of time," Coomaraswamy said.

If the rapists continue to escape punishment, it could push the region to reconsider the liberties given to women since the fall of the Taliban regime. Even Khan suggested that the easing of Taliban-era restrictions that kept women at home might be making girls easier prey. "These days all these young girls are going to school and coming out of their houses. These criminals chase after them," he said. "When these criminals come, they commit rape as well."

Jafery says he's lost confidence in the system because while the lawmaker's son has been arrested, he is being tried as a juvenile after producing papers showing his age as 16. Jafery says the man is in his early 20s.

Another family that went public with a rape last year has since been shamed into fleeing the country, according to Hakim of the women's rights group. And in another northern province, Kunduz, police say a man arrested for allegedly raping a nine-year-old girl escaped last week after three days in jail. He had not been tried.

But Khan says he will wait for Karzai. He had to talk his sister's family out of collective suicide, persuading them to travel to Kabul to demand government action. "This is like a revolt against the warlords by my family," he said.

Heidi Vogt with contributions from Rahim Faiez, The Associated Press, "Rape Allegations Force Afghan Government Crackdown," 11/08/2008.

BARTERING BOYS

Afghan parents are selling their sons to wealthy women unable to have their own. The trade in children is a result of the country's battered economy and the failure of foreign aid to reach beyond the coffers of the central government in the capital Kabul. While girls are rarely traded, boys can fetch substantial sums—at least in the eyes of the poor couples who give up a child simply to allow the rest of the family to survive.

Mehran Bozorgnia, a cameraman working for Channel 4 News, witnessed the sale of an eight-year-old boy, Qassem, to Sadiqa, a wealthy woman from Kabul, outside the northern city of Mazar-e-Sharif. As the meeting began, the boy's father, Nek Mohammed, knew he only had a final few moments with his son. Sadiqa was business-like. "Kiss your father and mother goodbye now—it is time," she said, before handing over $1,500. Mr. Mohammed began to weep.

The translator accompanying the cameraman said, "Sadiqa, this is wrong!" "Yes you're right. It's cruel," she replied, before claiming, "But I have two aims here. First, to give this boy a bright future and a good education. And second, to save their other children. The winter's coming and I've given them money so the children don't die of hunger."

Mr. Mohammed said, "I sold a piece of my heart to stop my four other children dying of hunger. I don't have an elder son. I'm also sick. My kidney is failing. My body is in pain." For Mr. Mohammed, selling a child was the only way to keep his other children alive. The plight of many Afghans is now so desperate that selling a child is increasingly routine.

But there is another threat to the welfare of the young—and their parents. Afghanistan's boom business is kidnapping. There were at least 180 documented abductions in the past seven months in Kabul alone. The going rate is around $71,000 to release the sons of the wealthy.

One kidnapper in Kabul who spoke openly about his trade said he had no problem targeting the rich. "We're not dealing with poor people," said the man, who claimed his name was Mateen Khan. "We are only going to kidnap people who have foreign money from all around the world and who have taken it for themselves. We are going to take their children. You see their six-year-olds sitting in the back seat of a Lexus—the latest models. People abroad couldn't afford these cars. So we kidnap these type of children to get the money off their families—the money they've stolen."

In a stable he showed off a teenage boy who was blindfolded and bound and plainly terrified. "We'll sell him or take his eyes out and bring him to the eye hospital and call his relatives. Or we'll sell him to the Taliban," said Mateen Khan. Although he said his gang had no formal ties to the Taliban, his admission that he did business with them appeared to confirm speculation surrounding the Islamist group's involvement in the trade in children.

His threats were all made within earshot of the teenager, whose fate is unknown.

Alex Thomson, "Afghan Parents Selling their Sons to Survive," The Daily Telegraph, December 23, 2008.

MORE ABOUT WOMEN AND CHILDREN

Kabul: A Woman Caught. Muhibi is an unusual Afghan in that she has just graduated from Methodist University in the U.S.—with the blessings of her father. Now the most educated person in her village, she has established the 100 Mothers Literacy Program to teach young mothers in rural Afghanistan how to read and write. But, like most young Afghan women, she's been betrothed to a man for many years. Her fiancé since she was seven years old lives with her family and works in telecommunications. Her parents now are insisting that she forgo further education to marry him. There is no answer yet. But as Muhibi says, "Somebody has to stop this, and somebody has to say, 'No. I respect you still and I love you still, and you are still my parents. But I don't want to marry this guy.' It should stop somewhere, and I am the one who I feel should do that."[1]

Eraq: School for Women. Literacy makes all the difference. Before, even going out shopping was impossible because it's impossible to tell currency apart. With literacy, the task is easy and the illiterate person gains the confidence to speak out. The effort of numerous NGOs to provide literacy training to Afghan women is paying off. In Eraq, in Bamiyan Province, for example, more than 3,000 women in nearly 200 villages have attended literacy circles over the past year and a half. Sometimes at great expense: Some women walk up to two hours each way to come to literacy class. Afghanistan's growing number of primary schools for boys and girls have reduced opposition to women's learning—especially if vocational training like sewing sweetens the pot.

Kabul: A Seminar on Women's Rights in Islam. In May 2009 Afghanistan's Minister of Women's Affairs, Husan Bano Ghazanfar, hosted a seminar on women's rights in Islam. The first time female Islamic scholars from countries around Afghanistan have convened, the program's purpose is to give Afghan women direct knowledge of women's rights and responsibilities according to the Koran.

Kabul: Art About Ideas. Medica Mondiale, a German NGO, has been teaching contemporary art to Afghan women at the Female Arts Center, part of Kabul's Center for Contemporary Arts in Afghanistan. This is a new avenue of expression for Afghan women, who tend to have little sense of inner life or imagination and are loath to express personal feelings or thoughts. Traditional crafts like embroidery or jewelry offer little room for personal expression. Emerging women artists find that through their painting they are able to address subjects still primarily taboo in Afghan society.

Takar Province: Speaking Out About Child Rape. "In our society, it is not the perpetrator of the act of violation who carries the shame of dishonor. It is the victim, who's condemned to an eternally cursed life." That's how it's always been in Afghanistan. But it's changing, partly because of Afghanistan's new and vigilant media. A 2008 kidnap/rape/murder case committed by the son of a member of parliament shows how Afghan society is changing. Rather than pushing this unfortunate family event under the carpet, the father of the eight-year-old spoke out on Afghan TV along with the families of other victims; the families showed themselves to the public and talked about their misfortune. The media's campaign for justice for child rape victims resulted in the dismissal of involved government employees, arrests and even public discussion by religious scholars condemning the sexual abuse of children as a "grave sin."

[1]Reid, Sarah A., "A Young Woman Is Caught Between Promises," Fayob Server, May 2, 2009.

EDUCATION

REBUILDING AFGHANISTAN ONE BOOK AT A TIME
THE LOUIS AND NANCY HATCH DUPREE FOUNDATION FOR THE AFGHANISTAN CENTER AT KABUL UNIVERSITY

The Dupree Foundation is an educational, scientific and cultural charity founded in 2007 by New Yorker Mary Anne Schwalbe. It aims to ensure the sustainability of the Afghanistan Center at Kabul University (ACKU), to raise awareness and broaden knowledge about the history and culture of the people of Afghanistan throughout the United States, and to support the cultural heritage preservation, information-sharing goals and research efforts of ACKU.

THE DUPREES AND ACKU

BACKGROUND

Americans Louis and Nancy Hatch Dupree met in Kabul, Afghanistan in the 1960s. Both were documenting the development of Afghanistan—he a former paratrooper and Harvard-educated archeologist, and she a social historian writing books on Afghanistan and its culture. In wildly romantic fashion, they fell in love and joined forces quickly. From that time onward, they worked together in the cause of Afghanistan and the Afghan people. The books they wrote about Afghanistan are considered classics—the gold standards—still unparalleled to this day.

In the late 1970s, just prior to the Soviet invasion of Afghanistan, the Duprees relocated from Kabul to Peshawar, Pakistan, a notorious frontier town near the Afghan-Pakistan border and Khyber Pass—a well-known hangout for spies, drugs and arms dealers, mercenaries and others involved in intrigue. This mix of characters was changing and swelling in number due to the influx of those fleeing Afghanistan—members of the aid community, political activists, journalists, exiled citizens, former government officials and refugees. The Duprees began to collect all of the material on Afghanistan that passed through this community—books,

Nancy Dupree conferring with supporters about the archive.

into a unique, detailed and accurate record of everything that happened in and around Afghanistan from then onward. Meanwhile, back in Afghanistan, such materials were being destroyed, forced underground and falsified. Therefore, the Duprees' collection became, in essence, the "national memory" of Afghanistan—the only accurate and complete record in existence about modern Afghanistan.

This collection continued to grow, even beyond Louis' death in 1989, with Nancy perpetuating the project. Today, Nancy Dupree is perhaps the world's foremost expert on Afghanistan, and has dedicated her life to this damaged but fascinating country.

THE AFGHANISTAN CENTER AT KABUL UNIVERSITY

In 2004, when she deemed the archive could be secure in Afghanistan, Nancy Dupree moved the collection of then 37,000 items to Kabul and established it as the Afghanistan Center at Kabul University (ACKU)—a resource and research center to be used in the rebuilding of Afghanistan and thereafter. Kabul University lent space in its main library to house the

Nancy Dupree introducing school girls to an ABLE library delivered in 2009 to their school. The library (in shelves and on table) is the first for this school of 6000.

reports, documents—as Louis would say, "…everything on Afghanistan," including the rare output of the Mujahedeen press. While the resulting collection was originally intended to create a resource center for all the different aid workers and Afghan experts who could no longer travel freely in war-torn, occupied Afghanistan, this growing body of information turned

collection and cataloguing facilities, and a garage in its transport sector for ACKU's administrative office. The ACKU collection has now grown to 45,000 items, as new reports, documents and literature are added every day. The entire corpus is currently being digitized so that it can be accessed not only in Kabul, but around the world.

While this collection is unique in the world, it is one of the two collections that comprise ACKU's archive.

The second ACKU collection is equally unusual and important—and this is the collection of books that make up the ABLE program. ABLE is a box library or mobile library scheme that provides books to communities in every one of Afghanistan's provinces. Many of the books that ABLE distributes are ones that are actually produced by ABLE itself. ABLE personnel identify topics of interest (usually practical topics such as homemaking, health and farming methods), hire an author to write the book, review the manuscript with the ABLE editorial board, publish it and then distribute it all over the country. ABLE books are written to the level of the newly literate, but not in a manner that is childish or condescending. Each book is issued in both Pashto and Dari, the most popular local languages in Afghanistan.

ABLE places a metal book box (mobile library) in a shop, a mosque or other community gathering place in rural villages. In most of these communities, the ABLE books are the only printed material available—there are no other magazines, newspapers or books. ABLE also supplies libraries to some high schools, and is starting a pilot program to supply libraries in provincial council headquarters.

BLE currently has published 160 titles. The most recent are two on democracy, one describing what a democracy is, and the second describing not only the rights an individual has in a democracy, but also the responsibilities one has. This is sorely needed in a country with a fragile new democracy, where citizens' rights and responsibilities in this form of government are poorly understood. ABLE has also just completed a book funded by the World Health Organization on tuberculosis.

ABLE has reached a phase of maturity where it is ready to add a number of new titles and reprint very popular titles whose supplies are depleted. Each ABLE book costs $1. An entire ABLE library (500 books) thus costs $500. Funding one of these titles or libraries is a remarkably good investment in the future of Afghanistan. It is something that donors can fund that is immediate and tangible. Putting these books in the hands of the people, helping them become literate, and disseminating helpful information is something that makes a difference here and now. It is harder for tyrants and despots to manipulate the thinking of people if the people can read and access information for themselves.

So these two one-of-a-kind collections—the large historical, political and cultural archive that underpins the research aspects of ACKU and the ABLE collection of original books to be sent to every corner of the country—make up one of the most unique libraries anywhere and the most significant library in Afghanistan. It will serve Afghans for generations to come.

A NEW HOME FOR ACKU AND THE FUTURE

ACKU is currently involved in the construction of a new home for its collections and activities, a purpose-designed landmark building on the campus of Kabul University. The construction of this building is being funded by the Afghan government. The building will include space for the archive,

a large reading room, conference rooms, a gallery, courtyard and office space for the staff of ACKU, IT and cataloguing space and a sizable area for all activities of the ABLE program. This new building is expected to become a prominent center for cultural events—debates, conferences and a significant stop on tours of Kabul. It will be a place where students, scholars, policy-makers, business leaders and journalists can meet to carry out research and to present points of view and craft approaches that will help build a free, democratic Afghanistan.

CONCLUSION

The Dupree Foundation is convinced that ACKU is a project for the generations. Its effects will be felt for decades to come. At the same time, it will have immediate impact. Every $1 book sent to the provinces will be passed around from hand to eager hand, and assist in educating the Afghan people. It is one way that donors can see their contributions put into immediate use for the lasting betterment of the Afghan nation. The Dupree Foundation proudly supports the programs of ACKU, and aims to sustain it in the years to come, when ACKU will continue to provide the historical identity of Afghanistan.

EDUCATING COMMUNITIES
GREG MORTENSON—CENTRAL ASIA INSTITUTE

Saida is a serious and quiet brown-eyed girl who has spent most of her young life amid war and poverty. But she knows the value of education.

"It is very important to learn and to know things," she said. "It helps to know how to read the signs, understand what we are told at the medical clinic. If we don't have knowledge, we have nothing. But if we get knowledge, then we will have something."

The oldest surviving child in her family, Saida prodded her father for permission to attend school after her brother, Gulmar, died in 2004. Gulmar had been herding goats near a Central Asia Institute (CAI) school being built in a village south of Kabul. He stepped on an old Soviet landmine, which exploded and killed him.

When Greg Mortenson, CAI's founder and executive director, visited Gulmar's grave to pay his respects, Saida was right there, "tugging on my clothes" pleading with him to help convince her father to allow her to attend school. "She's really earnest, really determined," he recalls.

Eventually, she prevailed. The family moved to Kabul in 2006 and enrolled Saida in CAI's "displaced girls' school" in a private home. The school caters to families who want their daughters to get an education, but fear for their safety in a more public venue. The space is donated by a family; CAI pays the teacher's salary and buys supplies.

The displaced girls' school is a customized solution to a unique problem. Most of CAI's Afghanistan schools are more traditional; the bulk of them in Badakhshan Province and a small but growing number in Kunar and Panjshir provinces.

The nonprofit organization, based in Bozeman, Montana, began in the early 1990s in northern Pakistan. Mortenson told the story in his book, *Three Cups of Tea*. In the years since, CAI has established more than 100 schools in remote regions of Pakistan and Afghanistan.

"Central Asia Institute's mission is not to put in hundreds of schools everywhere. That is the job of governments," Mortenson said. "Instead, our focus is in areas where there are little or no education opportunities, which generally are in three locations: areas of extreme physical isolation, areas of religious extremism or religious intolerance, and areas of conflict and war."

Key to CAI's formula, too, is that the schools are truly community based, he said. "All our schools are initiated, implemented and managed by local communities," Mortenson said. "We do not use 'outside' contractors. CAI provides skilled labor, materials, school supplies and, most importantly, teacher training and support. The community matches that with free land, free resources like wood, and free or subsidized manual labor equal to up to 50 percent of the CAI contribution. In addition, all schools have a local education committee that oversees the school."

Achieving all that means building relationships, which can take years. But Mortenson has long held that the solution to Afghanistan's overwhelming problems lies in working within the country's provincial, tribal structure.

CAI expanded into Afghanistan in 2001, when Mortenson and Sarfraz Khan, CAI's Pakistan-based operations director, met with tribal leaders in Badakhshan, a mountainous and isolated region where schools, electricity, good roads, safe drinking water and healthcare are all scarce. But the region has, as the World Bank noted, "a strong history of community participation."

Camel taking load to Bozoi Gombad, Wakhan Corridor, 2007.

And that's what has made CAI such a good fit. But such work can be time consuming. And logistics can be daunting.

In Bozoi Gombad, a remote village in the eastern Wakhan Corridor, it took Khan two years of meetings with community leaders to decide on the location, size and type of school that would mesh with the nomadic Kyrgyz lifestyle. Once the deal was sealed, CAI's masons had to walk for three days carrying heavy loads of tools and equipment. Materials were trucked in on an old Soviet tank trail from Tajikistan. The masons spent the summer of 2008 hammering rocks to create stones for a two-room school.

Further west is CAI's biggest project in Badakhshan, the Ishkashim Girls High School, which opened in 2008. The 12-classroom school accommodates up to 1,800 girls in two shifts each day, double the capacity of the local government school.

"The hilltop school vantage is stunning," Mortenson said, "with the tower-

The Sitara School in Sarhad Village—first CAI school in Wakhan.

ing Pamir range to the north, the rugged Hindu Kush Mountains to the south. And it's amplified by the hope and joy the young women have to be able to realize their lifelong dream of education."

In Badakhshan, as it does everywhere, CAI emphasizes girls' education. Some schools are girls only, others, especially in places where there are no other schools, are co-ed.

CAI recently built two girls' primary schools in Panjshir. CAI staff traveled to the area in 2008 and met with provincial education officials.

"They said there was a need for dozens of schools," CAI field consultant Doug Chabot said. "They said there were teachers and students, but no buildings. The children were being taught in the dirt. And we said, 'We can probably help you out with that.' We explained CAI's interest in girls' schools

148

Rubina, widow in Wakhan Corridor, spinning wool.

… and they were very open to girls' schools."

In Afghanistan, focusing on girls' schools may seem like a dangerous proposition. Yet CAI's schools remain safe—for two basic reasons. First, the attacks tend to take place in places where CAI schools are not. Second, CAI works hard from day one to ensure that there is resounding community support in any village where it builds a school. Sometimes that takes years. But the payoff is that once a school is built and students enrolled, the villagers protect the school with their lives.

Although such work comes with a certain amount of risk, Mortenson said no other investment is more effective for reaching development goals than educating girls. It is something he learned growing up in Tanzania, the son of Lutheran missionaries. "It goes to the African proverb I learned as a child: 'If you educate a boy, you educate an individual. But if you educate a girl, you educate a community.'"

But education alone isn't always enough. Other, seemingly peripheral projects have proven key to CAI's success. "CAI takes pride in the fact that it tries to make sure, as much as possible, that there is clean drinking water in the schools and good latrines," Mortenson said. That means drilling a well, piping water from a nearby spring or erecting a water tank. "This is particularly important in order to attract girls to school."

Health and sanitation are also built into the CAI curriculum, which generally mimics the national curriculum: standard reading, writing, arithmetic, science, geography, English, Dari and/or Pashto, Arabic and Islamiat studies. But a unique program teaching hygiene, sanitation and nutrition begins in the early grades.

Education will always be CAI's focus, but Mortenson said the schools inevitably become a community hub, which has led to other projects.

"They become catalysts for adult literacy centers," he said. "In some cases, they are a central location from which the community can start revenue-generating projects, like poplar tree plantations and poultry farms or vocational centers for women, where women are taught sewing, knitting and embroidery skills."

In Kabul, in addition to the displaced girls' school, CAI tried something new: a computer center. Wakil Karimi, CAI's program director in Afghanistan, came up with the idea and its success has exceeded everyone's expectations. In addition to young people seeking computer literacy, language and math skills, the center's nontraditional students include business owners, doctors and other professionals. "Already more than 1,000 people have graduated, about half of whom are female," Mortenson said.

"People are coming from distant cities in Afghanistan, from Jalalabad and Kandahar," he said. "One benefit is that it is not in central Kabul, where office space is cost-prohibitive and security and other issues become a concern. That in turn makes it accessible to the average Afghan."

The program has been so successful, in fact, that CAI expects it will soon be self-supporting, perhaps even generating money for other CAI projects in Afghanistan.

SCHOOLS.
BUILD US SCHOOLS.
JOURNEY WITH AN AFGHAN SCHOOL
BY JULIA BOLZ
A SEATTLE ATTORNEY

When my American colleagues and I first started working in north-central Afghanistan in January 2002, we spoke extensively with community leaders. Time after time, we heard, "Schools. Build us schools." They clearly understood that education is a building block to eliminating poverty, oppression, and extremism.

Julia Bolz and students.

When I returned to the U.S. after my first trip to Afghanistan, I thought of the kids and communities constantly. It was as if they had become etched on my heart. There were no schools, no teachers, no books, no pencils. Nothing. Everything had been destroyed by decades of war. Those kids fortunate enough to attend school after the Taliban had been removed from power often sat in a dirt field writing on a blackboard that leaned against a mud wall. Others sat in tents open to the elements. Afghanistan was truly the poorest of the poor. It led the world in child and maternal mortality, homelessness and landmine victims. Life expectancy was 43 years of age. And, in our region, the literacy rate was 6.5 percent. There was no hope or opportunity, especially for women.

Together with friends and family, I founded a project called "Journey with an Afghan School" to build and supply schools for kids, particularly girls, as well as build bridges of understanding between our countries. To date, we have built (or rebuilt) and supplied 30 schools and two teacher training centers, serving over 25,000 Afghan students and hundreds of teachers. We also have provided schools with clean water; distributed textbooks and supplies; provided teacher trainings, libraries and computer centers; and facilitated cultural exchanges.

Every few years, I conduct a study to understand what is working (and not working) within the schools. Are we actually making a difference? The results we found were not simply good but phenomenal:

• Education decreases harmful traditional practices, like early childhood marriage and female genital mutilation, as well as child slavery. In our case, girls were no longer getting married at seven or nine. In fact, we have a number of students who are now in their late teens and early 20's. Further, kids were no longer being sent to Pakistan or Iran to work for pennies.

- Education leads to longer and healthier lives. We found that fewer children were dying of preventable diseases like dysentery and dehydration. Suicide and depression had vastly decreased as well.
- Education leads to lower birth rates. If I asked a girl, "How many children did your mother have?" many said 14. Then I asked, "How many do you want?" Most said two. Interestingly, we also saw that boys wanted fewer wives.
- Education teaches much-needed leadership skills, civic responsibility and life skills. And it is paramount for freedom and democracy. We found families participated more fully in the political, social and economic development of their communities, and more women ran for office and voted than in almost any part of Afghanistan.

I could go on and on. Former Secretary General of the United Nations, Kofi Annan, once said that, if you educate a child, you educate a family. To educate a family, you educate a community. To educate a community, you change a country. I saw this firsthand.

Another thing I found was that education brought hope and opportunity. When I had spoken to kids several years ago and asked what they wanted to do when they grew up, there was silence. Nobody had a vision for their country or their future. They were focused on survival. Now almost every student talks about the future. I especially remember the responses of three girls:

One said, "I want to be a teacher so I can improve my community and make my country less dependent on foreign assistance." Another said, "I want to be a teacher so I can make sure that girls are taught about math, history and science. Not just the Quran." The last said, "I want to be a teacher—NO, I don't want to be a teacher—I want to become the Minister of Education so I can ensure there are schools for not only boys but girls!"

I also interviewed the Minister of Education in one of our districts. I asked, "What do you think has changed the most in the communities since we started building schools?" Without hesitating he smiled and said, "HOPE. You've given us hope again." I'd love to share one short story with you to illustrate this:

It took place back in 2002. It happened at that first girls' school we built. You have to imagine the excitement in this community on the day the school was opened. There was a huge celebration with music, songs, speeches and a feast. It was something that the community will remember for years to come. Some 420 girls showed up that day. Everyone went home with new school supplies.

Despite the new school, there were a number of girls in the community who were not at the ceremony. Their fathers did not believe that girls should be educated. One was a little Afghan girl who was about nine. I don't know her name, but I'll call her Parvana. While all of her friends started the first grade, she was ordered to stay home.

You can just imagine Parvana with her long black hair and twinkling brown eyes. Day after day, she saw her classmates walking into school, each wearing a new black school uniform with a white chador over her head.

Seeing the excitement of her friends, she started sneaking into school. Realizing the danger, Fatima (the principal) pulled Parvana aside one day and warned her of the severe consequences if she were caught. Although she could have been publicly whipped or stoned for disobeying her father, Parvana simply asked the principal not to tell her father. She felt that education was so important to her, she would take the risk.

Days went by and Parvana continued to show up at school. Then, one day, as dreaded, Parvana didn't show up at school. Fatima feared the worst.

Well, this is what happened. Earlier that week Parvana's father had received a letter from a relative in Pakistan. He was illiterate; he couldn't read it.

Nor could anyone else in his family. Subsequently, this little girl bravely came forward and told her father that she could read it for him. Instead of beating her, he embraced her. Although he was shocked, he was proud. She was the first person in three generations to read in his entire family.

This story reverberated throughout the district. Our girls' school went from 420 girls and eight teachers to almost 1,000 girls and over 20 teachers. Soon afterwards, other girls' schools in the area started and blossomed as well. This one little girl had caused an amazing ripple effect.

I could go on and on with my stories. Children who used to carry weapons and fight in school yards are now playing soccer together and learning a common language. Parents from multiple ethnic groups, who fought for decades, are participating in Parent Teacher Organizations. Putting aside the three R's (reading, writing and arithmetic)—what these schools are doing is nation building and creating peace within Afghanistan.

The Afghans have a lovely way of saying thank you. They put their right hand over their heart and say "*tashakor.*" It's like I'm saying thank you from the bottom of my heart. On behalf of the thousands of Afghan children and families that I have come to know over the past eight years, *tashakor* to all of you for helping make a difference in Afghanistan.

Uniquely, some 50,000 citizen diplomats across America support "Journey with an Afghan School." They come from public and private schools, family foundations, book clubs, giving circles, various religious institutions, businesses and nonprofits, like National Geographic Society and Rotary. To learn more about Julia's work, go to www.ayniedu.org.

BUILDING BASICS
ORGANIZATION FOR THE ADVANCEMENT OF AFGHAN WOMEN

The oganization for the Advancement of Afghan Women (OAAW) was founded by a group of professional Afghan-American women working and residing in New York and New Jersey. The board members and staff work as volunteers in the U.S. and Afghanistan. Currently OAAW has two projects in Afghanistan, Aymini School and Moshwani Clinic.

Aymini School is located in Chilstoon, a western suburb of Afghanistan. The school was built from the ground up with the help of USAID. It has 20 modern classrooms, which accommodate 4,000 students in three separate shifts. The school, which opened its doors in March 2007, has a library, health center and a canteen, which was built by OAAW.

The Aymini school in 2004 was a group of classrooms in a ruined building.

The new Aymini school, opened in 2007, is a model modern school.

Moshwani Clinic is in the Kalakan region of Afghanistan. Thirty-five miles north of Kabul, the clinic provides primary healthcare to nine villages in the area. It is registered with the Ministry of Public Health, and OAAW is in the process of opening a vaccination center and family planning program for local women. The Organization for the Advancement of Afghan Women is sole financial supporter of this clinic.

READING... LEARNING... RESPECT
AFGHAN INSTITUTE OF LEARNING

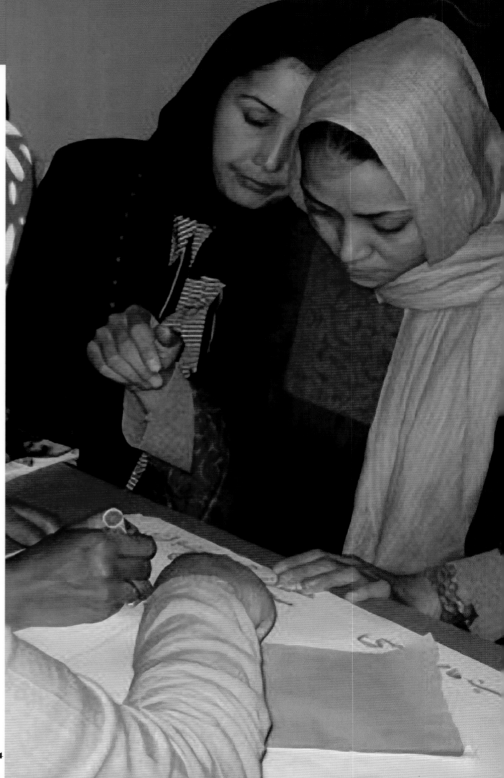

The major goals of the Afghan Institute of Learning (AIL) are to provide a holistic education for Afghan women and children, train teachers in interactive methodologies and provide human rights and leadership training to Afghans. AIL pioneered the concept of community-based Women's Learning Centers (WLCs) and has supported over 150 WLCs, providing education for 150,000 Afghan women and children since 2002. AIL's concept for WLCs has been replicated throughout Afghanistan. In addition, AIL has trained more than 16,000 teachers in interactive student techniques—a program initiated by Dr. Sakena Yacoobi. These teachers now provide a higher-quality education, based on critical thinking skills, to 500,000 children annually. The 5,000 Afghan women who have received human rights and leadership training through AIL are now leaders in their communities.

A few years ago, AIL began offering "fast track" classes in its centers to shorten education time. These classes allow girls who missed schooling to catch up and mainstream into a regular schools.

An equally important purpose of the fast track classes is to offer educational opportunities on an accelerated basis (fast track) to women and girls who are not allowed into schools because of their age or marital status or because there is no school in their area. Included in the curriculum of all fast track classes are messages on health, human rights, peace and leadership. The positive impact of the fast track classes, particularly in rural areas, has been astounding.

Malika's story is typical of older students in AIL's rural centers.

My name is Malika. I am now 27 years old and a student and teacher in the AIL center in my village. It has been wonderful for me and my family. My family did not think a woman of 21 with children and the heavy workload that every woman in the village has to perform could be able to learn new things.

My hand was not used to holding pen and chalk. I had never seen anyone in my family write or read when I was with my parents. It was hard for me in the literacy classes to write a word or make a sentence but my teachers encouraged and helped me. They said not to believe the old ideas "that older people can't learn how to read or write." I wanted to be literate so I can help my children with their lessons.

Six years have now passed and I am in the sixth grade. I have not only become a literate person but know many things like famous poets, writers, Afghanistan history, geography, religion and Pashtu language. I have knowledge about the human body and health. I have learned math and geometry. I help my son who is in first grade and also my daughter in fourth grade. We both try to help each other with our lessons. I learned to sew and I earn good money from my sewing skills. I use that money on my children's education and if there is any left over I help my family. I also completed the Holy Quran class and am able to teach it to my children. Do you know— since I have had all this success I am eager to learn more and more.

Recently AIL started the CHW program in our village. I started this training and now know about diseases and prevention of disease. I give advice to women on reproductive health. I know first aid and can do dressings and give injections. I can prescribe for common illnesses.

Last year, our center needed another teacher. I was chosen as a first grade teacher and received training from AIL.

I am able to do all of this because I am literate. I am respected in my community now. I am extremely grateful to AIL and its people who caused my life to be changed. If AIL was not in our village I would have remained as an illiterate and useless person and I would never have been able to serve my people. Now I can have an effect on others. I learnt from AIL and now I help others to learn and that is the new meaning in my life.

Malika's story is similar to the story of many of the women who come to AIL's fast track classes. The success of AIL's centers is now having a larger impact: When other communities see what their neighbors have done, they come and ask for support for a center in their community.

The Afghan Institute of Learning is an Afghan women's non-governmental organization which was founded in 1995 by Dr. Sakena Yacoobi to help address the problems of poor access for Afghan women and children to education and health services, their subsequent inability to support their lives, and the impact of this lack of education and health on Afghan society. AIL is an organization run by Afghan women that plays a major part in reconstructing education and health systems capable of reaching the women and children of Afghanistan—whether in refugee camps or in their homes in Afghanistan.

AIL has offices in Kabul and Herat as well as one in Peshawar, Pakistan. Serving 350,000 women and children annually, AIL is run by women and annually employs about 480 Afghans (over 70 percent women). AIL offers pre-school through university education and training opportunities to over 25,000 women and children annually and healthcare to 200,000. AIL has been project partner with Creating Hope International (CHI), a 501(c)(3) non-profit in the U.S.—since 1996. Through a long-term technical assistance agreement, CHI provides advice, training, financial management and fundraising assistance and acts as fiscal sponsor for AIL upon request. AIL's founder, Dr. Sakena Yacoobi, has won numerous awards for AIL's work including, most recently, the Henry R. Kravis Prize in Leadership for her outstanding work.

OTHER ACTIVITIES AIL SUPPORTS THROUGH ITS WOMEN'S LEARNING CENTERS INCLUDE:

- **Teacher Training**. AIL has trained over 16,000 teachers in student-centered teaching techniques, dramatically improving educational quality for hundreds of thousands of Afghan students.

- **Human Rights and Leadership**. Afghan women have learned how to advocate for their basic human rights and developed leadership skills through AIL's Human Rights, Leadership and Democracy workshops—all culture-based, grassroots-oriented, participatory and dialogical trainings.

- **Home Schools**. Through its Home School Project, AIL kept education for girls alive during the Taliban years, providing underground education for girls in grades one through eight.

- **Health Programs**. AIL has four basic health clinics and mobile health clinics that serve over 10,000 Afghans each month. The clinics also provide health education to over 10,000 women and children monthly.

In the words of Habiba Sarabi, the governor of Bamiyan Province, who was trained as an AIL Teacher Trainer:

It was AIL that trained me and was sending me to camps in order to hear and feel the problems of my poor countrymen. That is why people in America call me "People Minister." The training and experience I received from AIL is unforgettable for me.

ACCELERATED LEARNING TO RECLAIM A "LOST" GENERATION

AID AFGHANISTAN FOR EDUCATION

Aid Afghanistan for Education (AAE) was founded in 1996 in the days of the Taliban when girls were permitted no education and women were confined to home. With a goal of empowering women and rehabilitating the education system in Afghanistan, its first projects were clandestine: Hassina Sherjan, AAE's founder, returned to Afghanistan from years in America to establish secret schools for girls. During those years Afghanistan's school-age population was 4.4 million, but enrollment in primary schools hovered as low as 38 percent for boys and just 3 percent for girls. As bad as those rates were, they dropped precipitously at the secondary and university levels. The sad result: Afghan youth have fallen behind the rest of the world, leaving Afghanistan with lots of catching up to do.

Now a not-for-profit registered in Afghanistan and the U.S., AAE has developed a strong two-pronged strategy to achieve its mission:

Accelerated Learning. In March of 2002, after the defeat of the Taliban, three million Afghan students returned to school: 48 percent of them were in grades one, two and three, and 35 percent of that group were "over-aged" girls. These numbers prompted AAE to embrace a program of remedial, accelerated learning instruction, a program geared to assist students to catch up on the six years of education they lost during the Taliban era and then integrate them into the regular school system. With accelerated learning, students are able to advance two grades in a single year. Originally working only with women and girls, AAE now also provides Integration for Boys in Need and has over 300 boys enrolled in the program.

27, she is about to embark on the next stage of her dream to be a surgeon. "I wish to be a surgeon and to continue my studies. I want to help the Afghan people and be able to support myself."

To ensure the quality of AAE instruction, AAE employs credentialed teachers and, going a step farther, gives each teacher bi-annual training. This strategy has resulted in the added benefit of helping the teachers move from rote-based teaching to a more participatory, thought-based method.

Throughout, AAE has worked closely with Afghanistan's Ministry of Education to ensure that AAE programs provide an avenue that will successfully integrate its students into Ministry of Education schools. AAE is now registered with the Ministry, and an agreement has been signed for AAE schools to be integrated into the regular school system as a program. The Ministry provides standard textbooks to AAE students and monitors AAE student exams.

A less formal aspect of AAE's education program is the creation of libraries, each with 200 to 400 books covering topics such as the history of Afghanistan, literature, geography and poetry.

• Over the past two years, AAE has graduated a total of 120 students from high school—the first time students have successfully graduated from an NGO program.

AAE students are encouraged to read and to participate in reading-based games such as "poetry fights" and student knowledge competitions.

Razia, a new AAE graduate, has been accepted into the medical faculty at Kabul University. "During the Taliban times my family went to Pakistan [where] I decided I would be a surgeon." Razia was attending 12th grade when the Taliban captured Kabul. She returned after their defeat and joined the AAE program. Now, at age

Vocational Training. Launched in 2009, AAE's vocational training program targets over-aged girls in grades 10 through 12. It provides instruction in office management, basic accounting, computer skills and English language. With this training, students have the option of going into the workforce if they decide against going on to university studies. This aspect of AAE's work is especially important for empowering the widows of

Afghanistan and helping them achieve self-sufficiency. Work for these women translates to survival, not only for themselves, but enables their children—Afghanistan's next generation—to continue their education, thus creating a sustainable future for Afghanistan.

Within the next two years, these key AAE programs will be integrated into the Ministry of Education's program in order to establish a system of education/vocation for Afghan women who wish to continue their education and become active members of their society.

AAE provides other programs geared to eliminate barriers to education and these, along with its core Accelerated Learning and Vocational program, are helping to resolve Afghanistan's critical shortage of skilled workers. At the same time, AAE is giving Afghan women a stronger voice in claiming their human rights while preparing them to participate in the social, economic and political life of their nation.

TRAINING FOR BUSINESS
INTERNATIONAL ASSISTANCE MISSION

The International Assistance Mission's (IAM) Business Development Project targets low-income families living in poorer areas of Kabul. BDS provides two types of training: (1) adult literacy, teaching women to read and write in Dari, and (2) very basic business skills, training in a "hands-on" way.

The literacy classes are designed for women who have some handicraft or tailoring ability but who have never been to school. These women live very restricted lives, hardly ever traveling further away than the immediate area around their houses. These literacy classes give them the rare chance for social interaction outside the family. They learn from each other and from their teachers. Literacy not only gives women the ability to read and write; it increases their status in society, providing the self-esteem to interact with the wider society, expands their understanding of the world around them and enables them to explore new opportunities with more confidence.

In response to student requests for more teaching about business issues, BDS teachers arranged an extra course that teaches the basic elements of business principles and practices. It specifically covers market research, marketing, understanding competitors, quality assurance, product development, pricing and other business skills in a simple way. BDS has also produced illustrated "picture book" training materials so women who are just beginning to read can develop their reading skills and at the same time gain further understanding about business-related issues.

As part of the course, selected students are taken into the local bazaar and through coaching, mentoring, encouraging, supporting and practical guidance, their IAM teachers help them compare quality and prices of materials available and talk to shopkeepers to learn what products sell and if they would buy from a new supplier. None of these women would have had the confidence or the initiative to approach shopkeepers without the help and support of their teachers.

One IAM student wove carpets at home but earned only about 50 Afs ($1) a day. She wanted to find markets for her tailoring skills. With IAM teachers taking the lead, she approached several shopkeepers. Eventually one of them said that he had many customers wanting to buy dresses with mirror embroidery as decoration, but was short of them in the shop. Our student said she could make those, and an agreement was reached that she would make a sample dress and bring it back in a few days' time. She actually made two dresses, and when she showed them to the shopkeeper he was so pleased with the quality and design that he bought them both and ordered another 10, paying her 350 Afs ($7) for each. When she calculated her expenses, she realized that she had made 260 Afs profit for three days' work—increasing her daily wage by 75 percent.

AIL works with individuals who struggle to live their daily lives, provide for their families and serve their community. The role of BDS is to give them the skills to help them move forward confidently into a better future: their own and also the future of Afghanistan.

IAM has worked alongside the Afghan people since 1966 and is known by many Afghans for its work in eye care. During the past four decades IAM has trained Afghans through its health and development projects. Currently IAM employs about 500 Afghan staff, many of whom now run IAM projects. IAM now has about 60 expatriate volunteer professionals and about 40 dependents who also volunteer their skills.

A SCHOOL UNDAUNTED
THE REBUILDING AFGHANISTAN FOUNDATION

The Mayar Elementary School in Wardak Province.

The situation in Afghanistan at a critical turning point—the Taliban were effectively expelled from much of the country and much foreign aid was beginning to flow towards Afghanistan's reconstruction. Alexandra and Elizabeth wanted to participate in this historic effort and, in particular, they wanted to bring assistance to Afghanistan's young women and girls who, for the first time, had a chance to receive a much sought after education. They were struck by the fact that these girls, many of whose mothers or aunts may have been teachers, doctors

The Rebuilding Afghanistan Foundation (RAF) is a New York-based 501(c)(3) determined to bring education to Afghan children by raising money in the private sector to fund U.S.-based charities building schools and developing educational programs in Afghanistan. RAF is committed to the idea that education is essential for Afghan society to flourish, for its people to be self-reliant and for the nation to exist as a free and independent state.

The Foundation's roots reach back to the spring of 2003. While on holiday in the Czech Republic, Alexandra Coolidge and Elizabeth Hartnett started to craft the very beginning of what would become known as RAF. They saw

or other professionals in the 1960s, had no exposure to any school books or learning. Like Alexandra and Elizabeth, they had a profound thirst for knowledge, but unlike them they were unable to realize their dreams.

Upon their return to New York, Alexandra and Elizabeth gathered together like-minded young New York professionals and hosted a fundraiser to benefit The Children of War's school for orphans in Kabul. The event, held at the Bryant Park Hotel in September 2003 and titled "An Evening in the Gardens of Babur," was a huge success and featured keynote speakers James Woolsey, former Director of the CIA, and Mansoor Ijaz, who is currently on the RAF Advisory Board.

Elizabeth Hartnett, Alisa Tugberk de Macedo and Alexandra Coolidge setting place cards for a dinner at Le Cirque to raise funds for Afghanistan.

A few short months after this, spurred by the success of the initial event, Alexandra and Elizabeth filed to form the Rebuilding Afghanistan Foundation as a registered nonprofit organization. This spring marked RAF's sixth birthday. The organization has grown from a fledging group to a highly regarded foundation attracting some of the most sought after speakers on Afghanistan. RAF's annual fundraising dinners have included General James L. Jones, National Security Advisor; Ambassador Husain Haqqani, Pakistan's Ambassador to the U.S. and Lt. General Brent Scowcroft, former National Security Advisor.

With funds raised to date, RAF's primary project has been the construction of the Mayar Elementary School in the province of Wardak, Afghanistan, which opened its doors on October 12, 2005 to 400 children in the village of Sheikh Yassin. The Mayar School, founded as a school for girls, is now co-educational. The curriculum is comprised of basic math, science, religion, geography and reading and writing. Since 2005, RAF has been the

school's only sustaining sponsor, funding approximately $26,000 per year of annual recurring operating expenses. RAF remains dedicated to supporting the school until the expenses can be financed by the Ministry of Education in Afghanistan.

The Mayar School, like many girls' schools across Afghanistan, has suffered through difficult times. The school has been attacked on three separate occasions. The first attack took place on the eve of the school's ribbon-cutting ceremony, when a security guard knelt down to pray and discovered a wire leading to a bomb laid under the school. Luckily the Afghan Army arrived in time to dismantle and remove it. The second attack took place during a wedding in a neighboring village, when village boys, who were jealous that the girls had a beautiful new school while their school was falling apart, lit a pile of desks on fire, burning the roof off the structure. RAF funded the roof repairs and learned from this experience that it was best to make the school co-educational, educating girls in the morning and boys in the afternoon. A third attack was launched in April 2006, when armed extremists tied up the school's security guards and fired missiles at the roof, burning the roof off once again and damaging the interior. Determined not to let the terrorists win, RAF stepped up to rebuild the school once again. RAF has coordinated with the local Provisional Reconstruction Teams to try to procure additional security at the school, and it has worked with the school's directors and local village elders to help end the violence at the school. Today, the school serves approximately 300 boys; approximately 100 girls are being educated through formal home schooling programs paid for by RAF. The local village elders ultimately decided to remove the girls from the school for their own safety. The girls are to be kept in the home school program until it is safe for them to return to their former classrooms.

Today, the Foundation's Co-Directors include Alexandra Coolidge, Elizabeth Hartnett and Alisa Tugberk de Macedo.

Students at the Mayar Elementary School, Wardak Province.

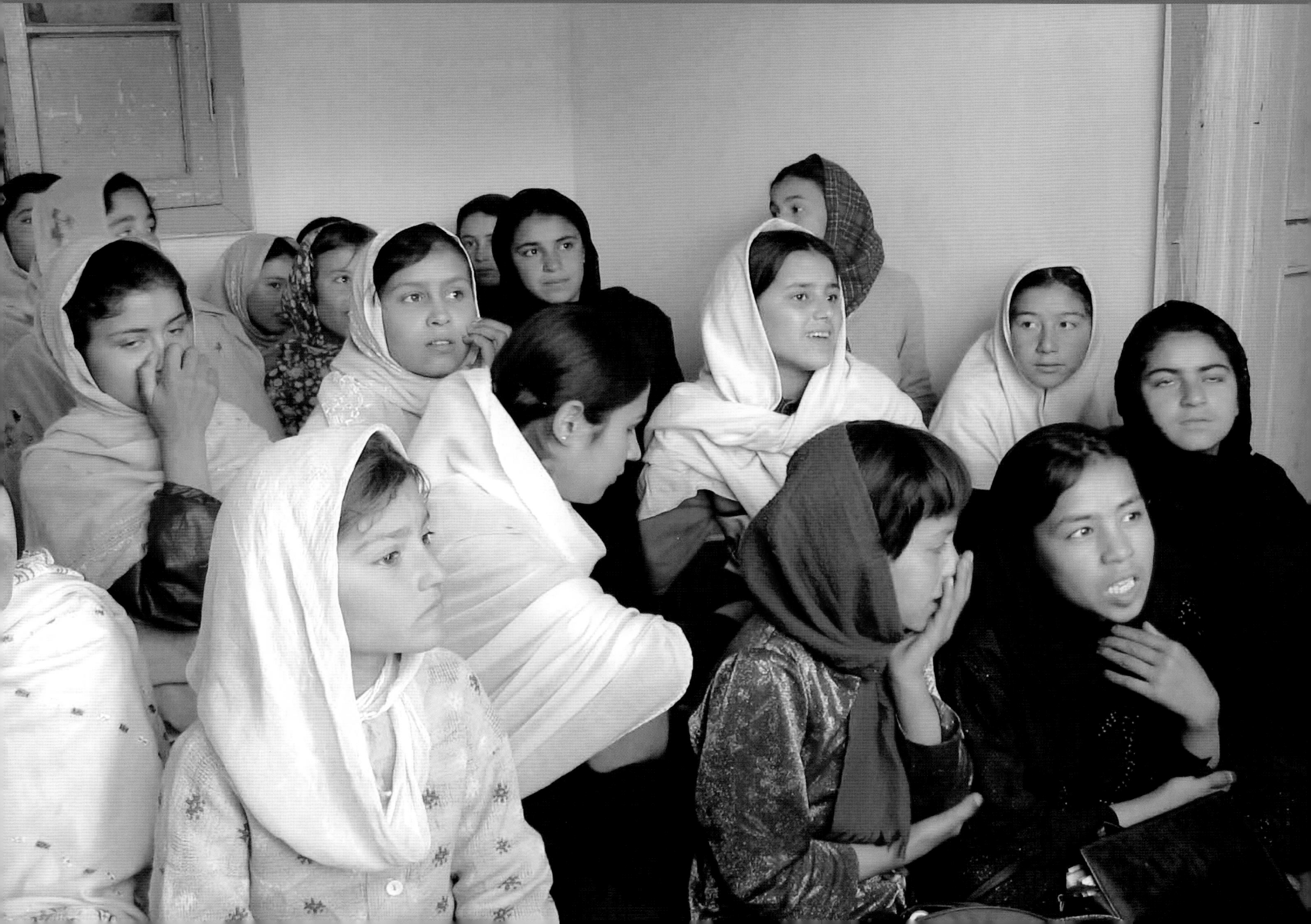

A CHAIR, A DESK, AN EDUCATION
POUND RIDGE COMMUNITY CHURCH

The Pound Ridge Community Church is continuing to expand its meaning of community by including the farthest reaches of the globe. Late last year members of the church decided to provide chairs and desks for students in the Hazarajat region of Afghanistan. To date the church has raised about $9,000 on the way to the $15,000 goal needed to provide school furniture and other supplies for about 400 students.

The Church World Service, a cooperative humanitarian ministry comprising 36 Protestant denominations, provides assistance to more than 80 countries. The church initiated a project a few years ago to supply water to the residents of a small village in Malawi, a small country in Western Africa, whose citizens were required to walk miles for water two times a day. The church helped build two wells in a village.

Working with Church World Service, the church also donates time, energy and money to Crop Walk, a hunger relief charity that raises funds every October and feeds the hungry of the world.

The Malawi project and Crop Walk engendered a good feeling among the parishioners in the church, according to Ken Swenson, a member of the church. The church's concern for all of humanity is the basis for many projects, "and there are many, but I think the difference of the Malawi project compared to some others was that it had length and it was done in a way that we could educate ourselves about a subject," Mr. Swenson said. "There was also a high level of confidence in Church World Service because of other projects that we had done with them over the years."

Mr. Swenson said several members of the congregation were asked to pick a project that interested them and where the efforts of the church would do some good. Many people liked the plan to supply chairs and desks because they felt that educating people in the region could have a very positive impact toward furthering democracy and in the process would educate members of the parish about that part of the world.

Marvin Parvez, director of Church World Service in Pakistan/Afghanistan, will talk Sunday morning during the 10 a.m. service in the Hazarajat region, which received the desks and chairs. "He knows this project intimately," Mr. Swenson said.

Chris Herlinger of Church World Service said that a school desk and chair are signs of dignity in Afghanistan, where poverty and illiteracy are commonplace. The Hazarajat region is especially isolated, politically unstable and subject to food shortages that make education a secondary concern after the fight for survival. Mr. Herlinger said that landmines should be added to the perils of the region. "To get from the capital of Kabul to Hazarajat, you drive through gorges and fields all sullied by mines placed during 20 years of war and upheaval," he said.

Din Mohammad, a school principal in the region, makes a connection between a desk and chair and the desire to attend school and learn. "When students were sitting on the ground, they weren't so eager to come to school," he said in a written statement provided by Mr. Swenson. The arrival of desks and chairs increased attendance by more than 150 students.

"That is not surprising," Esehaq Zerak, a director of support programs in Ghorband, Afghanistan, said in describing conditions in correspondence received by Mr. Swenson. "Chairs and desks can be an incentive for a community to improve their schools."

A school in Ghorband, a community in Hazarajat, educates about 400 girls compared to over 1,750 boys. The boys have a larger space to learn, while the girls are crowded into a much smaller area, and yet the girls display a greater eagerness to learn and are grateful for the desks and chairs, according to Mr. Herlinger.

Din Mohammad said that the schools are in need of repairs that must be accomplished before the country can progress. "The foundation of Afghanistan's reconstruction will be education," he said.

Captain Evan Swayze, the son of Ebie Wood, a member of the Pound Ridge Community Church, is a doctor in the United States Air Force who was deployed to Afghanistan twice during Operation Enduring Freedom. He said his most recent tour took him to a remote region in the southern mountains of Afghanistan, where he worked with area residents on projects that included road construction as well as well-digging and medical services.

"Providing care for local nationals was very rewarding, but also frustrating due to the limited services I could provide in such a remote region, where people live in mud huts and cook over an open flame," Dr. Swayze said in a letter addressed to the church. "I so often wish I could do more."

"In part, the Christian message is learning to love God and our neighbors, and our neighbors are not just those that live next door, but they live at a distance and may even have quite a different background or lifestyle than we do," Mr. Denton said. "That puts us in touch with people not only in Pound Ridge, Mount Kisco and New York City but also globally."

He said the difficult conditions in Afghanistan were brought home as he looked out his window and saw the million-dollar project that enhanced the Pound Ridge Elementary School and thought that for $38 a student, much good work could be done.

"Because of the disruption caused by the Taliban and the military intervention more recently and the need for education, it was thought that we should do something positive in the area," Mr. Denton said. "My hope is that there may be some town folks that say, 'Yeah, that makes sense to us,' and they would join with us in helping us to reach our goal."

Those wishing to donate can make a check out to the Pound Ridge Community Church and mark it for the Afghanistan Fund. For more information, contact the Rev. Frank Denton at 764-9000.

Thank you for donations to the Pound Ridge Church's Afghan Schools Project.

July 2009. In an update to the story, Ken Swenson, member of the church, reports that the Pound Ridge Community Church did, indeed meet its target and provided all 400 desks and chairs plus some teacher education and school infrastructure updating. The Pound Ridge Community Church did a variety of projects in their community to raise the money, including an "apprenticeship program" where individuals could hire a knowledgeable neighbor with skills in areas such as computers, photography, golf, etc. to give them training; a table set up at Scotts Corner Market; Christmas "gift cards" that took the place of presents; and other creative fundraisers to bring in the needed cash. The Afghanistan project was part of Reverend Frank Denton's strategy of "helping others while educating ourselves." The project's education extended all the way from church members to the entire Pound Ridge community and, ultimately, all the way to Afghanistan.

By Don Heppner, The Record-Review, Pound Ridge, NY, May 20, 2005

CITY AND GUILD CERTIFICATES
AFGHANISTAN-INDIA VOCATIONAL TRAINING CENTER

The Certification Ceremony of Afghanistan-India Vocational Training Center, Kabul, was held on April 23, 2009. Upon the successful completion of four months' training and a certification test conducted by the internationally known organization "City and Guild," certificates were awarded to 490 trainees in the fields of carpentry, tailoring, welding, masonry and plumbing. Along with the certificates, tool kits funded by the United Nations Assistance Mission in Afghanistan (UNAMA) were distributed. Participatory Certificates were given to all the 625 trainees in the program.

The Afghanistan-India Vocational Training Center was set up on June 26, 2008 by the Confederation of Indian Industry (CII) at a cost of $1.4 million

under India's assistance program for Afghanistan in the skills building sector. Under the project, CII trained master trainers in the five fields of carpentry, tailoring, welding, masonry and plumbing, who in turn provide training to the new trainees under the overall guidance of the CII team. Personnel trained were from Kabul and adjoining provinces. UNAMA has provided tool kits to the successful candidates as per their trades in order to equip them to be independent medium-level entrepreneurs.

Capacity and human resource development has been accorded a special focus under India's assistance program, which has been identified as the top priority by the Government of the Islamic Republic of Afghanistan. Every

year 500 long-term university scholarships by the Indian Council of Cultural Relations (ICCR) and 500 short-term Indian Technical and Economic Co-operation (ITEC) training programs for Afghan nationals are awarded. India's Self Employed Women's Association (SEWA) has set up a Women's Vocational Training Center in Bagh-e-Zanana for training Afghan women in garment making, nursery plantation, food processing and marketing. In addition to these, India is involved in assistance programs in infrastructure, humanitarian, capacity building and small development projects all over Afghanistan.

At the ceremony, Minister Bashiri expressed his sincere appreciation for India's assistance in all the sectors for the development of Afghanistan. Indian Ambassador Prasad reiterated India's strong commitment to the reconstruction and development of Afghanistan, in particular in the capacity development of the Afghan people and its institutions.

MORE ABOUT EDUCATION

Kabul: Schools Reopen. At the opening of the 2009 school year, the Ministry of Education announced that 11,000 schools had reopened and that the Ministry had bought 30 million textbooks for the new academic year. Efforts of tribal and community leaders were credited with the high number of school openings, despite continued violence, especially in the south.

Afghanistan: Private Schools. While the Ministry of Education has opened thousands of schools and boasts that enrollment of both girls and boys is up, it continues to confront tough barriers. Deputy Education Minister Patman noted in May of this year, "We still need 7,000 new schools. We need at least 5,000 school laboratories. Many of our students still sit on the floor. We need desks and chairs for them. We need new buildings. We have to train qualified teachers. All of these require money and Afghanistan cannot finance this without international assistance." Some parents are finding private schools a good alternative to the troubled public system. There are now some 300 private schools in Kabul and throughout the provinces. Though enrollment fees, at $15 a month or more, are well beyond the means of most Afghans, many parents are sacrificing to put their children in these usually secular schools with better facilities and more qualified teachers. The thirst for education is great and, while still violent in some areas, general resistance to girls' education is diminishing. As with many other developments in Afghanistan, positive change is clearly happening. But it takes time.

Eal Keshan: Photos Build a School. Concern Worldwide, along with Concern Afghanistan, has taken an unusual route to raising funds in the U.S. to build a school in Afghanistan: They sent the children in the town of Eal Keshan disposable cameras. The Afghans, most of whom had never seen a camera, were shown how to use the cameras and proceeded to pho-tograph their town and their current school—a tent with no insulation and no plumbing. Their pictures were returned to the U.S., developed, displayed and sold at an event in Chicago. With funds from the sale, Concern is now building a permanent school in Eal Keshan that will educate some 800 girls and boys immediately and for generations to come.

Kabul: Long-Distance Classes. "Duty" sometimes takes us to unexpected places via surprising routes. For a group of teachers in Athens, Georgia, it has meant starting up Internet-based midnight classes for partner teachers and students in Afghanistan (all of whom have to show up for class at the sparkling hour of 7:30 a.m.). The program, designed by the Athens-based Women to the World and supported by funds from the U.N. Development Fund for Women (which supplied computers and Internet connections) has had its bumps. After all, getting one computer working perfectly can

be a challenge. Linking some two dozen computers with cameras, microphones, etc. in a country halfway around the world with basic power supply problems is nothing short of miraculous. But, technical frustrations aside, a growing group of Afghan women are learning basic job skills from teachers a world away.

Afghanistan: School Sanitation. Afghanistan's children are streaming to schools these days. By May of 2009, over 6 million school-age children are enrolled in the country's 10,000+ schools—an impressive achievement for a country that in 2000 was educating well under 20 percent of its children. But the success is not without lagging indicators. Only about 60 percent of schools have on-site water supplies, though the Ministry of Education reports it continues to dig wells for schools, planning another 5,000 this year. Basic sanitation facilities, too, are still unsafe in about 75 percent of

schools. UNICEF continues to work closely with Afghanistan's Ministry of Education to promote good drinking water and sanitation facilities for all Afghanistan's schools.

Kabul: Music School. If music can, indeed, soothe the soul, Afghanistan is at last on its way to peace. The savagely plundered Kabul Secondary Vocational School of Music is about to be transformed to a world-class National Institute of Music for Afghanistan. With the help of multiple donor governments, music schools around the world and individuals and manufacturers of musical instruments, the new Institute is now hiring teachers and planning practice and performance spaces. Ahmad Sarmast, one of the main advocates for the school, enthused, "In eight or 10 years we should have the first symphony orchestra or a well-qualified brass band."

MILITARY AND POLICE

A LETTER TO MY FATHER

BY RUSH MCCLOY

Rush McCloy is a Lieutenant in the Navy who has been serving in Afghanistan since January 2008. He is the founder of Channelstone Partners and a graduate of the University of Virginia and Wharton Business School. This is an email he sent to his father, John J. McCloy, on Wednesday, September 24, 2008.

Dad,

I hope everything is great at home. I really love what we are doing here and there is a part of me that will truly be sad to leave this country when I re-deploy. I cannot tell you how much I appreciate the package you and Mom mailed me. Receiving a care package with Mom's handwriting on the box made me feel like I was back in summer camp on mail day. I received the articles you sent to me. It is hard to refute that the violence has accelerated. The fact is not flawed, but the tone does not capture the essence of what we see here and what we are doing for the country. In the last seven months, we have invested almost $15 million in projects throughout our area of operation here. Our provinces have not only gained access to schools, clinics, women's shelters and wells, but also gained necessary road projects that increased the economic development and security. Everything we do hires local nationals; many projects intentionally hire young nationals to help them learn a trade; and some hire women, a breakthrough in many regions.

We weave these efforts into the training and development of the Afghan National Security Forces. The community support of the local government through the combined ANSF and infrastructure development is paramount to the counterinsurgency fight. We are turning former insurgents into supporters and the anti-government elements are naturally fighting back be-

Rush McCloy and Afghan friends.

cause they are losing territory. Much of the violence we see is linked to the projects we build for the communities. Violence is not necessarily a negative reflection of the campaign here, but a reflection of the immense efforts we are putting into the communities. I believe there is a natural spike prior to the decline.

Additionally, too many articles focus on friendly casualties. The burden of any casualty, friend or foe, is a heavy weight. Unfortunately, readers of the tabloids do not read about the people we capture when we are ambushed, work with them, help their communities and then gain their support. I have looked in the eyes of and worked with people who shot at me and their

Police Mentor Team Faryab—Ghormach, Badghis Province, Afghanistan, 2008.

groups are helping us now. It is fairly typical that the stories from the field do not make it to the tabloids because the men and women in the field are focused on the mission with a sense of patriotism and selflessness that does not include self promotion. The friends we all have made with the local nationals are inimitable. If it were not for the distance and travel restrictions, they would be lifelong. I would like to think they are, but I have to be realistic. I remain hopeful and the memories and the lessons I have learned from them are unquestionably steadfast.

I know I have gone on a long tangent, but I just wanted you to know that what we are doing is really working in areas and a spike in violence does not necessarily mean the situation is slipping. Quite the contrary. I do believe we need more support here and more investment into the infrastructure. It will take time and it is not World War II. Those who think it is taking too

long have not looked at all the angles of this incredibly complex campaign. If only they could see how people are changing and how much we are giving to future generations. Also, if only they could have the patience my parents have and, in my case, Brooke has had in pushing off our marriage until I finish this tour. I do feel blessed for having had the opportunity to serve here. Man, it has given me a great perspective and a great sense of what is important.

I love you so much and please give Mom my love… dogs too. I cannot wait to meet Snipe. I will slip him a piece of turkey under the table at Thanksgiving when Mom is not watching.

Love,

Rush

RAMBO HELPS KEEP U.S. BASE IN AFGHANISTAN SECURE

KABUL, Afghanistan—A taxi stops near the front gate of Camp Phoenix on the outskirts of Kabul. Within seconds a short, stocky man wielding a pipe starts to approach the vehicle. The man with the lead stick means business.

"Move the car," he demands in a language anyone could understand. "Move the car. Now!" The occupant hastily pays his fare and the taxi driver wastes no time backing away. With the way clear, the Afghan man U.S. soldiers call "Rambo" returns to his post just inside the gate to resume his vigil.

A person would be hard pressed to find anyone in the camp who doesn't know or hasn't heard of Rambo, so named by troops in the 10th Mountain Division. "He's definitely a legend in this camp," Sgt. Michael Sweet said. While Sweet, an Indiana National Guardsman, is a shift sergeant, it's abundantly clear that Rambo is the primary gatekeeper.

In June 2003, when U.S. forces first rolled up to the front gate of what was then a Russian-Afghan transport company, Rambo was waiting. He hasn't left. Stories of Rambo permeate the base. Some are factual. Others are not.

"This is my hooch," he says through an interpreter as he opens the door to a small, cramped room immediately off the front gate.

His real name is Jamal Udin, born in Kabul "maybe 41 years ago," he said, to parents who moved to the capital from northern Afghanistan. For many Afghans, details such as years and dates aren't all that critical.

As a teen, he said, he served as a conscript in the Afghan army, which, at the time, was under the thumb of the Russians. After military service, Udin got

Noor Rahman carries on the "Rambo" tradition, guarding the entrance to an installation of the National Police Department in Kabul.

a truck-driving job with the transport company. His trips took him all over the region: Iran, Turkmenistan, Uzbekistan, Tajikistan and Pakistan.

It was during this time that he married his wife, Shahgull, who was a couple of years younger than he was. By Afghan standards, Udin had a good life. He had a steady job, an apartment, six children and a wife he adored.

The turning point for Udin, he said, came several years ago when a rocket-propelled grenade apparently fired by a Taliban soldier slammed into his apartment, killing his wife. Udin remembers the time of day—10 or 11 a.m.—but not the year. The Taliban captured Kabul in September 1996, but were beating back counterattacks for sometime afterward, so it could've been 1997. "We loved each other," Udin said of his wife, "which is why I will never remarry."

Udin took his brood—four sons and two daughters—to Pakistan, where Shahgull has family. They remained there for about four years.

"While I was in Pakistan, I saw President Bush and his wife on TV," Udin said. "They said, 'We will help Afghanistan. We will rebuild Afghanistan.' That's why I like Americans and why I like to work for them."

That commitment to his country prompted him to return to Kabul. Because Udin had sold his apartment, the only logical place to go, he figured, was his old workplace. His bosses didn't have a driver's job open, so they assigned him to the front gate—and he's been there ever since.

"He takes a lot of work off our hands," said Spc. David Young, who, like Sweet, is with Company C, 151st Infantry Battalion. Udin has an incredible capacity to remember faces, Sweet said. He always knows who belongs on base and who doesn't. If a stranger approaches, the man they call Rambo steps forward first to sort things out. And his lead pipe, wrapped in red tape, rarely leaves his hand, sending a subtle but convincing message not to cross him.

The guy is dependable, too. Udin typically works from 5:30 a.m. to 8 p.m., every night. Last year, he can recall taking only two days off. Every fourth or fifth night, he'll visit his brother's house to see his daughter Zamina, who is now 10.

While Udin frets about his daughter, the troops worry about him. Udin's room is filled with gifts from well-meaning young Americans. A general's driver from the previous rotation gave him a TV; a sergeant from the Indiana Guard bought him a space heater; and another current occupant of the base, a female soldier, presented him with a blanket, gloves and a black wool hat with the name "Rambo" stitched across it. And that's only scratching the surface. There are several 12-pack soda boxes, instant soup, snacks, sunglasses and even a bottle of bubbles, the type that kids like to play with.

Udin also has his own camouflage uniform. "They are always taking care of me," he said. The attention, he added, "makes me work harder and harder for them."

For months after the Americans arrived, Udin refused to accept money. His company was already paying him and he saw no reason to double dip. When his company quit paying him, he accepted the Americans' offer. Today, his monthly salary is $420, plus meals.

"Have a good day, Rambo," Spc. David A. Pranger said after he delivered lunch to Udin. "He's not really military, but we bring him breakfast, lunch and dinner," Pranger added. "He's a cool guy. He's always here to greet us." Indeed, whenever a military vehicle—U.S. or coalition—enters or leaves the compound, the occupants inside get saluted.

Udin patrols the area outside the gate with a vengeance because the area tends to attract locals looking for work or handouts. The compound is also situated along a busy street. Terrorists, he explained, "might attack the front gate with a car bomb."

A couple of months ago, an Afghan fired on a French military vehicle. Udin sprang into action immediately and charged the armed man. Before he could disarm him, the French shot the man themselves. "I'm not scared," Udin said. "I feel like I am in the Army, so if I die, no problem."

"Rambo is one of the most honest, genuine persons I have ever met," Sweet said. "He's worth every penny they pay him. He never complains."

Udin hopes soon to get an apartment so he can move his five children back home. The pay he receives from the Army has helped him immeasurably, but he states he has no intention of abandoning his post any time soon. "Whenever the Americans leave, I will leave," he said. "As long as they want me to stay, I will stay."

Article by Kevin Dougherty. Used with permission from The Stars and Stripes. © 2005.

U.S. SOLDIERS TEAM UP WITH ROMANIAN TROOPS FOR AFGHAN MISSION

HOHENFELS, Germany—When it comes to getting ready for the fight in Afghanistan, the 1st Battalion, 4th Infantry Regiment does things a little bit differently than other U.S. Army units.

The unit is preparing to send a company in the late summer to Zabul Province, but unlike other Army units, they won't be part of a U.S. battalion. The 1-4 attaches to a Romanian army battalion when it deploys. The unit also deploys for six- to eight-months, rather than the 12-month stints most units are accustomed to. But the 1-4 always has a unit rotated into Afghanistan, said Sgt. 1st Class Robert Hartfield. "To me, working with a foreign unit, once you learn each other, it is a lot easier," Hartfield said.

"It does paint a good picture of what they are capable of," Capt. Kyle Wheeler, the commander of the 1-4's Company A, said about the joint training.

When 1-4 soldiers aren't in Afghanistan or training to go there, they are simulating the Taliban or other insurgents to train American and allied countries' forces.

To gear up for this coming deployment, the 1-4 has been training with their Romanian counterparts at the Joint Multinational Readiness Center in Hohenfels. And earlier this year soldiers from the unit went to train in Cincu, Romania. The troops are now at Hohenfels for a mission rehearsal, Hohenfels spokesman Maj. Sean Fisher said. "It's about building a team early," Fisher said. The Romanians are proficient in English, he said.

The joint U.S.-Romanian force's mission in Afghanistan will be to keep Highway One, a vital roadway, secure to keep military supplies and units flowing to where they need to be, Fisher said.

The joint arrangement with the 1-4 helps to tip the fight in NATO forces' favor, said Romanian army Capt. Cimpeanu Rares.

From left, U.S. Army Staff Sgt. Kenneth Beutler and Chief Warrant Officer Two Tom Mirto work with Romanian army Maj. Vale Roman and Romanian army Capt. Dan Huduma to train in a simulated Tactical Operations Center before they deploy to Afghanistan together in the late summer.

Rares is one of the officers who will be coordinating and planning missions with the 1-4 from the Tactical Operations Center (TOC) in Afghanistan. He is part of the Romanian Army's 280th Infantry Battalion based in Focsani, Romania. "We got things to learn from them. They try to understand the way we work and our procedures," Rares said.

The upcoming deployment will be the second time that U.S. Army Staff Sgt. Joseph Rivera has worked with the Romanians. This time he will be working with them in the TOC. He said the units won't conduct joint patrols, but can work together in the field, for example, by having a Romanian mortar unit support U.S. forces if needed. Soldiers said that during training the Romanian unit proved to be highly skilled mortar men.

"The biggest thing for me was knowing that if I needed mortar support from the Romanian mortar team it would be there and it would be accurate," Hartfield said.

Article by Mark Abramson, Used with permission from The Stars and Stripes. ©2009.

WARMING HEARTS AND HOMES

FRENCH SOLDIERS FROM REGIONAL COMMAND CAPITAL (RC(C)) CIVIL MILITARY COOPERATION TEAM HELPED PROVIDE HEATING TO 450 AFGHAN FAMILIES FOR THE COMING WINTER SEASON

Some 62 tons of charcoal were distributed to all the families from Bariq Ab—"refugees camp"—a village that is the home of families coming from Kabul's ghettos. The soldiers teamed with the 13 district chiefs—the "Maleks"—of Bariq Ab to identify the needs in heating resources. In total, more than 800 bags of charcoal were delivered, including 600 to Bariq Ab, 200 to Heshneh Ye Karuti and 20 to the police station. Each family received three bags worth, for cooking and heating during three months.

While the area, with its wells and homes, gives the families a place to settle, living conditions remain difficult. There are no medical facilities or economic activity. Only four teachers are educating the 500 schoolboys and girls of the village in a rundown tent. A weekly Shura helps the Maleks to discuss these daily difficulties. A representative from the French RC(C) team attends these meetings.

Bariq Ab may simply survive because of charcoal donations this year; however, many believe that the community will thrive soon. About 5,000 families are expected to move to the village in the next few years. Aside from coal supply, a French battle group is also doing daily patrols in the area, and many other reconstruction and development projects are in progress to help ensure that the quality of life continues to improve in the village.

Source: North Atlantic Treaty Organization, December 17, 2007.

MORE STORIES FROM ISAF*

THE FOLLOWING STORIES ARE A FRACTION OF THE REAL STORIES HAPPENING DAILY IN
AFGHANISTAN—BY THESE AND OTHER TROOPS STATIONED AROUND THE COUNTRY

Australian Army. Sometimes two civilians a week are injured by landmine explosions in the Bagram area. These people are so desperately poor that they'll venture into the minefields to scavenge or to pasture their animals. Major Dave Bergman, an Australian Army officer in charge of the Mine Action Center (an international military organization focused on demining the Bagram area), decided something needed to be done. He joined with Hemayat Brothers Demining International (HDI), the first Afghan company in the mine action industry, and together they developed a demilitarization program that hires locals to recycle munitions from the minefields in a safe manner and a carpentry program that teaches new skills and provides new products for the community. It is hoped that with alternative employment opportunities, local residents will stay safely away from the minefields.

British Army. Private Jason George Williams, 2nd Battalion, The Mercian Regiment, a resident of Worcester, gave his life for Afghanistan. . . for an Afghan. The 23-year-old, known for his ever-present smile and cheerfulness, lost his life—less than a year after joining his regiment—while on foot patrol east of Gereshk in Helmand Province. The day he died, there had been an attack by insurgents and three Afghan National Army Warriors were killed. When the fighting stopped, one of the dead Afghans could not be found. Private Williams and his platoon were looking for that lost man so the insurgents couldn't seize and desecrate the body. The platoon was successful in its search for the Afghan, but lost Private Williams when he set off the home-made bomb that killed him. To the Afghan National Army, Private Williams is now a hero. He was honoring the ancient code of warriors: leave no man behind. His actions made it possible for the slain Afghan warrior's family to pay proper honor and respects to their fallen son. The British Secretary of State for Defense honored Private Williams saying, "He was doing a vital job, living and working alongside the Afghan National Army to bring security and a better future to the people of Afghanistan."

British Army. Major Nick Clarke is staying. Though his tour in Helmand Province was due to end in March, he elected to stay on until the end of August to work alongside his local regiment 2nd Battalion, The Mercian Regiment—to provide continuity for the Afghan soldiers. Working with an Operational Mentoring and Liaison Team training the Afghan National Army (ANA) at Camp Shorabak in Helmand Province, Major Clark said, "It was important for the continuity of the training of the ANA." Noting that training the ANA is a challenge, "… not only have you got a different language but illiterate people as well," he says the job satisfaction when you've taught someone to write and see he's "got it" is basically why he's staying. Having personally helped train some 1,000 Afghans, he's positive about the ANA: "The ANA is very capable, with the right grounding of training. And we are in the process of 'training the trainer'… We are getting some very encouraging results."

British Army. Major Sean Birchall was based at Lashkar Gah in command of IX Company 1st Battalion Welsh Guards. His job was to bring peace and security to the surrounding area. He was brave in leading his men and concerned about the progress and welfare of the Afghan National Police in the area. His biggest concern, though, was getting a wall built around a local school. He wanted to protect the kids in the school from the nearby minefield and the Taliban insurgents. He want-

U.S. troops in Afghanistan being transported via helicopter.

ed to be sure the Taliban didn't win and take the possibility of an education away from those children. And with the $10,000 price for the wall, he worried about whether it could ever be built. In the end, Major Birchall gave his life in Afghanistan—hit by a roadside bomb. He was an inspirational leader, loved by his family and respected by the Afghans with whom he worked.

Canadian Army. The Zharey district of Kandahar now has an irrigation system, thanks to the Canadians. In November 2008, the first canal opened. A second canal construction project was in process and a third project, improving the culverts along the main road, was planned. The projects' goals are to help local farmers improve crop yield. In the process, some 160 local Afghans were hired to do the construction work on the projects. Improved farming conditions plus new jobs raise hopes that ex-residents of the area will come back to their land and resume normal life.

Canadian Army. Colonel Ian Anderson, a trauma surgeon, did everything to save Marzya's leg. Though usually handling wounded soldiers at the Multinational Medical Unit in Kandahar where Anderson works, they found the time and room to treat wounded children as well. In late November last year, Marzya had been leaving her uncle's shop when an insurgent's rocket-propelled grenade landed nearby. It was impossible to save Marzya's leg. But the medical team did its best to provide TLC and encouragement and to provide her with an adequate prosthesis. Her life will be tough, requiring many more surgeries and adjustments to survive with difficult economic, social and cultural challenges. Marzya, undaunted, simply says, "I am tough."

Canadian Army. Even Afghanistan's conservatives have recognized the value of female soldiers. While Canadian women soldiers carry out security tasks like searching women at checkpoints, they have overcome initially strong opposition and are successfully working as mentors to male Afghan police and army officers.

Danish and British Armies. A team of 12 Danes and six British soldiers are working in partnership in a Military Stabilization Support Team (MSST) to coordinate the military effort in the Upper Gereshk Valley in Helmand Province. Their mission includes funding small projects like bridges and wells. Larger projects include building water towers, roads and parks and refurbishing schools, clinics and hospitals. The MSST meets regularly with the municipal mayor—who is enthusiastic about the development but lacks technical know-how—mentoring him on project management. Because Gereshk has become one of the most stable areas in Helmand, many see it developing into the new economic center of the province.

Dutch Army. The Dutch Operational Mentoring and Liaison Team (OMLT) has been training Afghan National Army personnel since July of 2008, teaching basic infantry skills. As Dutch Royal Marine Capt. Tim noted, "Working with the ANA is rewarding; you almost instantly get back what you put in. We are trying to build an army that is effective and capable to operate by itself. We are providing security and stability in this region so the people can build up their own country." The Dutch soldiers live with the ANA and accompany them on combat missions. Brigadier General Abdul Hamid, ANA 4th Brigade commander, observed, "Our people and our soldiers have knowledge about the territory, about the culture, about the language of our people. The Dutch people have good technology and good technique. If we mix these, it will make us strong."

French Army. In January 2009 six French soldiers gave their blood to save an Afghan civilian injured in the January 17 suicide bombing in Kabul. The bombing victim suffered perforations of both liver and lung and had a critical need for blood—before he could undergo an operation to repair the damage. Each soldier donated some 450 milliliters of blood, gifts that contributed to saving the life of the Afghan victim.

German Army. In a country where the average lifespan is 44 years, finding someone 91 years old is rare; providing them medical treatment is even more unusual. German Navy Major Klaas Oltmanns at the medical facility at Camp Marmal did just that in February of this year. Din Muhammad, one of the oldest Afghans living, was treated for asthma and coughing, released and is doing just fine. Din Muhammad, a farmer for 20 or 30 years, then a restaurant owner, observed, "I want a calm situation. Everybody wants that for their own country. And I do too. I want the world to feel this feeling." He added, "I have good memories of ISAF."

ISAF. Volunteers from the ISAF (International Security Assistance Force) Headquarters in Kabul donated more than 550 kilograms of rice to residents of a temporary refugee camp on the outskirts of the city. The project was led by U.S. Navy Lt. Cmdr. Yevsey Goldberg, founding member of ISAF's Volunteer Community Relations and Resources Group. Dr. Goldberg donated nearly half the money for the donation himself, saying, "It's all part of my love for the people of this country. These people have so little, it's good to give them something, especially with the winter coming."

Romanian Army. The people in Shajoy district, Zabul Province received a December 2008 donation of food, winter clothes, blankets and school supplies donated by the Romanian organization Save the Children. Abdul Qayoum, district leader, said at the donation ceremony, "We want to thank you for your help; it is very good to have the joint forces here in Shajoy to help our people. We are supportive of the Afghan government, the ANSF and ISAF because they provide stability and security in our district."

Spanish Air Force. In December 2008 the Spanish Air Force presented more than 50 tons of food, clothing, baby supplies and other essential items to the Afghan people of Herat. All supplies were collected by the Spanish Air Force with contributions from several Spanish companies. General Jose Jimenez Ruiz, Spanish Air Force Chief of Staff, stated, "Our presence here in Herat is like a bridge that connects the Spanish society with the Afghan one. It is a good explanation of our citizens' commitment to the social welfare of this country."

Turkish Army. The Turkish Provincial Reconstruction Team (PRT) in Wardak is providing modern policing methods training. The PRT completed building and furnishing a Police Training and Education Center in Maidan Shahr, Wardak in January 2008. Able to handle 30 boarding and 80 nonboarding trainees for full-time training, the Center has already graduated 267 Afghan National Police officers with an additional 40 now in training.

United States Army. It's a matter of security—long-term. The story's been repeated over and over again: coalition forces drive the Taliban out, congratulate themselves and leave; the Taliban return. American Marine Company C has learned from experience in Anbar Province, Iraq that it takes more. Their strategy: to win over a critical mass of the local population, then empower them to stand up against insurgents. Winning the population means really listening to them, building trust with them and giving them confidence that they can gradually take over their own security. Sharp observation, information from locals and control of transportation routes all reduce the risk of the Taliban's return.

*International Security Assistance Force.

PISTOL-PACKING DEPUTY, WIFE AND MOTHER

Meet Malalai Kaker, wife, mother and pistol-packing deputy police commander. Malalai Kaker wears a headscarf and a shoulder-holstered pistol. A broad leather belt holds up the trousers of her stock issue blue-grey police uniform—clearly not designed for a female's contours and most especially not a female who's barely five feet tall. Shucking off the scarf impatiently, Kaker fires up a cigarette and inhales deeply. It's the first time I've ever seen an Afghan woman smoking. But Kaker is a woman of many firsts.

The first girl—just 14 years old—to enroll in the Kandahar Police Academy, her police officer father and five officer brothers watching proudly. The first female detective in the province. The most senior female officer in all of southern Afghanistan, now deputy commander of the Kandahar city police department, with a squad of 10 female cops who report to her.

Until two years ago, Kaker wore a burqa over her uniform but finally and firmly took it off. For most male colleagues, it was the first time they'd ever seen her face. "Now I wear it only when I'm not working, when I'm shopping at the bazaar, when I'm not armed. There are Taliban around who would kill me if I were recognized out of uniform." Or in uniform, for that matter, which is why Kaker lives in a protected compound and is driven to work every morning by one of her brothers.

Increasingly, she and other female officers here have been receiving "night letters" from the Taliban, warnings to quit their jobs, stay inside their homes. "Sometimes, they phone me. They have my cell phone number, even though I keep changing it. Last month, my son was threatened by someone who said: 'Tell your mother to leave her job or we will kill her.' I won't let them scare me away. But I do worry for my family."

A Kabul police "sister" of Kandahar's Malalai Kaker.

KAKER IS 38 YEARS OLD, an attractive woman with laugh lines crinkling around intense brown eyes, mahogany hair, bronze lipstick matching her nail polish and an utterly self-confident nature. She was, presciently, named after Malalai, the Afghan heroine from the Battle of Maiwand during the second Anglo-Afghan war of the 19th century who used her veil as a banner to encourage Afghan soldiers in their fight against the British.

During the Taliban era, forbidden from continuing as a cop, Kaker fled to Pakistan where she met and married a UN worker she describes as a "modern man." They have six children. With the fall of the Taliban she returned to Kandahar, to her vocation, more dogged than ever about continuing in a non-conventional, for women, career. It's not just about being a female detective in a man's world, in this most conservative, Pashtun domain of Afghanistan; it's about being a detective who investigates, where male colleagues won't: crimes committed against women by men.

Captain Nodera, a 37-year-old veteran of the Afghan Police, works in the family unit of the 4th District of the Kabul Police Department.

"Women don't usually complain to male police officers if they're being beaten by their husbands or if they've been raped. And male officers can't investigate those claims because they can't go and interview women—they can't look at their bruises and injuries. Some of them also still believe that men have the right to abuse their wives or their sisters."

In one notorious case a couple of years ago, Kaker broke down the door of a local residence to find a widowed woman and her children being kept in a cage, fed little more than bread and water for eight months, the family enslaved by a brother-in-law.

But there have been many other incidents, if not quite so horrific, of domestic abuse, busted open by Kaker and her team. "What we do is apply the law in the right way. Our constitution is supposed to protect women's rights, too."

Practicing body searches.

The squad room commonly becomes a refuge for women fleeing violence, hovering about, anxious to brew tea or clean up, anything to make themselves useful.

Yet women, Kaker reminds, can be criminals, too, involved in narcotics, committing theft and murder, abusing children. "I've found guns on women while investigating cases. But at least I'm allowed to touch and search them, under the burqa. Male officers can't do that."

Not that Kaker investigates only women. As a senior cop in the department, she frequently participates in raids targeting male criminal gangs. A male suspect once bit her on the arm—she carries the scar still.

But an AK-47—which she also has been issued—is a great gender equalizer. "For men, it is particularly insulting to be arrested by a female officer. Too bad." During Mujahedeen days, there were no female cops anywhere in Afghanistan, though some women fighters. (There is still, in fact, one female warlord in northern Afghanistan.) During Afghanistan's communist era, the Soviets were keen on expanding female representation in police forces. They were all sent packing by the radically misogynous Taliban, of course.

But the ranks of policewomen have been on the rise since 2002. There are now about 250 female officers, according to the Ministry of the Interior, with most of them working in the police hospital, with passport control and at checkpoints for searching women.

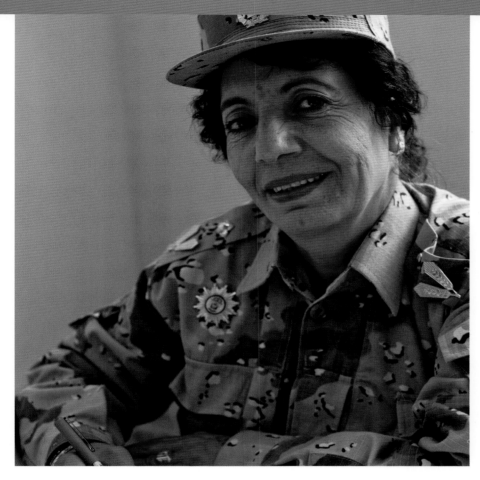

occurred a couple of years ago during an ambush by Taliban gunmen where Kaker was left with only a handful of male colleagues to repel the attack, other officers fleeing the scene. After being rescued by reinforcements, she returned to the station livid with her cowardly colleagues, hissing at them: "You have long moustaches, but you have no bravery."

The security situation has palpably worsened in the last two years. "Day by day it gets worse. I don't know how we can improve things in Kandahar, except the tribal leaders should get more involved with supporting the central government. I think the people might listen to them if they spoke out against the Taliban, if they said Islam forbids suicide bombings and the killing of law enforcement officials."

Kandahar cops make about $100 a month, which isn't much for daily risking one's life. And, in the case of women, being routinely subjected to harassment and ridicule. Of late, Kaker has been kept away from routine city patrols, with the renewed and more emboldened threats against female officers. "Even my father is afraid for my life now and he has always supported me. It's a very dangerous job, whether you're a man or a woman. But if you're a woman, you have to put up with so much more. People have small, narrow minds. It will take a long time for many people to accept us in this position. But I want to show other women that it can be done, even here in Kandahar."

She has been, over the course of her career here, through seven police chiefs, most removed for corruption. And Kaker genuinely believes she might make chief some day. "Oh yes. Why not? The men I work with respect me now as an equal."

In the interim, she would like two other things so far denied her, even after all these years and all these promotions: a brimmed police hat to replace the scarf and her own vehicle. "They won't let me drive," she says. "It's not allowed for women."

In the past, Kaker has gone out on the streets, buttonholing women, urging them to join her in law enforcement. Many considered her insane.

On top of all other crime, common to any urban center, Kandahar is gripped by an escalating insurgency that adds another layer of brutality and peril, most particularly for cops, who bear the brunt of front-line ambushes. When the *Star* flew into Kandahar last week, there were a dozen incoming officers from Kabul on the flight, sent as immediate replacements for 13 cops slain in a disastrous encounter with the Taliban a few days earlier.

A fortnight ago, Kaker was part of a unit that became involved in a firefight with insurgents at the edge of town. Her most frightening experience

DiManno, Rosie, "She's a Top Cop…," Toronto Star, June 8, 2008. Reprinted with permission— TorStar Syndication Services.

MORE ABOUT POLICING

Paktya Province: Mine Removal. The U.S. Department of State announced in April 2009 that it will give an additional $5 million to six humanitarian demining groups to enable 34 new mine action teams to remove more mines across Afghanistan. Implementing partners, five Afghan NGOs, are Afghan Technical Consultants, Demining Agency for Afghanistan, Mine Clearance Planning Agency, Mine Detection Center, Organization for Mine Clearance and Afghanistan Rehabilitation and The HALO Trust. They will clear three square kilometers in 19 communities. The U.S. has contributed more than $20 million for mine action and conventional weapons destruction to Afghanistan in F.Y. 2009.

Kabul: Female Police. More than 40 women graduated from Kabul's police academy in May 2009, joining a force of some 350 female police posted throughout the country. Dozens more are being trained. Afghanistan's Interior Ministry recognizes a core need for female police officers in the country.

Kabul and Herat: Emergency 119. August 2008 saw the launch of Afghanistan's first emergency hotline. Kaka Nijat, or "Uncle Rescue," is its TV spokesperson. For the first time, Afghan citizens of Kabul and Herat have a way to fight illegal activities and contact police directly—24/7—and good encouragement to do so. Within a few months, Emergency 119 was receiving 4,000 to 4,500 calls a day. The Uncle Rescue ads, paid for by NATO's International Security Assistance Force, have encouraged Afghans to be more involved in thwarting terrorist attacks. The 119 system ultimately will be extended to all of Afghanistan's 34 provinces. An Interior Ministry spokesman indicated that the hotlines have reduced illegal activities, and police performance has improved with the implementation of a special quick-response unit backing the hotlines.

Kandahar: Anti-Narcotics Progress. British Brigadier-General David Hook believes that Afghan farmers will be able, gradually, to abandon poppy cultivation with the improved security, better market for other agricultural crops and improved highways that characterize Afghanistan in 2009. Current climate conditions and poppy eradication along with world food prices are also encouraging Afghans to look to legal crops for prosperity.

Helmand Province: Drug Bonfire. In May 2009, six-and-a-half tons of drugs—opium, herion and hashish—were burned in a spectacular bonfire marking the work of Afghanistan's counter-narcotics police in raids across the country. In making the drug seizures, the unit also arrested some 1,100 individuals including international drug dealers. Afghanistan has seen some successes in countering its poppy problem. Public information campaigns along with soaring prices for wheat have reduced poppy cultivation. But, bottom line, experts in Afghanistan say that stability is the real key. It will take the establishment of the rule of law in major producing areas before the battle against the poppy will be won.

Kabul: Policing the Streets. It's a dangerous job: Casualties among Afghan police are quadruple that of Afghan soldiers. Despite the danger, over 5,000 young men have graduated from Afghanistan's national police academy. Kabul's Criminal Investigations Department, led by General Ali Shah Paktiawal, oversees the city's frontline against both crime and terrorism.

Kabul: Neighborhood Watch. The Supporters of Peace Guards, a neighborhood watch system, was developed in Kabul in the fall of 2008. Designed by the Interior Ministry, the program encourages cooperation between the police and residents in

City police officers stand or sit under intersection umbrellas with a small white "STOP" sign to control traffic.

precincts throughout the city in hopes of reducing both crime and terrorist attacks.

Nangarhar Province: Drugs Seized. April 2009 saw the seizure by Afghan police and coalition forces of some 3,000 kg of morphine and 580 kg of chemicals used for opium production.

189

COMMUNITY

Ehsan Bayat and poor Kabuli children that live in the huts and tents in the background.

140 PROJECTS AND COUNTING
THE BAYAT FOUNDATION

Since 2005, the Bayat Foundation, led by Ehsan and Fatema Bayat, has contributed to over 140 projects to improve the quality of life and enable the lives of Afghans by providing for basic human needs, constructing new facilities and infrastructure, organizing sporting events, promoting health, education and economic programs and preserving Afghanistan's cultural heritage. In 2002, Chairman Bayat launched

Afghan-Wireless Communication Company, www.afghanwireless.com, the first wireless service and Internet service provider in Afghanistan, followed by the 2005 launch of ARIANA Television Network (ATN), www.arianatelevision.com, with international reach, and ARIANA Radio (FM 93.5). The independent USA-based 501(c)(3) Bayat Foundation, www.bayatfoundation.org, partners with the non-governmental Bayat Foundation in Kabul,

Students gather in front of the Saleha Bayat Building at the American University of Afghanistan in Kabul.

Afghanistan, www.bayatfoundation.org.af, to provide advocacy, outreach, education and engagement to promote the well-being of the Afghan people through the support of its donors. The Bayat Foundation-NGO partners with other NGOs to support Afghan humanitarian activities. Email info@ bayatfoundation.org for more information or to sponsor a program.

AFGHAN FAMILY SPONSORSHIP

The Bayat Family Sponsorship Program matches donors with Afghan families with the greatest needs in Afghanistan to provide monthly financial support and encouragement. Through the War Stories program aired on Ariana Television and Radio, families who have suffered from war and conflict are introduced to potential sponsors. Family sponsors make a commitment to contribute 50 dollars per month to a designated Afghan family, thereby enabling the head of the household to purchase items needed most, including food, clothing and medicine. The sponsored family is also given a mobile handset and SIM card by Afghan-Wireless Communications Company in order to receive calls of encouragement and support from the sponsoring family.

Bayat Foundation Afghan Family Sponsorship program recipients.

WINTER AID

The Winter Aid Program is an ongoing annual program of the Bayat Foundation serving families in need with basic food and clothing during the harsh winter months. In its inaugural year, 2006, over 13,500 families received aid. In 2009 over 2,500 families were served in spite of the challenges of the delivery route in remote areas and unsecured territories with bumpy roads, the chilly winter climate and threat of avalanche. In January and February 2009, Bayat Foundation Winter Aid, consisting of blankets, winter clothes and foodstuffs, was distributed to people in greatest need in the northern provinces, Maimana City, Baghlan Province, Wach Tangi Baysood District in Jalalabad Province, Badghes Province, Gardez Province, Herat Province, West Kabul (Dashti-barchi), Kapisa Province, Boldak and Qalat.

MATERNAL CARE

The Bayat Foundation is committed to improving the quality and availability of maternal care and education throughout the provinces and has built a 150-bed hospital in Mazar-e Sharif, a 20-bed hospital in Tora Bora, a 50-bed hospital in Daikundi, and a 50-bed hospital in Faryab. The Saleha Bayat Maternity Hospital extension in Mazar-e Sharif served 2,931 patients in January and February 2009, improving the quality of life, if not saving lives, for mothers and newborns in an area that previously lacked adequate maternity facilities.

BUILDING GOOD GOVERNANCE—
ONE VILLAGE AT A TIME
NATIONAL SOLIDARITY PROGRAM

The National Solidarity Program (NSP) was created by the government of Afghanistan to develop the ability of Afghanistan communities to identify, plan, manage and monitor their own development projects. NSP promotes a new development paradigm whereby communities are empowered to make decisions and manage resources during all stages of the project cycle. The program will lay the foundation for a sustainable form of inclusive local governance, rural reconstruction and poverty alleviation.

The NSP is executed by Afghanistan's Ministry of Rural Rehabilitation and Development (MRRD) with funding from a variety of sources, including financing from IDA and JSDF, financing from the Afghanistan Reconstruction Trust Fund (ARTF), which provides funding to NSP from various donors (Australia, Belgium, Canada, Czech Republic, Denmark, EC/EU, Finland, Germany, Norway, Sweden, UK DFID and the United States), and bi-lateral funding, which has come from Norway, Denmark, New Zealand, Italy, Switzerland and Netherlands directly to NSP.

The NSP/MRRD has contracted 28 NGOs and one UN agency (UN-Habitat) called Facilitating Partners (FPs) to work directly with targeted communities to implement NSP activities at the local level. Currently some 5,000 Afghans are employed by NSP in all 34 provinces.

Assisted by its Facilitating Partners, NSP has laid the foundation of good governance structure at the community level called Community Development Councils (CDCs). These are elected, inclusive and consultative decision-making bodies in villages. CDCs have

been adopted in more than 22,148 communities, covering nearly 35,436 villages throughout the country.

As the largest community-driven development program in the history of Afghanistan, NSP has paved the way toward improved access for the rural population to basic infrastructure and services through financing and tech-

culturally acceptable manner to identify and address their priorities, giving them the opportunity to make joint decisions on their collective needs. It has not only ensured sustainable socioeconomic development at the community level but also has promoted gender equality and strengthened unity and cooperation with and between rural communities throughout the country. "I am extremely happy today because all men and women came together in order to elect and vote for their representatives," said Miss Fatima, head of the CDC in Fakhr Razi Village, Karokh District of Herat Province. "It is our duty to serve our community by taking an active part in all affairs together with our men."

CDC, in fact, is the gateway for a social and development foundation at the community level. It is responsible for implementation and supervision of development projects including water supply and sanitation, transport, irrigation, power generation, education and human capital development, among others. CDCs are also forums that represent communities to government and non-government organizations. CDCs are considered to be the most accountable, transparent and cost-effective local governance bodies at the community level. The World Bank estimates that implementation of projects by NSP are on average 30 percent cheaper than those implemented by other national and international organizations. "This is our money, so all the time we are checking whether it is spent correctly," Mr. Ibrahim, a local teacher in Langar Khana Village, Nahr Shahi District of Balkh Province said.

nically supporting CDCs to improve their prioritized sub-projects. "Thanks to NSP for construction a school building in our village," a sixth-grade student, resident of Baba Jee village, Enjil District of Herat Province, said. "Before this, we used to study in a tent under burning sun."

The NSP indeed is the flagship development program of the government of Afghanistan that has structurally involved both rural men and women in a

Reports and statistics show that NSP has contributed considerably in reducing poverty and empowering people by establishing sustainable community-level governance bodies, promoting skill and capacity, generating sources of income and ensuring inclusive participation in the development process through implementation of basic infrastructure and human capital development.

SOCIAL DECISIONS LEAD TO SOCIAL COHESION

Rabat Abdullah, a village located in Enjil District about six kilometers to the east of Herat City, is composed of 400 families. Although its residents live a semi-urban life, they haven't thoroughly overcome their problems.

The latest development initiatives of its residents are, indeed, good examples for other populous communities in Afghanistan. The local CDC, with the assistance of NSP, was able to construct a social center in the middle of the village. The greatest financial sacrifice constructing this building was the contribution of one *jireeb* (acre) of agricultural land by Haji Ghulam Mahboob, the head of the CDC.

Asked why he contributed his valuable agricultural land to the social center, Haji Ghulam Mahboob said, "It's a great pleasure for me when I see my villagers come together and share their thoughts with each other. Villagers who were previously dispersed in many houses on sad or happy occasions are now coming together in this building. The first story is allocated to men, whereas women use the second storey of the building. Prior to this, the villagers did not share problems nor did they meet each other on a regular basis."

The beauty of the building catches the attention of people because it has been designed with numerous facilities. A number of halls, toilets, literacy classrooms for women, a stockroom and a huge kitchen for local ceremonies have been constructed in both upper and lower stories of the building. The building was completed at a total cost of Afn2,593,306 (equivalent to $51,866) of which only 10 percent was community contribution.

Adds Haji Juma Gul, a resident and an influential elder of Rabat Abdullah Village, "In addition to social and moral benefits, the construction of the

social center has also helped us avoid spending too much money both on cultural and religious ceremonies. Most of our villagers used to hold their wedding parties at hotels where they had to spend hundreds of thousands of Afn. Due to long-distance difficulties, most of the villagers couldn't participate either in tribal or social gatherings. Providentially, we no longer make use of hotels because currently we have a properly equipped social building in the middle of the village where we can economically celebrate our ceremonies."

In addition to participating in the collective decision-making process, approximately 20 to 25 women of Rabat Abdullah Village regularly receive education in the social center. Some of the women attend literacy classes, whereas a number of them attend tailoring training that will benefit their families a lot in the future.

ROADS, SCHOOLS, HOSPITALS, COMMUNITY COUNCILS...

INTERNATIONAL RESCUE COMMITTEE AFGHANISTAN

The International Rescue Committee began conducting aid programs in Afghanistan in 1988. In recent years the IRC has focused on education, economic development, reintegration of returning refugees and support for community-level governance.

I n rural areas, the IRC establishes community-based schools, trains teachers, and sets up local school-management committees. Between 2004 and 2009, over 550 of these schools were integrated into the government education system. An IRC program helps children with hearing and visual impairments attend mainstream government schools.

These girls attend an IRC-run school in Logar Province near the capital, Kabul.

T he IRC is a leading partner of the Afghan government's National Solidarity Program, which helps communities plan and manage their own development projects. By February 2009, the IRC had helped establish 1,475 community-elected Community Development Councils in four provinces. With a total budget of $168 million, the councils carried out over 1,500 projects, ranging from the construction of roads, schools and hospitals to the creation of literacy and vocational education classes. Afghan citizens account for 98 percent of the IRC's staff in Afghanistan.

MAKING AFGHANISTAN'S FUTURE BRIGHTER
NOORISTAN FOUNDATION

BACKGROUND

The word *noor* means "light" in Dari and represents a new beginning for the people of Afghanistan based on education and development. The Nooristan Foundation (NF) is a U.S. 501(c)(3) nonprofit charity that provides assistance to rural areas of Afghanistan. The organization began its goal to support educational, healthcare and humanitarian aid projects in the Nooristan region in 1999. It was one of the first U.S. NGOs to provide support to these rural areas of Afghanistan. As it grew, NF expanded and has provided assistance to projects in Kabul, Bamiyan, Logar, Laghman and Takhar provinces.

The Nooristan Foundation's hallmark has been planning and implementing projects with local communities. It has been able to implement successful educational, water supply and small infrastructure projects with this approach. NF believes that NGOs should not wait just for government or international donors to provide assistance and should also be leaders of positive change for communities that have suffered tremendously through war and poverty.

APPROACH

The Nooristan Foundation's guiding principles include:

- Requiring independent monitoring and assessment to obtain objective feedback.
- Including local communities in planning and implementation of projects.
- Partnering with local NGOs or non-Afghan NGOs with successful track records.

- Keeping overhead low and working to get resources to the "village level."
- Obtaining visuals of project implementation so that donors can "connect" to the individuals they are helping.

The priority of NF is to utilize resources as efficiently as possible to get assistance to the village level. Afghans must see tangible results in their lives in order to support the new political system. Involving beneficiaries in project implementation and maintenance provides a vested interest for local communities in the success of a project, and also increases its sustainability.

GOVERNANCE

NF is governed by a Board of Directors that oversees the work of the organization. Action committees focus on specific projects. The Board and committee members all serve as volunteers. NF utilizes a small number of paid staff in Afghanistan to implement and monitor projects, and partners with other organizations in order to utilize donor resources efficiently.

PROJECTS

The Nooristan Foundation started its work in 1999, through donations from Afghan-Americans who believed in the importance of education for Afghanistan's development. The Foundation began by supporting two schools in Nooristan Province, which had received no assistance from other organizations. NF was formalized to a 501(c)(3) organization in 2003, after its founder, Dr. Nadir Atash, went to Afghanistan and identified great needs in rural areas.

America's Fund for Afghan Children. In 2004, NF was awarded $100,000 as part of Red Cross America's Fund for Afghan Children program and successfully implemented over a dozen key projects. NF also distributed school supplies on behalf of the American Red Cross.

Chaman Hoozoory Wells. Two wells were constructed in Chaman Hoozoory, a densely populated area of Kabul, providing safe drinking water to approximately 4,500 residents as well as soccer players in an adjacent soccer field.

Istalif Well. This well provides clean drinking water for approximately 1,500 Istalif inhabitants, including 250 children.

Nilaw Water Supply. Materials were provided for building a water supply fed from a spring for the village of Nilaw, located in western Nooristan. Approximately 17,000 residents benefit from the water supply.

Paprok Irrigation. Located in eastern Nooristan, this irrigation project provides safe drinking water and water for farming for approximately 1,000 people.

Frashghan Irrigation. For this remote, economically depressed village, NF provided materials for the community to begin building irrigation canals.

Dowab-Mondol Road. NF provided materials and transportation to support construction of a road to this isolated area of western Nooristan and completed preliminary design work for a bridge.

Frashghan Road. In 2003, NF mobilized the community to participate in building a road to connect Frashghan to Doulatshah, a distance of about 12 km (eight miles).

Micro-Hydro Electric Projects. NF completed three micro-hydro electric projects (10KW-25KW) in the villages of Gezeen, Pacha and Ameesh in western Nooristan.

Teacher Training. NF brought 30 teachers from Nooristan to Kabul for training in science, math and technology in 2004.

Sarasyab Kindergarten. NF provided equipment, furniture and toys for 100 children attending the Sarasyab Kindergarten in Kabul.

Bargematal Boarding School. NF provided support for the building of a boarding school in eastern Nooristan, providing educational opportunities to students from villages all over Nooristan.

Nilaw Primary School. In close collaboration with community leaders, NF helped to obtain a parcel of land for building a primary school for both boys and girls in the village of Nilaw and supported its construction.

Youth Recreation. Because the youth of Kabul have only limited access to sports facilities, NF assisted in rehabilitating tennis courts as well as two soccer fields and provided two soccer teams with uniforms, balls and trainers.

Bamiyan School. In 2004 NF supported ImagineAsia, a nonprofit organization started by National Geographic photographer Steve McCurry. With NF's assistance, ImagineAsia distributed supplies to schools in Bamiyan.

Give to Live. NF's Give to Live campaign promotes projects that provide direct support to the needy in Afghanistan.

ChangeMakers: NF also has a "ChangeMakers" campaign, through which fundraising events are held to support NF's programs. Through events in 2008 and 2009, NF was able to start "New Beginnings" and support "Midwife Training" in Takhar Province and "Pasigam Village School."

STORIES OF TIMUZ
GARY MOOREHEAD—MARIGOLD FUND

Fifteen-year-old Kareem, one of many fatherless kids in the village, would often come out to greet and guide Gary Moorehead during his monitoring visits of Shelter for Life (SFL) projects at Taka Timuz. Drinking tea there one day in March 2004, the head mullah told Gary that Kareem's mother had died of tuberculosis the day before, leaving him and his younger siblings orphaned and young Kareem as head of their household. It is Gary's friendship with this young family that begins the story of the Marigold Fund.

Gary made inquiries after their health; the mullah suggested that they were not doing so well, that they had minimal help from extended family or neighbors who were themselves very impoverished and in the process of returning from refugee camps abroad. After getting the mullah's and a few scattered relatives' permission, he visited the children the next day in their tiny 8 x 10 foot piled-mud room and brought them to the hospital to be examined, where they were found to be sick with several diseases. After initial treatment, he took Kareem to the bazaar to purchase new household items, clothes, food and clean bedding for the kids. After a couple of follow-up visits to doctors in subsequent days and weeks, the children recovered. In subsequent months, Gary came to enjoy the friendship of these and other little ones from the village and learned more about how to appropriately give them help and encouragement needed to carry on with life.

The pocket money used to help these children was the seed money symbolically planted in Afghanistan that has grown into the Marigold Fund.

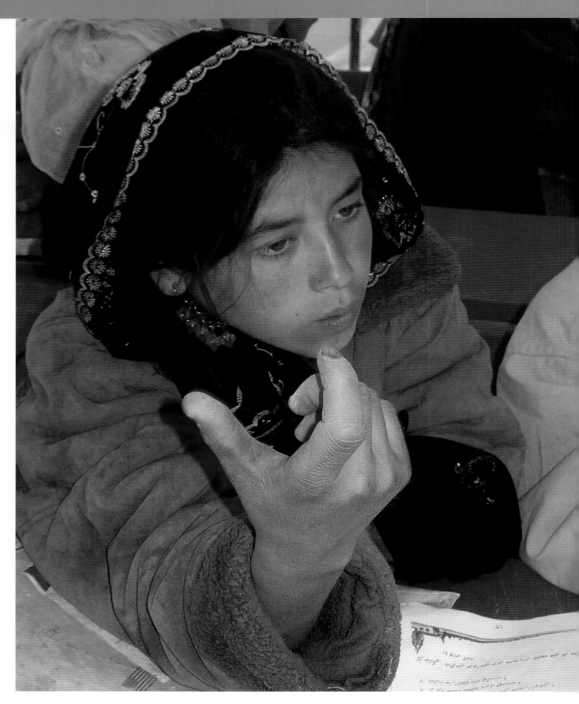

SIGN LANGUAGE AND LITERACY

Around the time of their earlier hospital visit, we learned that two of the five children were deaf. The youngest, Uzra, was practically a little Afghan Helen Keller, clever but quite wild. The middle child, Alim Khan, was clearly a bright young fellow who had contrived his own simple manual vocabulary, but was (like his young sister) entirely illiterate and adept only at marginal communication with others. Marigold began to consider how these children might be helped.

After consultation with the Ministry of Education and SERVE, an agency with experience with deaf education in Afghanistan, and with help from new Friends of Marigold (common folk from the U.S. and the U.K.), we made arrangements with the village school to allow a special class to be held. The program featured literacy and Afghan sign language training for deaf children and their hearing siblings of the village, as well as a school lunch program. About a dozen children enrolled in the class. A search was made for a qualified Afghan sign language teacher; one was found and hired.

The program has continued for four years now, with ongoing help from Marigold. Kareem's family has been attending this special class and has been catching up with classmates in the main school. Alim Khan is now one of the star pupils of the class. For him and this family, Afghan Sign has become a second household language. The oldest sister, Nusrat, attends the class and has begun to realize and articulate her desire to be a teacher at her village school, a formidable challenge given that if she can reach her goal she would be the first female teacher in the history of their village. We have recently found an older female teacher from the town who is beginning a mentoring relationship with Nusrat. The importance of her having positive female Afghan role models is one of the keys for her to attain her goal of being a teacher.

In the midst of our regular contact and growing relationship with both this family and their village, their larger-scale needs became evident. One such pressing need involved the difficulty of accessing the main road to town.

THE BRIDGE AT TAKA TIMUZ

The sun began to set one night on the old bridge at Taka Timuz when we began eyeballing it for a refit. Even decades before, it was a fairly rickety skywalk of misshapen boards and logs atop alternating stones and concrete, and over subsequent years of war and use, it was reduced to a state worthy of any bridge in an Indiana Jones adventure. Many thousands of humans and animals have used it, and from time to time pedestrians have fallen off and been killed or injured; a few years ago, for example, a boy was bumped off by a passing animal and he died.

The Marigold Fund began working with the locals and the provincial government in late 2005 on a plan to revamp the structure and deck of the bridge. The project took a bit more than a year, as the work was done almost completely with weekend labor from among the six villages that use the bridge. The story of this community project is worth sharing, as is the metaphor that draws Afghans together with Westerners.

We removed the three sections of the old bridge and strengthened the central stone and concrete support pillars, as well as the ledge-support of the far river bank. Large wooden beams were purchased in the market, brought to the worksite and prepared for fashioning into larger beams, four beams stacked to form "super-beams."

One of the interesting and gratifying parts of the project involved the design and making of metal hardware and tools. We were introduced to a German metal craftsman, Georg Westermayer, who has lived in Kabul for more than 33 years. Georg and his team devised some very creative solutions for our hardware needs. With his assistant Rajab Ali and others, Georg fabricated metal parts needed for the job.

After the 'super beams' were constructed with the timbers and metal fasteners, they were hauled into place by teams of village men on two different occasions. One beam-moving also featured a large crane that we rented for the day, a rig which was otherwise employed in the construction of the

who spent many hours on the basic timber-frame design of the bridge. Many others gave advice on ways to enhance the design or enable the placement of the beams, including folk such Tom Harris and his staff from Architectural Timber and Millwork of Amherst and Hadley, Massachusetts, and Marigold Fund friend Rich Plotczik of Amherst Woodworking.

The villages took a strong managing role in the project, coordinating with Marigold in various aspects of the work. Periodic planning meetings took place to review and plan each phase, work details were scheduled, and changes in design and implementation were processed in meetings. The villagers experienced excitement and a sense of justifiable pride in the work they'd done.

We sought to embed this work project in an educational atmosphere so the knowledge to build and maintain the bridge would remain long after the bridge was complete. The passing of time will measure the level of success of this goal. As future maintenance needs arise and other projects are conceived and undertaken by the people, they hope to apply the knowledge gained from the bridge project.

We had no qualms about appropriating some designs (split rings, large fastening hardware, bearing plates) that are used in the West for construction, but opted to reproduce them out of locally available materials rather than importing them. All of what we used was available from local markets, including the large wooden beams that come from Russia or the Central Asian republics north of Afghanistan.

main road that was also in the process of being rebuilt; this is the road off of which descends the path to the Taka bridge. Beam-moving days were exciting and enjoyable, and thankfully no one was hurt.

The building committee from the village, as well as others from the U.S., Germany and other countries, spent time and effort in figuring out how to assemble and place these beams. Chief among them is a fellow from upstate New York named Robert Curtis of Engineering Ministries International,

The bridge building is actual, but it is also a metaphor for a larger task the West is faced with in the world today… and Marigold is seeking to carve out its part in this labor. One of the things we hope for in our mission is that common folk from different countries connect across cultural and political

Gary Moorehead with his young friends from Taka Timuz.

More than a tactical or strategic political and humanitarian undertaking, this is about the lives of common Afghans and common Westerners coming in genuine contact, both giving and learning from each other. The involvement of our New England carpenter-guests at the end of this program, as well as the financial support many have given from the U.S. and the U.K., and just the general interest expressed by many in the welfare of those Afghans needing the bridge, are examples of how we can deepen the sense of the personal and the grass-roots, "common-folk politics" of these kinds of projects.

As the final stages of construction approached, it was well known that the bridge wouldn't be complete until the last board was nailed down, which would not take place until the final ceremony. We were able to create and present a deeply meaningful gift as a symbol of friendship for the occasion. From a few pieces of shrapnel, unfortunately plentiful in this valley, a long spike was made by a Friend of Marigold in the U.S. to be the last nail in that last board. It was presented as a gift from the West to the people of Taka Timuz in the spirit of the Hebrew prophet who said that there would be a day when the people would "beat their swords into plowshares," taking implements of war and redeeming them for peaceful purposes.

gulfs, that friendship and peace are sought and perhaps gained. One of the ways Marigold seeks to do this is by enabling groups of international guests to occasionally come to Afghanistan to volunteer for a short project, to work with Afghans, visit them in their homes, to drink tea and break bread with them. So, for this project, we were excited to host a small team of skilled carpenters from Massachusetts in early November 2006. They gave their time and skills to help finish the bridge.

We have an opportunity to resume unfinished business here through many projects and efforts of the international community, and to consider how the welfare of Afghans may be linked to our own. May God help us to manage this with love, with effectiveness and with a growing understanding of how this all matters very much to the unfolding of the American story.

ENABLING THE REBUILDING OF COMMUNITIES
SHELTER FOR LIFE INTERNATIONAL

Shelter For Life International (SFL) has directly impacted the lives of more than 1 million people in Afghanistan since 2001 and through its program activities is helping to win the war against poverty, illiteracy, disease and housing needs in Afghanistan. SLF's mission is to demonstrate God's love by enabling people affected by conflict and disaster to rebuild their communities and restore their lives in tangible ways.

EDUCATION

SFL has just successfully finished work on 32 new schools, funded by USAID, giving the gift of education to over 20,000 Afghan children. Randall Olson, the President and CEO of SFL, states: "There is, in fact, no greater gift the U.S. government can give to the Afghan people than the gift of education." In addition to the schools, SFL built 20 clinics and, according to USAID Afghanistan, almost 100 Afghans visit each of the clinics on a daily basis. Since 2001 SFL has completed over $25 million in construction projects, including schools, clinics and houses destroyed by natural disasters. Afghanistan has one of the lowest literacy rates in the world—only 36 percent. Only one in five women can read. The impact of literacy on the issue of health alone is staggering! With 165 deaths per 1,000 live births, Afghanistan ranks only behind Angola, having the second highest infant mortality rate in the world.

By supporting the education, health and housing sectors in a country once devastated by conflict, terrorism and disaster, the American people and organizations like SFL have begun laying a foundation that promotes security, peace and prosperity in Afghanistan. This year, thousands of children, including young girls, are able to attend school for the first time in their

lives and will have an opportunity to receive an education that will impact the country for generations to come. As the literacy rate improves, many basic health problems can be addressed.

The fight against illiteracy, disease and poverty in Afghanistan is far from over, but significant progress has been made since the fall of the Taliban. Last year, when the President of SFL visited project sites in the Lowgar Province, community leaders of one village pointed proudly to their newly completed school. For the last 20 years, the village has been without a school, and teachers were forced to hold classes under trees. Now they have a clean, safe learning environment.

Our efforts to bring education and healthcare have also come with a cost. Six schools built by SFL in the south of the country have been targeted and burnt by the Taliban. Three of the six schools have already been repaired, and the fight for a brighter future for the Afghan people continues.

INCOME GENERATION

Shelter for Life International's work extends beyond schools, as the story of Safir Mohammad—just one of thousands—illustrates. He is an old, unskilled laborer who until recently was working on an SFL bridge construction project. After falling ill and being operated on in the Taloqan hospital, he related the following story:

When I got sick I was not so afraid because I had saved some money from working on the bridges. Many people have died in our village because they do not have the money to go to the hospital. A few months ago when SFL distributed hens, my family was not on the beneficiary list. I was disappointed like many poor people who live in this village and did not get anything. Everyone is poor here and expects something. However I told myself that if Allah wants he will help us in other ways.

I was in Taloqan hospital for one week. When I was discharged I came back home and found my children and my wife were very happy. They told me we now have two goats with two kids, and they drink the milk every day. My wife seems happier than everyone in the village. She says she will take care of goats until they multiply into a flock. She says she now can sell the milk and get cash to solve many of our money problems. We also have good news that someone will buy the goats' wool. The staffs from SFL and the agricultural department have taught the women how to collect wool.

Before this project everyone thought we were all going to die. Many people sold their donkeys for $5 only. We did not have alternatives. We were considered the poorest village in Takhar. Now we have the goats, chicken, roads, bridges and we have work, people in the neighboring villages think we are richer.

CONTRIBUTING TO CIVIL SOCIETY
COUNTERPART INTERNATIONAL

Over the past five years, through the USAID-funded Initiative to Promote Afghan Civil Society (I-PACS), Counterpart International has been actively engaged in strengthening civil society in Afghanistan by creating a network of support organizations that reaches all 34 provinces and provides a range of services to strengthen the ability of 210 civil society organizations (CSOs)—including NGOs, Shuras, *jirgas* and community development councils—to directly improve the quality of life for ordinary Afghans. To this end, civil society organizations receive a menu of training for organizational strengthening—from management and fundraising to government relations and project design. To promote democratic decision-making at the community level, CSOs are trained to mobilize communities to identify, prioritize and address development needs through grants that support projects that demonstrate buy-in and investment by all community members, including local government and religious leaders—*ulema* (scholars) and mullahs.

Through radio and television talk shows and dramas, videos, roundtables, workshops and *jirgas*, Counterpart has been able to reach up to 6 million people at a time to convey the value and positive impact that civil society organizations are having in improving citizens' access to education, healthcare, improved sanitation and improved social infrastructure (*e.g.,* clinics, schools, sanitation facilities, roads). Linking the core values of civil society to the core values of Islam is embedded in much of this programming and resonates with religious leaders and citizens alike—demonstrating the shared values of participation in problem solving and community service, acceptance and tolerance, accountability to others, and the valuable role that women play in society.

Gender mainstreaming and empowerment is a priority of I-PACS. Fifty-one percent of all grant support has gone to support women's organizations and women's issues—from education and health to gender-based violence and employment. Among the project's milestones is the First Women's Council held in October 2008, organized with the Ministry of Women's Affairs, with funding from USAID. This historic gathering in Kabul of 400 women from 33 provinces provided a unique opportunity to dialogue on the challenges women face and strategize how to meet those challenges in conformance with multiple conventions supporting women's empowerment as well as the National Action Plan for the Women of Afghanistan, which focuses on security, legal protection and human rights, leadership and political participation, economy, work and poverty, health and education. Most significantly, this event gave a unique opportunity to the women of Afghanistan to have their voices heard as they presented a list of short-term achievable priorities to the President of Afghanistan, ministers, international dignitaries, donors and other key governmental and civil society actors.

DINING OUT IN KABUL WITH A CRITICAL EYE

Most Westerners think any foreigner traveling to Kabul is in mortal danger from Taliban suicide attacks, improvised explosive devices and firefights as soon as they arrive. The Afghan capital is obviously more dangerous than London or Berlin, and the tense security situation does limit the lives of foreigners living in the city.

But they still have to eat. A lively restaurant scene has grown in Kabul and is scrutinized by Rosemary Stasek, the country's only restaurant reviewer.

These days, the dozens of restaurants in Kabul have something for almost every foreign taste: curry at Lai Thai, falafel at Tavern du Liban, an oven-fresh baguette in Le Bistro, pasta in Bella Italia or Kabuli pilaf rice in the Afghan Sufi.

Unlike in many European capitals, diners can smoke in every Kabul restaurant, and Westerners can wash away the dust of the Afghan capital with a glass of wine or a cold

Afghans have such fun at a party. Even one guest is an occasion for cake and green tea.

beer before reading the menu. Muslims are not allowed alcohol in Afghanistan but non-Muslims can get it in licensed restaurants. Some unlicensed restaurants sell alcohol under the counter. On the bill, those drinks are then listed as "special soup."

Besides numerous kebab stands and snack bars like Afghan Fried Chicken, which has borrowed the name and logo of the U.S. chain KFC, there are

plenty of restaurants at the upper end of the price scale. Their customers are mainly foreigners who work for aid organizations, embassies or the media. Soldiers eat at the military bases.

Restaurant managers have erected high walls topped with barbed wire and installed metal doors flanked by Kalashnikov-armed guards to comply with UN security rules. Stasek has invited us to her favorite Chinese

In the summer, diners eat outside in the restaurant's enclosed yard.

The verdicts can be crushing—the "service sucks," Stasek writes or extremely positive—"the best lamb chops in the world." Stasek readily admits that being a reviewer is not her main job. She used to be mayor of the California town of Mountain View.

Numerous Afghans live there. In 2002—just after the Taliban regime was toppled—Stasek traveled with a delegation to the Hindu Kush for the first time. "I fell in love with this place," she says.

When her term as mayor finished at the end of 2004, she wanted to go to Kabul for a few months. She founded an aid organization for women, got to know a South African, married him and now has no plans to leave Afghanistan.

"One of the most common questions newcomers to the city ask is where can you have a good meal," says Stasek. She decided to put the answers on her website.

restaurant—Golden Key—complete with sandbags and automatic weapons out front. "Please keep your weapon inside," signs on the lockers in the corridor say.

In the garden, roses bloom, songbirds chirp in a cage and *shisha* pipes wait to be lit. The plastic swans are supposed to help the decor, but it is the menu that persuades the guest that this is a good restaurant. It offers duck with pineapple for $14 or lobster with ginger and spring onions for $28. The "mutton in hot pot" and the "iron platter beef" taste excellent. Stasek, a U.S. citizen, has tested 37 restaurants in Kabul so far and published the results on the Internet. The 45-year-old's reviews hardly meet the standards set by the internationally renowned Michelin Guide: They are short and to the point and help diners get their bearings fast.

On her website she says you can die a violent death in Kabul. But "the most likely cause will be getting plowed over by a Blackwater [a private US security company] convoy." Stasek says people in the West have a false picture of Kabul and that she in fact lives a mostly ordinary life there. In the morning she gets up, feeds the dog and goes to work. When she arrives home in the evening, she sometimes cooks and watches television with her husband. Other times she goes out to eat with him. "Very little of my life involves the Taliban," she says. (Internet: http://www.stasek.com/rrr)

DPA, The Earth Times, May 31, 2009.

MORE ABOUT COMMUNITY

THE WESTERN PROVINCES

Disaster Relief. It's not just the lingering impacts of war that make life in Afghanistan challenging. Spring 2009, for example, brought serious flash floods—the result of spring rains and snow melt from the mountains—earthquakes (two at over 5.0 magnitude in Nangarhar Province) and severe food shortages. With coordination from the Afghanistan National Disaster Management Authority and the help of the Afghan Red Crescent Society, U.N. Office for Coordination of Humanitarian Affairs, various NGOs, NATO-led Provincial Reconstruction Teams (PRTs) and Russian food aid, relief has made its way to impacted areas with greatly improved efficiency. Help to Baghland, Balkh, Badakstan, Bagdhis, Herat, Parwan, Faryab and Tekhar provinces has included tents, jerry cans, wheat, oil and salt. To help mitigate starvation in areas of food shortage, Russia has shipped in over 18,000 metric tons of wheat.

KABUL

Food Insecurity. In April 2009 the U.S. government and the City of Kabul announced a temporary employment project designed to help the growing number of Kabulis unable to feed themselves or their families. Some 50,000 men and women will be given temporary employment on public works projects—repairing the drainage system, surfacing roads, rehabilitating parks, etc. This project is one step toward solving an under-reported aspect of Afghanistan's problems: 4 thousand Afghans die a year from hunger and poverty—25 times the number of deaths due to violence. And the number has grown from 30 percent of the population to 35 percent since 2005. Afghanistan continues to suffer severe drought, which has led to a catastrophic drop in wheat production. Humanitarian organizations working in Afghanistan are calling for greater spending on agriculture-related development as a sustainable strategy for addressing Afghanistan's persistent food shortages.

Buses. After a 17-year absence, electric buses will be back on the streets of Kabul before the end of 2009. The initiative is seen as a blessing by residents of Kabul, as the buses running on batteries will not increase pollution in the city but will make it easier for residents to navigate their city.

MAZAR-E-SHARIF

Airport. Construction of a new airport in Mazar-e-Sharif started in April 2009 with funds from the German and UAE governments. To be completed by the end of 2011, the facility will have a fully equipped modern terminal, hangars and parking facilities.

AFGHANISTAN

Surrendering Weapons. Early 2009 saw the voluntary surrender of weapons by former Mujahedeen in Badakhshan, Logar and Kabul provinces. The commanders, who fought hard for Afghan freedom in the past, now declare themselves ready to work for peace and national cohesion. They hope their move will strengthen the reconstruction process. More than 4,000 weapons have been recovered in Badakhshan alone. A newly formed council of former commanders believe they can play a key role, through consultation with tribal elders, in resolving conflicts in Afghanistan.

HERAT PROVINCE

Taliban Surrender Weapons. Early 2009 also saw three Taliban commanders and their followers—some 40 men—lay down their arms, return home and become ordinary citizens. One leader said the fighters are simply eager to lay down arms and join the government of Afghanistan.

HERAT

Mass Wedding. Some 2,000 relatives were there that day in August 2008 when 50 couples held a joint wedding. The mega-wedding seriously reduced the often astronomical cost of weddings and simultaneously made everyone feel more secure.

AGRICULTURE/RURAL LIFE

the first step is hope

hope *worldwide*

It is through directly impacting the Afghan people so that their lives are made better that lasting changes can be made.

Since 1991, HOPE *worldwide* has been fulfilling its vision: to bring hope and change to the lives of the world's most poor, sick and suffering. It changes lives by harnessing the compassion and commitment of dedicated staff and volunteers to deliver sustainable, high-impact, community-based services to the poor and needy. An ambitious vision, and one particularly well-suited to the needs of Afghanistan, where HOPE *worldwide* has developed a broad range of programs that supply humanitarian support and, more importantly, deliver competencies through education and training, jobs through construction projects, and understanding through research and community involvement.

Highlighting just a few of HOPE *worldwide*'s current activities:

• At the Malalai Maternity Hospital in Kabul, HOPE *worldwide* has worked with the Afghan Ministry of Public Health to develop a fellowship program for Afghan physicians. A mentoring-focused program that also uses classroom instruction, the fellowship program is now training 13 fellows who have all completed their medical training and residencies in Afghanistan. They will participate as fellows through November 2009.

When there's enough water, Jawzjan Province produces magnificent cauliflower.

216

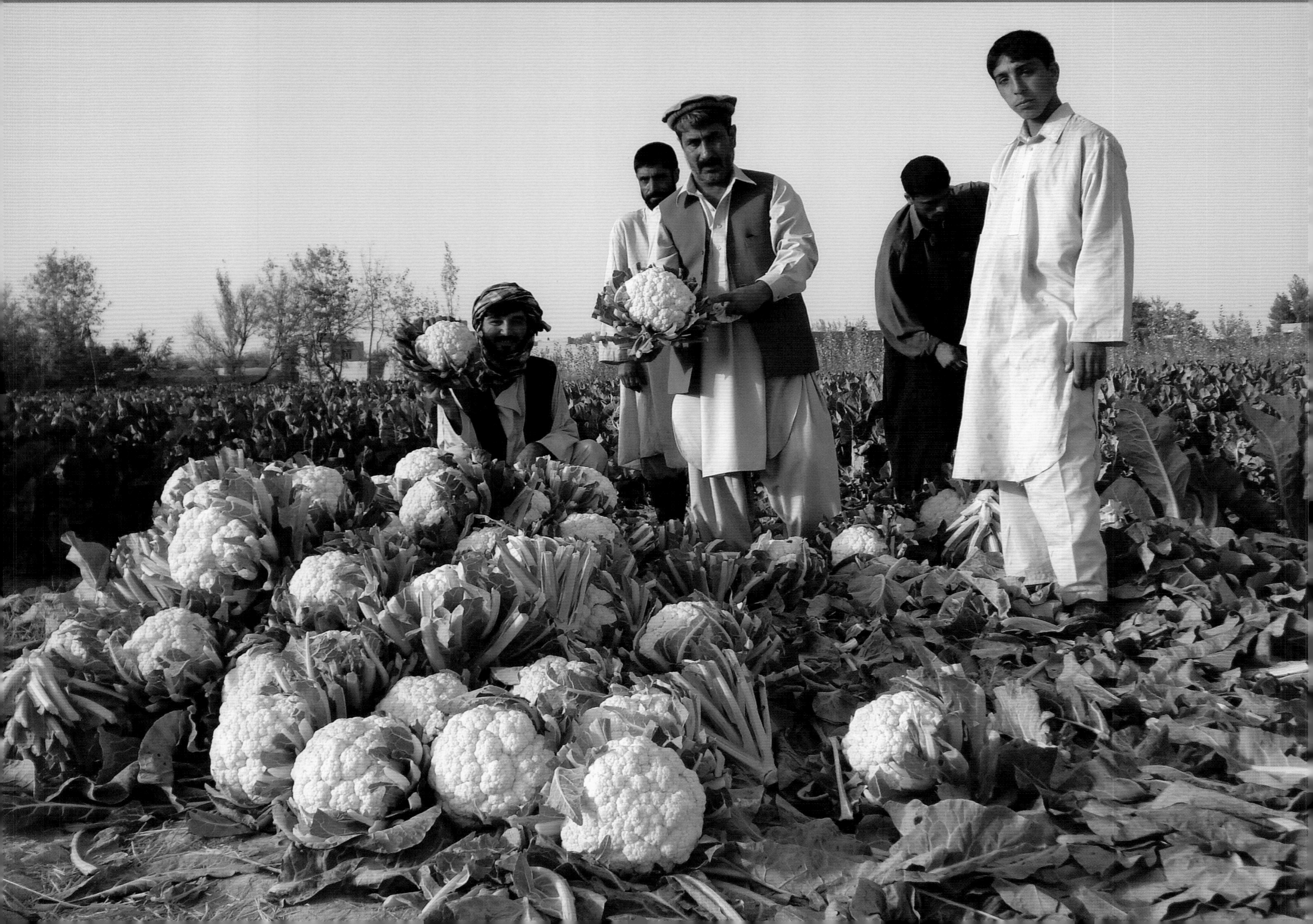

• HOPE *worldwide* has recently won a research grant from the Afghan Ministry of Public Health, sponsored by the Global Alliance for Vaccines and Immunization. With this grant, HOPE *worldwide* will investigate how to effectively encourage families throughout Afghanistan to use established health facilities to deliver their babies and also to complete their young children's DPT3 vaccination routine. This work is crucial to improving Afghanistan's infant and maternal mortality rates— still the second worst in the world.

• In keeping with its goal of sustainability, HOPE *worldwide* is helping its Afghan staff —some 90 members strong—to continue their education. Seven are currently enrolled in degree or diploma courses while HOPE *worldwide* is sponsoring others for training seminars to increase their capabilities in humanitarian aid work.

Of all its various projects in Afghanistan, its community-based irrigation rehabilitation is perhaps the most illustrative of HOPE *worldwide's* work to bring hope—and the tools to ensure its fulfillment.

These projects have created jobs for our people and at the same time it is helpful for our agriculture. Now we have enough water for irrigating our lands, generating electricity and operating our flour mill. I

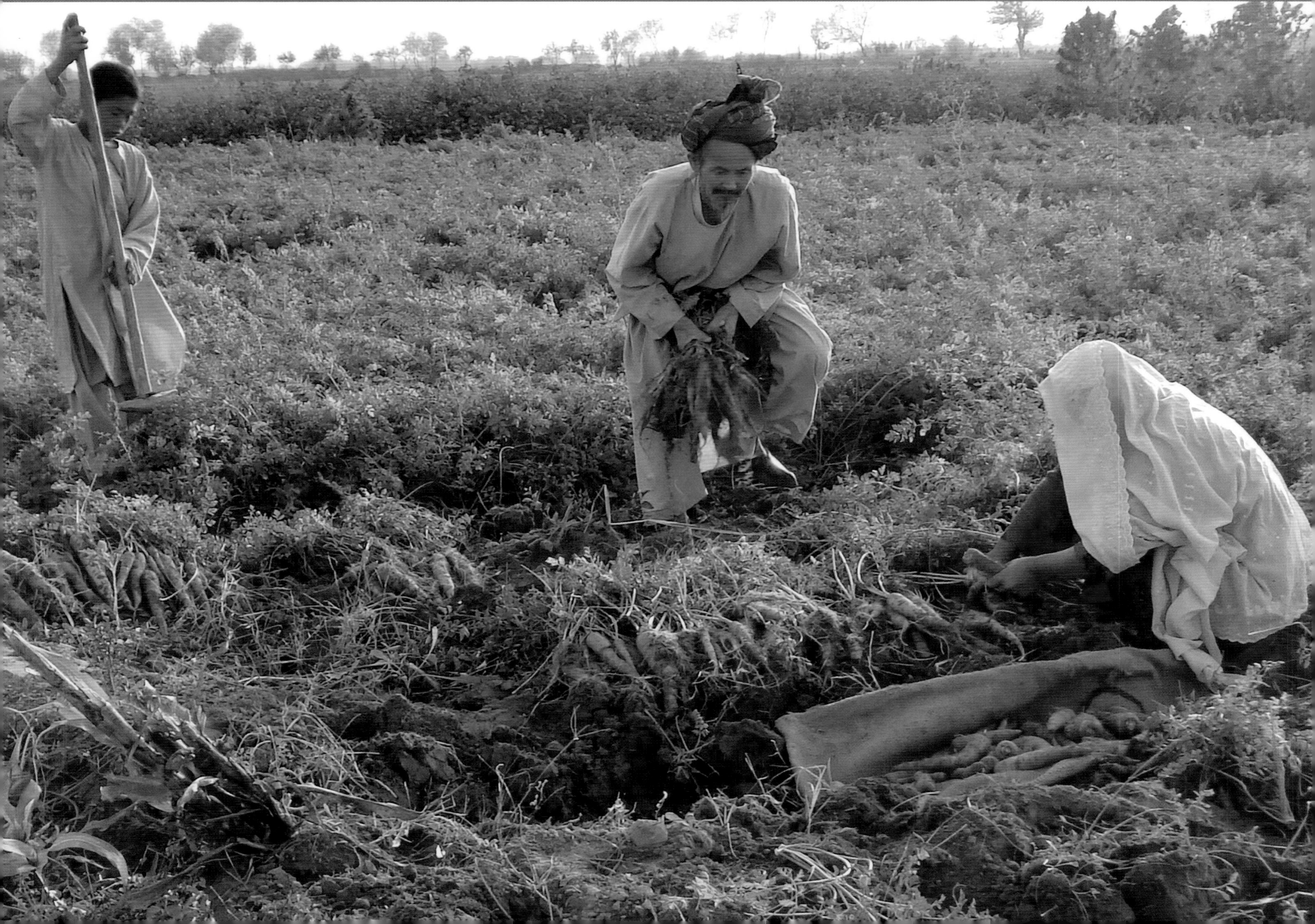

would like to send our voice to the government of Afghanistan that they should know that this project not only benefits or builds this village—it means that Afghanistan is benefited and built. These projects are helping people who are working here and at the same time they are building their country, and with the receiving of the money for projects like this they are feeding their families.

Mr. Amir Khan—Saripul Province

The community–based irrigation program is now in its final stages. This $5,000,000 program is sponsored by the Asian Development Bank (ADB) with funds provided by the Japanese government. Already 41 projects have been completed in northern Afghanistan. The dramatic importance of this program is in its "community-based" nature. This means that these projects are not "top down" (forced upon the villagers). These are projects that have been requested by the villagers themselves and are implemented locally as well. In the process, the village leadership has learned or been trained in several key areas:

- Decision-making regarding the usefulness of various kinds of local projects.
- How to manage the overall project process.
- How to manage construction projects in particular.
- How to keep accurate financial and accounting records for a project.
- Conflict management training.
- Agricultural management training.
- Water management and conservation training. In this regard, each village council signed a Water Management and Conversation agreement with the Ministry of Rural Rehabilitation and Development, outlining new ways of managing the available water resources and agreeing as a group to cooperate in its use.

Already these projects have made a major impact on the affected villages.

Here is how these projects are perceived by other local villagers:

This project that was implemented through the HOPE worldwide organization has been a very useful project. In previous years we could not utilize water for all our lands. Only about 500 acres could be irrigated. Now, due to the current project, around 5,000 acres can be irrigated.

Mr. Abdul Rahman—Faryab Province

Previously, our village had many problems in that we had to work 40 to 50 days each year repairing the canal that brings water to this village. Now this canal has been fixed and around 3,000 acres can be irrigated.

Mr. Azizullah—Faryab Province

Everyone knows that during the previous years of our fathers and grandfathers that they had problems with this canal and distribution canal. Our water was going to waste and they were not able to control the water. When the floods would come it would destroy the channel. But now, with the deep attention of the MRRD and HOPE worldwide it has helped us so much. Our people are very happy and we are so thankful for HOPE worldwide which worked with so much concern and sympathy for our people and the 700 families in our village.

Mr. Shah Mohammad—Saripul Province

Beginning in June 2009, HOPE *worldwide* will oversee the implementation of 34 more projects spread across three provinces. Thousands more people will be impacted—creating jobs, more usable farm land and a stronger connection to the central government. It is our hope in the future to help implement further community-based projects such as these in other parts of Afghanistan.

Farmers in Jawzjan Province at training.

Water distribution BEFORE Hope worldwide's irrigation projects.

Jawzjan Province farmers drawing pictures of their land in relation to other farms to determine how to best distribute water.

Provincial authorities join Hope worldwide and villagers for ribbon-cutting ceremony.

Water distribution AFTER Hope worldwide's irrigation projects.

Shepherds in Jawzjan Province bring their livestock to drink from the newly constructed channels, helping the shepherds without drawing water away from farmers.

MINES TO VINES ... AND THEN SOME

Roots of Peace is a California-based humanitarian nonprofit organization founded by Heidi Kuhn. In September 1997, following the death of the late Princess Diana, Heidi Kuhn embarked on a journey to transform MINES TO VINES—replacing the scourge of landmines with bountiful vineyards worldwide. Roots of Peace works to unearth the dangerous remnants of war in Afghanistan and empower the local communities by working to build sustainable crops on lands which are too dangerous to traverse—this is how we transform the scars of conflict into the roots of peace.

Seen here, Heidi Kuhn, who has a very hands-on relationship in all that Roots of Peace does.

The Roots of Peace Penny Campaign is the educational component, which is a student-to-student initiative engaging youth, as over 30 million American "pennies" have been raised by the international community to build/rebuild schools and soccer fields on former minefields. The mission was founded by ABC7 News Anchor Cheryl Jennings, Heidi Kuhn and her daughter, Kyleigh, as they launched this initiative on September 11, 2003 in the San Francisco Bay Area. Together, the three women traveled to Afghanistan to see firsthand the challenges and seek ways to restore the dreams of Afghan children—providing mutual goals and fair play for future generations. Today, there are schools on the former frontline of the Taliban in Mir Botcha Kot and reaching high into the mountainous regions lating significant local investment in improved agricultural inputs for high-value crops as well as the entire value chain involving processing, storage and marketing. With these investments in the land by the local Afghan people, coupled with technical training to improve their skills and to produce and process agricultural products, Roots of Peace has effectively linked farmers, weavers, input dealers, small-scale processors and many more stakeholders to market. Ultimately, we have empowered thousands of Afghan communities—both men and women—by working in 17 of the 34 provinces.

Harvesting apricots.

of Bamiyan, where a school for 600 girls is currently under construction—all raised from "pennies" from the hearts of children worldwide with a vision for a better tomorrow.

Our best practice has been to pioneer a development model that both promotes the grassroots community and identifies agricultural products with Afghan partners as a generator of increased income to small-scale farmers. We then connect these farmers to merchants interested in expanding their sales of the targeted product, and assist merchants in purchasing high-value/high-quality crops directly from the local Afghan farmers and/or their associations. The Roots of Peace model has proved effective in stimu-

Afghan farmers contribute to the cost of the agricultural materials, which they receive through Roots of Peace funding from private donors, foundations, USAID, USDA, DOD, ADB, EU and the World Bank.

Such investment increases the agricultural adoption rate of the training that Roots of Peace provides because the farmers are actively engaged—providing rapid incentive among fellow farmers.

In 2003, Roots of Peace pioneered the trellis grape vineyard technique with our sub-contractor, U.C. Davis, through the USAID/RAMP program. Now this innovative program is being replicated, as it allows farmers to prune the vine and double the yield. Thus, the ultimate result is a high-value crop that provides sustainable alternative agricultural crops to poppies—replacing the "seeds of terror" with the "seeds of hope" as we literally turn MINES TO VINES and POPPIES TO POMEGRANATES.

Roots of Peace aspires to return the legacy of Afghanistan to the "Garden of Central Asia." By planting cherries in Badhakshan, almonds in Mazar-i-

Sharif, sweet oranges in Jalalabad, pomegranates in Kandahar and grapes in the Shomali Valley, we are restoring community development by creating fertile grounds for peace. We are seeking additional funding to leverage our program throughout Afghanistan—a country which is 80 percent dependent upon agriculture—as Roots of Peace has pioneered a replicable model for agrarian societies. Also, we are seeking matching grants for our Roots of Peace Penny Campaign—Making Change Work! Today, 44.6 percent of the total population of Afghanistan is under the age of 14 years, and investment through the foundation of education provides "roots" for future generations to grow.

Wife of Afghanistan's ambassador to the U.S., Shamim Jawad, Heidi Kuhn and President Karzai.

MORE ABOUT AGRICULTURE

C rops are growing again in Afghanistan, making food instead of drugs for Afghans and the world:

Saracha: Fish. Nangahar Province has a strong governor, alternative crop cultivation, growing security and strong disincentives—all requirements for eliminating poppy cultivation. And it's working. Once second only to Kandahar in poppy cultivation, Nangahar today is nearly drug free. A program that's helped is fish farming. Fish have been scarce in land-locked Afghanistan, especially since drought, along with grenade "fishing" during the war years, wiped out most wild fish. But today a farmer can dig fish ponds, buy fry from Pakistan, grow them to maturity in about eight months and sell them at a profit to an enthusiastic market of Afghans who have a special love for the taste of fish. Who knew?

Kandahar: Fruit, Nuts and Herbs. In 2006, Kandahar reported an 85 percent increase over the previous year in the export of fruits and herbs from Kandahar and surrounding provinces. Exports of dry fruits and nuts—raisins, pistachios and almonds—worth over $23 million were regional—to Pakistan, India, Bangladesh, Saudi Arabia and the UAE—and wider ranging, to include Malaysia and Japan among others. Growth of these markets brings cash to farmers and, through a better economy, greater hope for local security.

Afghanistan: Pomegranates. By 2007, pomegranates marked "Kandahari Pomegranates. Export Quality. Products of Afghanistan" were becoming common on the streets of India and Dubai while a few even found their way to London and other Western countries. Part of a USAID-funded Alternative Livelihoods program, more than a million pomegranate trees have been planted, resulting in exports of between 30,000 and 40,000 metric tons of the fruit. This made it clear that farmers exporting fruit could make as much as poppy farmers per acre. The next step: creating enough security so more farmers have access to the export markets.

To have grapes year-round, newly harvested grapes are packed in clay pods to preserve them. In the winter, the pods can be broken open, presenting good grapes for cooking and eating.

Kunduz: Dried Fruit. Opening the door to trade with Europe and the U.S., the Afghan Chamber of Commerce in Kunduz, working with the U.S. Department of Commerce, held a three-day seminar to teach Afghan businessmen how to package dried fruit to meet international trade standards. More than 60 traders participated in the event.

Asadabad: Tea. The Ministry of Agriculture and Livestock has donated tea shrubs to Kunar Province, brought in from Pakistan. Initially introduced in 1965 when visiting Chinese specialists recognized that the province's climate and geography were suitable for tea cultivation, a promising start of tea cultivation was abandoned during Afghanistan's years of conflict. The hope now is that the new shrubs are the beginning of an industry that will make Afghanistan—a country where tea is a daily staple of conversation—self-sufficient in producing tea.

Lashgar Gah: Wheat. As part of its program to eradicate poppies, USAID is providing seed, fertilizer and improved irrigation to farmers in southern Afghanistan. It's a program that seems to be working: Opium cultivation dropped about 20 percent between 2007 and 2008 while the number of poppy-free provinces increased from 13 to 18. More than $22 million in USAID programs has also resulted in repair or construction of irrigation and drainage canals and roads needed to get crops to market. But clearly, these efforts have another important benefit: security and stability. As one farmer noted, "If you can just help the people of Afghanistan in this way, the fighting will go away."

Nengarhar: Honey. The honey industry started out small: In 2006, Mission East gave 20 women in Badakhshan Province, northern Afghanistan, one beehive, protection gear and training. Now, in spite of having no land for crops, those women have steady incomes and can support their families. In an update on honey production in Afghanistan, 2009 saw the opening of Afghanistan's first honey processing plant in Nangahar Province. This huge step will enable honey farmers to sell their product beyond local markets. A recent international agriculture exhibition in India was impressed with the high quality of the Afghan honey presented. The processing plant employs some 15 people and produces about 400 kilograms of honey a day.

Nooristan: Reforestation. In February 2009, the government of Afghanistan initiated the planting of three million trees in Nangarhar, Kunar, Nooristan and Laghman provinces in a reforestation program.

Badam Bagh Farm, Kabul: Agfair. Some 50,000 people participated in the 2009 Kabul International Fresh Fruit and Vegetable Agfair in May. The event featured Afghan produce—from pomegranates and grapes to cauliflower and spinach. In addition, much like a Stateside state fair, there were hundreds of international and national businesses displaying their wares in booths and tents along with seminars introducing new growing methods from greenhouses to food safety standards and harvesting techniques. An important venue for business-to-business meetings, the event drew representatives from around the world ready to buy Afghan goods or hoping to sell agricultural equipment and technologies.

Kabul: Afghan Conservation Corps. Since 2003, the Afghan Conservation Corps (ACC) has been involved in numerous projects to recover and protect natural resources: its Forest Management Committees in Samangan and Takhar provinces and rehabilitating and managing pistachio woodlands; improving tree nursery and seed storage facilities and recovering native grasses and other plants. Teacher training and workshops have provided instruction on improved reforestation techniques and forest management.

Afghanistan: Bumper Wheat Crop. The Afghan government announced in June 2009 it expects its biggest wheat harvest in three or four years, which will make Afghanistan nearly self-sufficient in wheat. Increased rain and snowfall are partially responsible for the improvement as are more farmland devoted to wheat, improved seed and use of fertilizers. Better roads also make it easier for farmers to get crops to market. Afghanistan also expects improved rice and corn crops this year.

INDUSTRY

MAKING LUXURY SOAPS FOR EXPORT
ARGHAND COOPERATIVE
BY JENNIE GREEN

Nurallah called me on Skype a couple of weeks ago to tell me that one of his male colleagues had left the Arghand Cooperative, possibly for good. What he didn't have to tell me was that Ali Shah's sudden departure left us with eight women and four men—scarcely enough manpower to cover the weekly production requirements. The women's portion of the work was likely to remain covered for the foreseeable future, but the men should total six, especially with Kandahar electricity down for the better part of most days, which meant they had no choice but to extract oil from the nuts and seeds with a hand-crank press. When I asked Nurallah if he had anybody lined up to fill the void, he replied, "I think, maybe …" He told me he would call back when he knew more.

My Skype phone rang again about a week later. "Jennie!" Nurallah shouted over a terrible connection—the result of meager bandwidth for which we pay a small monthly fortune. "I find one new guy, name is Kahn. He comes this Saturday to start work." I told him this was great and encouraged him to call again soon to let me know how the integration of a new member had gone. He called back sooner than I would have expected with surprising news: Kahn had lasted precisely one day.

"One day!" I bellowed. "Why?"

"He tells me this work is not good," Nurallah said. "He says he is too busy, this and that. I tell him okay, no problem. But I know why."

Arghand's double batched, hand molded luxury soaps.

231

I could tell by the way his voice lowered and then trailed off exactly what he was thinking: Kahn was scared.

When Sarah Chayes founded the Arghand Cooperative in 2005, she had several goals: She wanted to contribute to the economic development of southern Afghanistan; she wanted to expand the market for licit agriculture in order to provide local farmers with an incentive to grow crops other than opium poppy; she wanted to highlight the legendary fruits and botanicals for which the region was renowned prior to decades of war and destruction; she wanted to create a fair and democratic workspace in which men and women could work side by side; she wanted to generate employment opportunities in a corner of the world that sorely needed them. Toward that end, she created a product—double batched, hand molded luxury soaps for export to North America—that was intentionally labor intensive. In the beginning, enthusiastic Kandahari's lined up outside Arghand's door with the hope of being selected for membership. But as time went by and the security situation worsened, that line evaporated. By the end of 2007 it had become difficult to recruit new members, and by 2008 the three guys who helped Sarah build the cooperative didn't even want to try because they didn't know who they could trust.

I visited Arghand for three weeks in September 2007, and during that time the nephew of one of our female members—a driver for the Afghan National Army—was kidnapped and subsequently executed. His crime: his affiliation with the internationally backed government of Hamid Karzai. A pall fell over the compound. We knew that Kandahar was encircled by Taliban controlled areas, but now the city was being infiltrated as well. Kidnappings, suicide attacks and bomb explosions were happening on an increasingly regular basis with most of the targets being Afghan citizens who had lined up with the so-called "occupiers." As a foreign-led initiative, Arghand had become a magnificent target.

Women extract seeds from pomegranates.

With the memory of a brutal regime still fresh in the minds of most Afghans, the Taliban made significant strides through their intimidation campaigns. Unfortunately, they were not the only group vying for power and the escalating chaos was further enhanced by corrupt government officials, warlords, drug traffickers and a largely fraudulent police force. It became easy to attribute any sort of violence to the Taliban; it became almost effortless to get away with murder.

Given the abject poverty in which so many Afghans live, coupled with the great demand for our wonderful soaps and body oils in North America, Westerners are invariably surprised to learn how difficult it is for us to staff and expand our business. But for the last two years Arghand members have been risking their lives to come to work every day. The women routinely change their walking routes and the men don't leave the compound unarmed. They work hard to stay under the radar and keep a cupboard filled with guns. It's possible that Kahn really was too busy or that the work didn't suit him … but if he did get cold feet about hitching his cart to Arghand's precarious wagon, then nobody would blame him. Most of our members are surprised not only that we are still in business, but also that they continue to be alive.

Not just alive. Dare I say it: They are thriving. Now that Sarah is based in Kabul and working as a special advisor to the commander of ISAF, our members have embraced the challenge of taking over all aspects of the production process and facility, and are running the cooperative without assistance. They're doing it, of course, because like people everywhere they need money to support their families. But their motivations are actually more complex. The cooperative has become a kind of accidental jihad against extremism, oppression, corruption and discrimination. A tiny bastion of tolerance and respect for basic human rights smack in the middle of a war zone, Arghand has indeed become more than a soap factory; it is a microcosm of the larger society in which its members someday hope to live.

Pressing seeds for their oils.

233

MINE VICTIMS CREATE NEW LIMBS
RED CROSS ORTHOPEDIC CENTER

Orthopedic specialist Najmuddin Helal has just one requirement for prospective recruits at Afghanistan's largest prosthetics workshop in Kabul.

Watching staff, from technicians to security guards to helpers in the center's physiotherapy sessions walk past with unsteady gaits, it's easy to spot. They are all disabled and nearly 80 percent of them are landmine victims.

"We employ only disabled," smiled Helal, director of the International Committee of the Red Cross Orthopedic Center in west Kabul. "It is a kind of discrimination, but we like to call it positive discrimination.

"There are good advantages. It is a way to give jobs to the disabled. They know the problems (patients face) because they have passed through them, and then they can teach other disabled easily," said Helal, who has a staff of 240 in Kabul. The center is always busy.

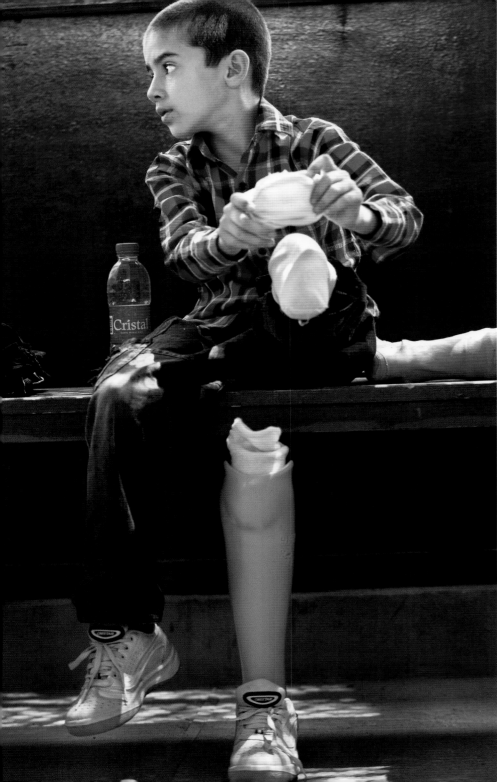

There are 60,000 surviving landmine victims in Afghanistan, according to the United Nations. Every month an average of 60 people are killed or wounded by landmines or explosive remnants of war in Afghanistan, which is estimated to have over 100,000 explosive devices still in the ground.

Nearly 80,000 disabled, more than 30,000 of them amputees, have registered with the ICRC centers in Afghanistan since 1988. Seventy percent of amputees who visit the centers are civilians, 30 percent are military.

The main center in Kabul produces around 4,000 prostheses, such as legs and arms and hooks to replace hands, and around 10,000 orthoses each year, as well as walking aids and wheelchairs, distributed to other provincial centers.

In one room, a worker assembles artificial elbow joints with a hammer and tosses the finished product into a box. He is blind.

In the next room, workers with artificial limbs make orthoses or medical supports like corsets and splints for polio sufferers.

On a board nearby, the products are neatly displayed: skin-colored plastic knee and elbow joints, metal braces, hand-replacing hooks in varying sizes—including small ones for young children.

A NEW LEASE ON LIFE

Sitting on a stool in one of the center's spotless workshops, 43-year-old former soldier Baz Mohammad carefully measures a stainless steel leg brace.

He is two feet shorter than he should be, having opted for short prosthetic legs after his own were blown off by a landmine in 1989 when the Afghan army was fighting against Mujahideen after the end of Soviet occupation. With both legs amputated above the knee, having a lower center of gravity makes walking easier. "I am happy working here. Not only can I support my family, I am also proud that I have the ability to work here and support other disabled people," he said.

Past the production line of artificial limbs is the physiotherapy wing, where male patients try out their new limbs, treading along yellow and red footprints painted on the floor—amputees on one side of the room, non-amputees learning to walk with braces on the other.

Behind a curtain, women—some wearing the traditional blue burqa—adapt to prostheses of their own. Already a stigma, amputation brings an additional curse for women, who are regarded as a liability when it comes to keeping house and so are spurned for marriage.

MINES STILL A MENACE

Twenty-one-year-old student Abdul Naser has come in for his first prosthesis. His leg was amputated four months ago when he stepped on a mine chasing after his goats on a mountainside north of Kabul. "I have just received this prosthesis. I hope it will change my life," he said, rubbing the reddened stump below his knee and trying on his false leg.

Over 80 percent of amputees who visit the center are adult males, because in Afghan culture they walk outside more than women and are the fighters.

The United Nations Mine Action Center for Afghanistan says it has cleared 300,000 landmines and explosive remnants of war from 1.0 billion square meters of terrain since 1989. That leaves around 700 million square meters still to be cleared.

"The number of prostheses needed remains steady, because they only last two to three years and need to be replaced," Helal said. "But the number of new landmine amputees is going down. There are now maybe two or three people injured or killed by a landmine per day."

It was a landmine blast that pushed 43-year-old Helal into the job in the first place—when his own legs were blown off at the age of 18 as he was driving along a Kabul riverbed. He was the center's 34th patient.

He still feels phantom pain, the same burning sensation he felt at the time the mine, possibly an anti-tank mine, blew the bottom of his car from under him. "I still think after 24 years … why should I lose my legs? Why can't I feel the grass on the ground with my feet? Why can't I feel my feet in the water of a stream? It's the same with everyone.

"But when I see amputees crawl to the center on the ground and leave walking, that is something very special for me."

By Simon Gardner, September 10, 2007 ©2007 Reuters. Reprinted with permission from Reuters. License#REU-5782-MES.

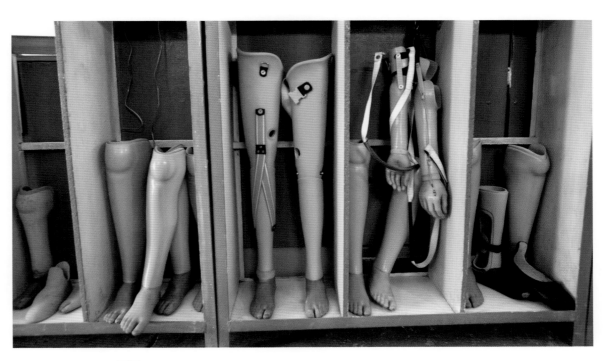

THE LAND BRIDGE OF ASIA
THE STORY OF THE MOST IMPORTANT ROAD IN ASIA

The idea of building a road that would circle Afghanistan's interior started back in the 1960s by the U.S. and Russia, in large part to make up for Afghanistan's lack of railroads. Expanding on that circle, this "ring road" would have secondary highways reaching out to all the provincial capitals and other major cities in the country. Its purpose was twofold: to make travel within the country easier and to open up new markets by linking China to Central Asia and Central Asia with Iran's seaports. For Afghanistan itself, it would mean easy transportation and expanded exports of fruits, nuts, rugs and other products to distant markets. But the Russian occupation and the wars came. New construction stopped and completed sections of the road were destroyed. Moving goods around or across Afghanistan became all but impossible.

With the fall of the Taliban in 2001, the idea of the ring road turned into a major development effort for the allies as a key part of their nation building for Afghanistan. Though admittedly a daunting task and expensive ($2.5 billion by June 2009 and counting), it continues as a key element in Afghanistan's struggle for security and statehood.

With 90 percent of the road complete today, finishing the final stretch through Badghis Province, Afghanistan's poorest, is proving particularly thorny. Security is poor. The Taliban presence is expanding and attacks on road crews and security agents are increasing; kidnappings in the area are not uncommon.

But the opportunities for commerce this project offers are impressive—as are the revenues it promises. Niklas Swanstrom, a specialist on Central Asia, sees the road as critical to all of Central Asia, estimating that the regional network of trade it will create could result in well over 700,000 permanent jobs in Afghanistan, Tajikistan, Kyrgystan and Kazakhstan as well as Pakistan and Iran.

Beyond commerce, the ring road is critical to Afghanistan's overall security. As Major General Michael Tucker, Head of Operations for NATO, put it, "Security in Afghanistan is ultimately defined by our ability to defend the ring road."[1] Or, to put it another way, "… every day that this road is not moving forward is another day that the Taliban and criminals think they've won."[2]

In spite of insurgency threats in Badghis, NATO's crews are determined to complete this backbone for Afghan commerce—even if it means redrawing the plan. In a recent move to outflank insurgents, road engineers have redirected the last link in the road from a route through the Murghab Valley to one farther north through desert land. While this is a less attractive route for local economic development, as it misses the most populous areas of Badghis, it offers safety. The canyons of the Murghab would make builders as well as truckers moving goods on the finished road easy targets for insurgents posted on the rims above.

The ring road is now scheduled for completion in 2010, transforming Afghanistan from a "land-locked" country to a "land bridge" for commerce to and from Asia. It's a notion that can be realized, but one that will need constant vigilance to ensure the safety of travelers and goods on what may, indeed, be the most important road in Asia.

[1]Smucker, Philip, "On Afghanistan's road to somewhere, Taliban block the way," McClatchy Newspapers, June 21, 2009.

[2]Ibid.

Other sources used for this story:

Hashimi, Anwar, "Ring-road will be finished by end of 2009," 28 April, 2008.

Jhanmal Zabihullah, The Afghanistan ring road project is 90 percent complete, 07 June 2009.

Synovitz, Ron, "Afghanistan: Ring Road's Completion Would Benefit Entire Region," Radio Free Europe/Radio Liberty, 10 October 2007.

Synovitz, Ron, "Afghanistan: Key Road Toward Pakistan to Improve Trade, Security," Radio Free Europe/Radio Liberty, 29 April, 2008.

EXCERPTS FROM

A BRIEF CULTURAL HISTORY OF AFGHANISTAN AND ITS HANDICRAFTS

BY MINA SHIRZOY

In all civilizations, magical powers have been ascribed to gems, and handicrafts, perhaps out of a need to explain their rarity and beauty.

Afghanistan is a land-locked country located in the heart of Asia. It is a land of harsh steppes of mountain valleys criss-crossed by irrigation channels sparkling in the sun like the landscape or the embroideries of Afghan women glowing with color like bright exotic flowers.

Afghanistan has always been a country proud of its culture, traditions and love for freedom, which its history speaks for itself. It is rough but very appealing. The hardworking and courageous women of Afghanistan express their talents and culture through their exuberant works of art.

Afghanistan's dramatic history, with successive waves of people bringing their own contribution and influence to the country, has fashioned and enriched the face of Afghanistan.

An important staging post on the Silk Road, it absorbed influences from Greece as well as from China, Persia and Central Asia and from Mongols and Turks. It retains a wonderful diversity of cultures, languages, traditions and crafts.

The richness of its history, the diversity of its landscape, everything conspires to make Afghanistan a stronghold of traditions and art forms. Each valley has its own cultural identity, its own originality. In a country where the main routes of communication were overrun by invaders, the mountaineers turned in on themselves. Access was difficult and uncertain, the valleys isolated. Each valley cherishes its individuality.

The embroidery of Afghanistan was mostly the work of women and young girls. In the privacy of their homes they decorated fabrics with threads of gold, silver and silk or wool. Women embroidered not only from pleasure of duty, but equally as a statement of their value and of their love for their family. Gifts to prominent guests marked the status of the donor's family.

It is not simply a craft but also expresses the soul of the family and enriches its history. It is for this reason that Afghan embroidery is so splendidly varied. Within each regional style, individual families embroidered variations on established themes, adding their own originality, fantasy and imagination. The longstanding isolation means that many villages have developed specific traditions that they have kept right up to the present. Each region, each ethnic group, almost each village had distinct customs, sometimes even a different dialect from one valley to another. This is still the case in Nooristan.

This explains the variety of clothing and embroidery in the past in Afghanistan. There are numerous techniques and styles of embroidery as well as a variety of shapes, colors and motifs for men and women.

EMBROIDERY IN THE SOUTH AND EAST. Pashtun women, whether settled or nomad, love rich, colorful and beautiful embroideries that shine. The women, who are more independent than their settled sisters, proudly wear all their jewelry. They fix jewels of silver and semi-precious stones and discs of multicolored beads onto their wide dresses. These are embroidered in the front of the dress and the wrists and are in red fabric for young girls and green or black for married women. The long shawl they wear on their head is embroidered in gold at the front and with large multicolored motifs on the back. Men in this area wear shirts embroidered with silk. They are long and made of cotton with the same color or white embroidery.

EMBROIDERY IN THE WEST. Baluch women of the provinces of Farah and Nimroz along the edge of the Seistan Desert wear wide trousers and a long dress with multicolored embroidery characterized by a large embroidered pocket below the waist with an upward-facing point. Baluch, influenced by Sind in Pakistan, stitch small mirrors held by threads onto the women's dresses and men's hats.

Herat has a great tradition of popular art: that of hunting cloths decorated with partridges. They are meant to ensnare with mythical animals.

EMBROIDERY IN THE CENTER. The embroidery of the Hazaras in the central region of the country is amazingly precise and fine. It entirely covers the background cotton fabric in a pattern of bricks or of multicolored zigzag lines. The items embroidered are small envelope-shaped bags, makeup bags, belts, bodice fronts for women's dresses and bigger bags to hold the Holy Quran.

EMBROIDERY IN THE NORTH. The Tajiks and Uzbeks of northern Afghanistan produce a particularly rich range of embroideries. Hats embroidered in multicolored silks or gold threads, women's dresses and men's waistcoats embroidered with flowers on a dark background. The women of the Tajik, settled agriculturalists long established in the region, embroider a lot of decorative articles for the house.

Patchwork (*korma dozi* or Afghan). Curtains and quilts are also made in patchwork when pieces of cloth of different colors are embroidered together. Traditionally the pieces were from the colored fabrics which the bride's mother offered to the guests at the wedding. The assembled piece was supposed to bring good luck and happiness.

CONCLUSION

For Afghan refugees made idle in the camps of Pakistan and Iran during the war years, it has been essential to find some occupation that would give them confidence in themselves and at the same time bring them some income. Workshops at Iran and Pakistani refugee camps have proven Afghan women's capacity for adaptation and organization. They accepted their new life and were encouraged to create magnificent works of art in Iran and Pakistan. They have ensured the survival of a traditional art of a very high standard.

The beauty of what women create through Afghan handicrafts will remain a source of pride to them and their country. It is to be hoped that these lovely creations will remain as diverse, as appreciated and as widespread in the country as once they were, for people of every nation need beauty, art and a sense of achievement in life. These handicrafts play a major role in the revival of the culture of Afghanistan after two decades of war.

TECHNOLOGY EXPLODES IN AFGHANISTAN

Policharkhe: Kuchi High Tech. Texas A&M University, along with the University of California-Davis, is introducing satellites, cell phones and spectrometers to Afghanistan's sheep and goat herders. With these tools—and the training to go along with them—herders are able to link into university models that predict plant growth based on expected rainfall and soil conditions. These show the herders where the best grazing will be and whether or not they should be purchasing feed supplements or selling their herds. Other analysis tools examine the manure of a herd, providing information on animal health. The American universities will be working with the Afghan Ministry of Agriculture and Kabul University to fully implement this program.

Kandahar: Cell Phones. In a country with few land telephone lines, cell phones are a panacea. For some businesses, the availability of cell phone

technology—never mind that the networks are still unreliable—is changing the way business is done. A cell phone call now replaces a trip on miserable, dangerous roads to neighboring Pakistan or Iran to place orders. For some, the cell phone IS the business: Enterprising Afghans are supporting themselves from fees collected from their "public" cell phones.

Kunduz: Fiber Optics. By March 2009 Kabul was connected to Central Asia with 8,000 fiber optic lines linking Kabul with Tajikistan and Uzbekistan. Fiber connections will be made with Pakistan in the near future.

Kabul: iPhones. Can modern technology break Afghanistan's 30-year cycle of war? Perhaps. Technologies, especially the Internet and cell phones, are giving young Afghans a different view of the world from their parents. About a quarter of Afghans now use cell phones. Roshan, the country's leading cell phone company, added more than 1 million customers in the last six months of 2008 alone. Kabul now boasts a shopping mall, complete with glass elevators, that features electronics stores bursting with all the hottest gadgets.

MORE ABOUT INDUSTRY

Herat: Investments. By late 2008, investors had set up some 45 new companies in Herat Province, and the value of foreign investment—from nine countries—was more than $23 million. In addition, between 2002 and late 2009, more than $1 billion had been spent on road construction and industrial capacity building.

Kabul: Investing. Looking to start up a new business? Afghanistan might just be the place to do it. The Afghan Growth Finance (AGF) Fund, started in April 2008, is investing in new small to medium-sized enterprises and focusing especially on businesses that add value to local raw materials, including mining, gold, marble and agro-processing. And because today Afghanistan imports some 90 percent of the goods it uses, there is a huge potential market. AGF has already provided credit to a steel processing plant and dried fruit and nut packers—so growers no longer have to send their fruit to India for packaging. According to Mustafa Kazem, who heads up AGF, "In the first half of [2009] we're going to invest more than we did in the entire 2008 as we're getting aware of the market we're expanding."[1]

Kabul: Milk. In spite of problems with electricity supply, the dairy industry has taken hold again and milk products are available in Afghanistan's cities. Production from a group of northern provinces increased 72 percent between 2002 and 2007. Improvements in industry infrastructure—processing and packaging goods—as well as better dairy stock are primarily responsible for the change. And while there is optimism that improvements will continue, Kabul's dairy union complains that more collection and processing facilities are needed and, of course, consistent electricity to keep the milk from spoiling.

Nangarhar: Carpet Processing. In 2009, for the first time ever, Afghanistan has its own carpet scissoring and washing factory: a facility that provides jobs to some 400 locals. The Provincial Handicraft Department initiated the project with funds from USAID. In addition to finishing carpets woven in homes and factories all across Afghanistan, the Nangarhar facility has its own weaving factory with modern equipment. While this factory does not entirely eliminate the need for weavers to take their carpets to Pakistan for finishing, it reduces the need and is a first step in ensuring "cradle-to-grave" production of this most lucrative of Afghanistan's exports. In a related development, the Ministry of Commerce has joined with Tanweer, a private investment company, to open a market for Afghan carpets in Dubai.

Afghanistan: Quraqul Hides. Those curly-haired sheep are back again! Quraqul sheep hides generated some $40 million in sales in 2008, making them Afghanistan's third-ranked export. An industry seriously damaged during the war years, Quraqul sheep ranchers have been recovering their herds. Afghanistan is rated as having some of the highest-quality Quraqul in the world; the sector will begin to really flourish when sufficient processing facilities for the skins are available.

[1]Motevalli, Golnar, Reuters, May 26, 2006.

ARTS & ENTERTAINMENT

MAKING KIDS LAUGH
MOBILE MINI CIRCUS FOR CHILDREN

MMCC, Mobile Mini Circus for Children, is an international nonprofit NGO that has been operating in Afghanistan since June 2002. The main objective of MMCC is providing educational and informative entertainment to children. This aim is achieved by identifying, training and applying Afghan talent and potential.

MMCC has a well-trained team of eight mobile Afghan senior artists who perform and run workshops all over Afghanistan. The mobile circus is equipped with props, animal costumes, puppets, a mobile stage, sound system and musical instruments. The artists are chosen through a number of auditions in Kabul. Since 2002, they have received training in theater and circus performance and have within their repertoire themes such as children's rights, peace and reconstruction, health issues, landmine awareness and social education. Each performance lasts for approximately one and a half hours.

MMCC's mobile artists have been performing in orphanages, hospitals, street children's centers and schools in Kabul as well as in a large number of provinces since 2002. So far, MMCC's mobile performances and workshops have reached half a million Afghan children in 15 provinces.

Since November 2003 MMCC has run a Culture House for Children in Kabul. Besides being an active creative space for children, the Culture House is more than anything a laboratory for new creative and cultural ideas to be developed in cooperation with the children themselves. The mobile artists then take the children's ideas to thousands of children all over the country as they tour with their performances and workshops.

The Children's Culture House is also the base for MMCC's 80 semi-professional junior artists. In the school season the children artists perform at schools in Kabul on a weekly basis. Like MMCC's mobile group of adult artists, the children's performances are a mix of traditional circus such as juggling, unicycling, etc. plus one or more educational performance piece. MMCC's very talented group of singing girls is an essential part of all performances. In 2005, 12 MMCC children artists performed in Germany and Denmark for two months. In 2006 another group was invited to Japan.

The teacher training workshops are an amazing opportunity for MMCC to introduce our creative educational methods to a large number of schools—and thereby help us fulfill MMCC's overall goal of spreading fun and joy to as many children in the country as possible. During a five-day workshop, teachers and school consultants create and work with a large number of creative objectives that are all very easy to implement in a classroom. In the second part of the workshop we help school consultants and teachers to implement the creative methods in school. This part starts with an educational entertaining performance by MMCC's mobile artists.

In the five-day implementation workshop, the school consultants and teachers each work with a group of children assisted by MMCC's artists. While one group creates their own educational theater play, others rehearse two or three songs or make a backstage curtain. On the final day, the children do their own performance assisted by their teachers—who now know how to do it again and again on their own.

REDISCOVERING AFGHANISTAN'S ANCIENT PAST

CHESHM-E-SHAFA, Afghanistan—Centuries-old shards of pottery mingle with spent ammunition rounds on a wind-swept mountainside in northern Afghanistan where French archeologists believe they have found a vast ancient city.

For years, villagers have dug the baked earth on the heights of Cheshm-e-Shafa for pottery and coins to sell to antique smugglers. Tracts of the site that locals call the "City of Infidels" look like a battleground, scarred by craters.

But now tribesmen dig angular trenches and preserve fragile walls, working as laborers on an excavation atop a promontory. To the north and east lies an undulating landscape of barren red-tinted rock that was once the ancient kingdom of Bactria; to the south a still-verdant valley that leads to the famed Buddhist ruins at Bamiyan.

Roland Besenval, director of the French Archeological Delegation in Afghanistan and leading the excavation, is sanguine about his helpers' previous harvesting of the site. "Generally the old looters make the best diggers," he said with a shrug.

A trip around the northern province of Balkh is like an odyssey through the centuries, spanning the ancient Persian empire, the conquests of Alexander the Great and the arrival of Islam. The French mission has mapped some 135 sites of archeological interest in the region best known for the ancient trove found by a Soviet archeologist in the 1970s.

The Bactrian Hoard consisted of exquisite gold jewelry and ornaments from graves of wealthy nomads, dated to the first century A.D. It was concealed by its keepers in the vaults of the presidential palace in Kabul from the Taliban regime and finally unlocked after the militia's ouster.

The treasure, currently on exhibition in the United States, demonstrates the rich culture that once thrived here, blending influences from the web of trails and trading routes known as the Silk Road, that spread from Rome and Greece to the Far East and India.

But deeper historical understanding of ancient Bactria has been stymied by the recent decades of war and isolation that severely restricted visit by archeologists. "It's a huge task because we are still facing the problem of looting," said Besenval, who first excavated in Afghanistan 36 years ago and speaks the local language of Dari fluently. "We

The ruins of Shar-i Gholgholaa in Bamiyan, with the Koh-i Baba mountains behind.

The opening up of Afghanistan did little to curb the treasure hunters. British author Rory Stewart, who made an extraordinary solo hike across the country in 2002, wrote how poor tribesmen were systematically pillaging the remains of a lost ancient city dating back to the 12th century around the towering minaret of Jam in western Afghanistan.

State control is a little more pervasive in Balkh but still patchy. The provincial culture authority says it has just 50 guards to protect historical sites across an area nearly the size of New Jersey.

Saleh Mohammad Khaleeq, a local poet and historian serving as the chief of the province's cultural department, said the guards ward off looters, but concedes the only way to safeguard Afghanistan's rich heritage is through public education. "People are so poor. They are just looking for ways to buy bread. We need to open their minds as they don't know the value of their history. We have to give them that knowledge and then they will protect it," he said.

know that objects are going to Pakistan and on to the international market. It's very urgent work. If we don't do something now, it will be too late."

Looting was rife during the civil war of the early 1990s when Afghanistan lurched into lawlessness. Locals say it subsided under the Taliban's hard-line rule, but the Islamists' fundamentalism took its own toll on Afghanistan's cultural history. They destroyed the towering Buddha statues of Bamiyan chiseled more than 1,500 years ago and smashed hundreds of statues in the national museum simply because they portrayed the human form.

Villagers hired as laborers at Cheshm-e-Shafa recall how they too used to be among hundreds of locals who would scavenge the site they are now paid 230 Afn ($4.60) a day to excavate.

"During the civil war everyone was involved," said Nisarmuddin, 42, who covered his face with his turban to block the dust that a stiff breeze whipped across the mountainside. Nisarmuddin, a farmer who like many Afghans goes by one name, said people used to keep their finds secret so the local militia commander would not claim them. They could sell items of ancient pottery and glass for a few dollars to antique dealers in the city of Mazar-e-Sharif, which lies an hour's drive down a bumpy track through the desert.

One of the Afghan culture officials working at the Cheshm-e-Shafa excavation was clearly anxious that media coverage could bring unwanted attention to the site, where archeologists have uncovered a two-meter-tall anvil-like stone believed to have been an altar at a fire temple originating from the Persian Empire period around the 6th century B.C. "Hezb-e-Islami and Taliban and other extremists might use explosives and blow up this stone," said archeology department official Mohammed Rahim Andarab.

Many archeologists remain wary of working in Balkh as Islamic militancy seeps into new regions of the country. Yet the sheer breadth of history to be unearthed is enough to lure Besenval and his colleagues.

They are also restoring an ornate 9th century A.D. mosque. Its stout, half-buried columns, decorated with abstract floral and geometric patterns in stucco, reflect local art but also influences from Central Asia, Buddhism and Persia. Chahryar Adle, a Frenchman of Iranian descent with long experience in Afghanistan, said

the mosque of Noh-Gonbad, or Nine Cupolas, is the oldest in the country and "undoubtedly it is one of the finest in the world of this period."

French archeologists have a long association with the region. They first visited in 1924 to excavate a fortress in the nearby town of Balkh. They hoped to find an ancient city of Alexander, whom history recounts married a local princess, Roxanne, in Bactria in 327 B.C., but left disappointed.

The mirage of Alexander also lurks over Cheshm-e-Shafa, about 30 kilometers away. The site had a strategic location at the southern entry point

into Bactria with fortifications circling an area of about 400 hectares, and its network of mountaintop lookout towers suggests it was well defended. A flat field the size of several football fields that may have been a parade ground or barracks lies on the plain below. And the local nickname, "City of Infidels," also suggests a foreign occupation at some time.

So could this have been Alexander's redoubt in Bactria, where he met the local princess Roxanne? The archeologist allowed himself a rare foray into the realms of speculation. "Who knows? Maybe they married in Cheshm-e-Shafa," Besenval said, smiling.

FROM MINEFIELD TO OUTDOOR FESTIVAL FIELD

AFGHAN GLASTONBURY BRINGS MUSIC TO MINEFIELD

More than 170,000 Afghans packed into the country's first pop festival this week, the biggest recreational gathering since the fall of the Taliban almost six years ago and a gig that could have been dubbed Glastonbury Afghanistan. It was a far cry from the misery of suicide bombs and house-to-house fighting and like Glastonbury, it shared an agricultural theme.

While the first ever Glasto rockers were treated to free milk, revelers at the Kabul festival were offered a free introduction to modern farming techniques and the opportunity to meet agri-traders from all over the country. The three-day event, on a reclaimed minefield, was ostensibly an agricultural fair, laid on at a cost of at least $1.5 million by USAID, the U.S. government agency which is a leading donor in the country.

But while plenty of people were doing business, most of the men, women and children at the landmark event were simply there to have a good time.

"I came to the fair because I love pop music," said Said Ahmed Rahik, a 17-year-old student from Kabul. "My father told me not to come because he wants me to study all the time. But I came without permission, because there is nowhere else to see music like this in Kabul." Headline acts included the winners of *Afghan Star*, the country's fledgling *Pop Idol* show, circus performers, stand-up comedians and traditional Afghan folk singers.

Marianne Walimi, 27, a photographer from Kabul, said, "Always Afghanistan has been at war. It is good to have something like this for a change. It is really fun."

The festival was housed on a farm. But Badam Bagh, in the northern suburbs of Kabul, has not been turned over entirely to music. Originally a government site, the 57-hectare farm fell into disrepair during three decades of war. It was mined, fought over and eventually claimed by Kabul's dog fighters. The government reclaimed the land last year and invested $1 million clearing more than 50 unspent munitions.

"It took a week to clear each mine," said Mohammad Haroon Zareef, the site manager. "There were more than 50 small bombs, rockets and mines. We had to clear rocks, build a reservoir and level the ground. Now it is the biggest party in Afghanistan. The farmers are coming and learning about new crops and new techniques, but they can have a fun time as well."

While tens of thousands of people danced and sang as the event was broadcast across the country, security was a major concern for the organizers. But the hundreds of soldiers, secret police and private contractors guarding Badam Bagh were not looking for people sneaking in without tickets. The whole event was free. And the festival, which ended last night, passed without incident, despite the threat from insurgents, even in Kabul, remaining very real.

Organizers claimed that the secret of a peaceful festival was giving more than 300 policemen lunch.

Jerome Starkey, October 27, 2007 © The Independent.

MISSION IMPOSSIBLE 2011
THE NATIONAL CRICKET TEAM: ONE DAY INTERNATIONAL STANDING

In May 2008 it was a crazy long shot: Afghanistan qualifying to play in the 2011 Cricket World Cup. Afghanistan? War-torn, conservative, sport-less Afghanistan? Against the heavies of cricket like Australia, India, Bermuda and Scotland?

- *May 2008, Afghanistan won the World Cricket League Division 5 tournament, beating Jersey and moving up to Division 4.*

Before Division 4 play, the Afghan team needed help, so they were off to Pakistan for a toughening-up session. As general manager Bashir Stanekzai noted, the sole good academy in Kabul could not provide stiff enough competition to give the team the mental agility it would need for the next level. Meanwhile, lots of Afghans began to closely watch their cricket team's progress. By January 2009, the team had aced Division 4 and had moved to Division 3.

Afghanistan has had help from the International Cricket Council, which has made it a regional focus for development. Today, the Afghan League is still in its infancy, has few clubs and little in the way of proper playing grounds. Yet its team is making unprecedented progress through cricket's professional divisions.

- *January 2009, Afghanistan plays the Division 3 tournament, winning a decisive final victory over Tanzania.*

By April 2009 Afghanistan could boast over 200 cricket clubs and the national team's successes were inspiring Afghan kids to take up the sport—in spite of poor playing facilities. The next 19 days of international play in South Africa would tell the tale for the national team. First, a win against Scotland, then Ireland and finally Namibia.

- *Alas! Afghanistan was knocked out of 2011 World Cup play in the final round of qualifying by Kenya and the Netherlands.*

Despite the loss, Afghanistan, with its fearless playing style, got all the kudos. With its unprecedented rise from lowly Division 5 play to the finals where they beat both Bermuda and Scotland, who played in the 2007 World Cup, the team wildly surpassed all expectations—even its own.

- *Now and for the next four years, Afghanistan enjoys "One Day International" standing.*

As team member Hamid Hassan commented, "I feel absolutely wonderful—it is a brilliant achievement for our country."

MORE ABOUT ARTS & ENTERTAINMENT

Kabul: **National Museum of Afghanistan**. "Tradition stays alive when its culture stays alive," so says the entrance to the National Museum of Afghanistan. Restoration of the severely war-damaged building (funded largely by the Greek government) is nearly complete and many of its displaced precious artifacts are finding their way home. By the end of 2007, thousands of ancient treasures had been returned to Afghanistan. Most notable, nearly 1,500 pieces were returned from Switzerland where they had been exiled for safety by the Northern Alliance. Remarkably, another trove of some 4,300 plundered pieces was recovered by Danish police some years ago and returned to President Karzai. Included in this return are items likely handled by Alexander the Great along with coins, weapons, jewelry and other pieces of artwork. Still, some 50,000 pieces—nearly half the museum's 1970s collection—are lost, probably forever. And, unfortunately, security at historic sites and excavations remains poor. Afghanistan hopes to create an archeological police force to eliminate the ongoing plunder of its national treasures.

Nangarhar: Hadda Museum. The Nangarhar Directorate of Information Culture is seeking funds to reconstruct the now-demolished Hadda Museum. Built by King Muhammed Zair in the mid-1960s, the museum, built on Shutir Tapa Hill, a site of historic excavation, was once known as the region's richest museum.

Istalif: Pottery. A pottery-making center for a good 400 years, Istalif was razed by the Taliban in 1996 after the Northern Alliance's retreat—a retaliation. Though burned to the ground, Istalif has seen the return of its craftsmen, and by early 2008 there were some 60 workshops operating—with new challenges. Deforestation has severely raised the cost of wood, making it expensive to fire the ceramic-ware, while potential buyers on the international market want higher-quality, stronger pots impossible to create in over-packed wood-fired kilns. Turquoise Mountain Foundation opened a resource center in 2007 to help Istalif's potters develop better product. A new gas-fired kiln offers cheaper and better firing that yields stronger pots. Experiments with new glazes and better clay processing are beginning to open new markets for Istalif's wares. Progress is happening but, as can be expected, change to age-old traditions will happen only over time in this conservative village steeped in the ways of folk tradition.

Kabul: War Rugs. It's an "oriental rug." But . . . what are those shapes around the border? Am I seeing … hand grenades? "War" rugs first appeared during the Soviet occupation of Afghanistan in the 1980s and were made by Afghans in refugee camps in Pakistan or Iran. Far from the tranquil "gardens" of traditional tribal weaving of Afghan carpet-makers, these were woven as a response to the dire, unsettling events that were part of daily life, and for propaganda purposes. Made for sale to tourists, soldiers and the international marketplace, these rugs feature the implements of war: Kalashnikov rifles, grenades where *bota* should go, tanks instead of *guls*, helicopters in the place of flowers. In more recent years, the rugs sometimes feature international icons such as the World Trade Center or carry slogans like "Tora Bora" or "The War on Terror." Soviet-era rugs are prized today; their more recent descendants sell to an interested market of American soldiers. Perhaps not so valuable for their historical or artistic merit, these rugs are helping to prop up the flagging Afghan rug industry.

Afghanistan: **Afghan Star**. For four years it's been the hit of Afghan TV and an important lesson in democracy. *Afghan Star*, a program much like *American Idol*, is a contest among performers; the judges vote by text messaging; the winner takes home a prize.

I t's one place in Afghanistan where a member of any tribe can win, where men and women compete against one another and where it's possible to lose without it being an insult to your tribe or clan. The show has its detractors, of course. There have been threats to Tolo TV, the broadcaster; the set is surrounded by armed guards and razor wire and the Afghan Council on Scholars has labeled the show immoral and un-Islamic. For all that, the show is overwhelmingly popular (viewership for the 2008 season was estimated at 11 million—or nearly half the country's population. As Havana Marking, a British filmmaker who has done a documentary on the show, noted, "What moved me most is that, despite all this, there is such kindness and strength. . . . the youth have such optimism and hope. They are desperate for the old culture that they hear their parents, or even grandparents, talk about—a liberal, cultured time, with strong universities and flourishing arts. You realize what a luxury it is to have a 'normal' peaceful life, where you can discuss TV shows and not how many people in your family are dead."

Kabul: Quran Idol. Facing potential restrictions or an outright ban of their hit *Afghan Star* series by the council of clerics, Tolo TV developed *Quran-Star*, a show that features contestants reciting long passages from the Quran. Like *Afghan Star*, its contestants are everyday Afghans—a shoe seller, a student, a laborer. And like *Afghan Star*, *Quran-Star* has broad appeal. Even the conservative Minister of Information agreed that *Quran-Star* is a good show.

K **abul: TV.** Less than a decade ago, it was illegal in Afghanistan to own a TV or listen to music. Today, though less than 20 percent of the population has access to electricity, Afghanistan boasts 13 private TV channels that run a variety of programs from Indian soaps to Hollywood movies and political analysis programs. And though the threat of censorship remains fluid, TV has become an important new mode of communication. The stations are careful to weed out material that

might offend—uncovered knees, nape of the neck, teens dancing together, a kiss on the cheek, references to religions other than Islam. Finding the balance of what is and what is not Afghan, what is and what is not acceptable is difficult. One genre that seems to survive the storms is satire and comedy. Not just spice for TV, they seem to speak to Afghan sensibility and are developing into a new and effective way to get things done. As an example, one program suggested that water bottles be made of soft plastic—so that when politicians throw them during heated debate they won't hurt anyone. Bottle throwing in the *jurga* stopped. The 21st century is using a very Afghan route to find its way into Afghan life.

Afghanistan: Girls' Football. Once again, against all odds, there's an extraordinary passion for women's football in Afghanistan. It's tough for the players to get good practice in Afghanistan—training has to be held on closed fields; international peacekeeping forces must be available for security; the Taliban are always a threat. But undaunted, the women's football team, led by a German "overseas coach," is dedicated to proving that football IS for girls. In 2008 the national women's team traveled to Stuttgart, Germany for training. Part of an effort to establish and nurture grassroots sports in Afghanistan, the hope is that the women's team, along with the men's, will soon be managed entirely by a local—Afghan—association.

Afghanistan: Olympics. For most Olympians, the chance to go to the Games is not only an honor but also a source of admiration from one's countrymen. Not necessarily so in Afghanistan. Mehboba Ahdyar, a runner, was to be the sole female on Afghanistan's team in Beijing. Training at night to avoid being seen, Mehboba suffered derision and even death threats. Though hopes were high for her performance, she disappeared from pre-Games training in Italy. She later turned up in Norway asking for asylum.

Afghanistan: Taekwondo. Hopes were high the summer of 2008 that Nisar Ahmad Bahawe, Afghanistan's champion taekwondo master, would win the gold for Afghanistan. The sport was brought to Afghanistan in the 1970s by an American master—and stuck. It's one of Afghanistan's favorite sports with some 700 clubs and 25,000 competitors. Bahawe's hopes were not just for himself. "Bringing home a medal would help people come together as a country whatever tribe or ethnic group they are from," he said. Taking a bronze medal home, Bahawe was Afghanistan's sole medal winner.

THE SONGBOOK PROJECT

CAN YOU STOP THE BIRDS SINGING

THE STORY OF THE AFGHAN CHILDREN'S SONGBOOK PROJECT
BY LOUISE PASQUALE

Afghan Children's Songbook Project begins … 2002.

For almost 40 years since my Peace Corps experience in Kabul, Afghanistan, I'd followed news stories. I read about the devastation, about the Communist coup, the defeat of the Soviets, the civil wars, the oppressive rule of the Taliban and the devastating loss of the ancient Buddha statues. With each new report my heart sank a bit more. I tried to imagine what was happening to the Afghanistan I came to know and love. I wondered what happened to the children I taught and the families and friends I'd made. Had they survived? I wondered about the music.

Then, about six years ago, I was rummaging around in my bookcase and came across my old copy of the children's songbook I created, in collaboration with Afghan poets and musicians, while in the Peace Corps. Now torn and faded I leafed through the pages, sadly realizing that I no longer could read the Dari and although I knew the melodies, I couldn't remember all the lyrics and had no easy way of translating them. As I stood in my living room, holding in my hands not only the songbook itself but all the memories that went with it, I came to the frightful realization, given the rigid decrees set by the Taliban, that perhaps these songs were in danger of being lost to Afghan culture forever. At that moment, I vowed to return them to the children, somehow, some way.

At that decisive moment, my thought process was simple. I feared the songs were going to be lost. They needed to be preserved. I needed to somehow return them. I had always felt that I gained much more from my Peace Corps experience than I had given to the Afghans, and had always wanted to somehow find a way to give something back. I never quite knew how to do that.

Louise Pasquale and friends in 1968—at the time, both children and adults were dressed in Western-style clothes.

Although I thought this was a credible idea I knew I needed to run the idea by Afghans. If, for some reason, they didn't approve or support returning the songs, I was willing to let the idea go. Once I began talking about the project to Afghans, I unearthed responses that went far beyond what I imagined. They wholeheartedly supported me and, in fact, were visibly moved by the idea, and thus I began the journey and at that moment the Afghan Children's Songbook Project became a reality.

Initially I thought I'd just copy my old songbook and send it back, but it soon became apparent that that idea was not feasible. My copy, not the original, was in terrible shape and I had, solely by ear, written the notation to each song. I was quite sure there were errors. I was also not sure if the songs represented the total Afghan population. It occurred to me that the best way to return the songs was to actually create a new songbook and include a recording of each song.

Children's Songs from Afghanistan
Qu Qu Qu Barg-e-Chinaar

To the children of Afghanistan,
May their hearts forever be filled with song.

قو قو قو، برگ چنار
سرود های مشهور اطفال افغانستان

NATIONAL GEOGRAPHIC
Washington, D.C.

After much searching I was introduced to Vaheed Kaacemy, a well-known and respected Afghan-Canadian musician living in Toronto. I told him about my project and he agreed to look over the old songbook. Vaheed is a musician and composer. Before moving to Canada, he was a kindergarten teacher in Kabul. He had the perfect combination of skills and background for this project. When I spoke to him on the phone about the project, he was thrilled and eagerly awaited the arrival of my songbook. I sent him a copy of the old songbook. His reaction—tears at seeing songs that had long gone from his memory. He immediately saw the urgency of the project. He jumped headfirst into it, hunting down the original sources for each melody and poem (something I had not originally done) and finding Afghan-Canadian children in the Toronto area to work on the recording. After he had recorded the first couple

Her own songbook has arrived!

of songs, he sent them to me. I was delighted—and hearing children sing the songs made it all come to life.

I headed off to Washington, D.C. to meet with the Afghan Ambassador's wife, Mrs. Shamim Jawad, whom I hoped would help fund the project through her organization, Ayenda, which I had read supported education. I shared my story and songbook idea with Mrs. Jawad, then gave her a pair of earphones and had her listen to the first two songs Vaheed had recorded. I had no idea how she'd react. I waited nervously as she put on the earphones and began to listen. Then she gasped—actually practically stopped breathing. With tears in her eyes she said, "I haven't heard that song since I was a child. I never thought about the power music can have. I thought we needed to send computers to the schools. This is what the children need. They need their music back." She enthusiastically agreed to support the project.

Vaheed continued to work diligently on recording all the songs and he very wisely suggested we include not only songs in Dari and Pashto (the two official languages) but songs in Hazaragi and Uzbeki. He also offered to write an Alphabet Song in Dari based on an old melody from Herat since, perhaps due to his training as a kindergarten teacher, he felt Afghan children needed an Alphabet Song!

The project moved forward and, dedicated to using Afghans in every part of the project, my next task was to find an Afghan-owned printing company. I was blessed to find Arsalan Lutfi who is the creative director of a printing, media and graphic design company—TriVision Studios based in Virginia and in Kabul. When I told him about the project, he too was incredibly moved and said he would do whatever he could to help. And that he did.

In March of 2007, Mrs. Jawad and the Afghan Embassy in D.C. hosted a release party to officially launch *Qu Qu Qu Barg-e-Chinaar: Children's Songs from Afghanistan*. About 200 Afghans attended the event. The first 5,000 songbooks had been printed and were being distributed to orphanages and elementary schools in Kabul and nearby provinces. Each songbook package

Wahid Qasimi, a famous Afghan composer and musician, with young children.

distributed to individual children includes a songbook with 16 children's songs, a CD and a cassette tape.

During this event, I told the story of the project, and at the end of my talk, I shared a DVD of the children from Toronto who recorded the songs, singing an old familiar song. They are singing the last song from the songbook—"Ma Mardume, Afghanaim"—which translates, "Afghan People." It's a familiar old folk song similar, in a way, to "This Land Is Your Land", speaking of the wonderful beauty of Afghanistan and how Afghans are united as one people in one land. It was the first song in my old songbook.

The DVD began to play and the room became silent. Then suddenly one woman in the crowd shouted out, "We all know this song. We should all be singing." Suddenly, all 200 Afghans in that room began to sing. I turned to look at the crowd, moved by hearing their voices in song, but what I saw

made my heart stop. Every person in that room was not only singing but had tears rolling down their cheeks. They were thrilled to hear their childhood songs once again.

THE PROJECT TODAY

To date (June 2009) thanks to the Ayenda Foundation, Bayat Foundation, National Geographic, the Flora Foundation and other funders and generous individuals, we have distributed 14,000 songbooks to 10 provinces. TriVision has reopened their printing business in Kabul and updated their equipment, so all the printing is now done in Afghanistan. This allows for hiring Afghan workers and gives the songbook much more exposure to the Afghan community. A few local businesses have offered to help support the next printing.

The distribution is coordinated through TriVision, and several NGOs and other small organizations support this effort. American Councils for International Education YES volunteers, in particular, play an instrumental role in distributing songbooks all across Afghanistan. They supply wonderful photographs and detailed documentation. The books are given to young children in schools and orphanages and women in villages where there are few resources. Distributors report that the songbooks are valued not only as a crucial connection to Afghan musical culture but also as a basic literacy tool.

PLAN FOR THE FUTURE

There continues to be an overwhelming need for more songbooks, and we are currently raising funds for another printing. As director and founder of the project, I will return to Afghanistan in October 2009 to assess the project and determine next steps. I plan to visit many of the schools that have received songbooks to evaluate how they are being used and how we can assist teachers in learning ways to use the songbook to enhance basic literacy. We hope to produce a second songbook in the near future and Vaheed has already collected the songs.

Songbooks being delivered.

Ah! The joy of holding her own songbook as she listens to the disc.

"Can you stop the birds singing?" Ustad Mash'al, one of Afghanistan's greatest painters posed that question in 1994 in response to the extreme music censorship that was occurring in Afghanistan in the mid-1990s. I recently asked my daughter, Jennifer, an ornithologist, that very question—Can the birds stop singing? She replied—"Yes. Actually. If young birds do not hear their own music, if their parents are silenced or disappear, the music is lost." The timing was fortunate. The songs are being returned during a time when there is still a generation who holds a memory of this music. They are now committed to passing those memories on and keeping the song alive.

There is a lesson to be had about the value music holds in a culture. It should be held dear and treasured. Despite the fact that music is often considered frivolous in this country, it's not. It's not only not frivolous; it's serious business.

Khaled Hosseini, author of *The Kite Runner* and *A Thousand Splendid Suns*, wrote about the songbook project—"This wonderful songbook is a small treasure that connects today's Afghan children with generations past. My own children have already memorized these songs, as I had when I was a child. With all the destruction that Afghan children have witnessed, it is my hope that this collection brings them a sense of joy, belonging and identity."

It is the intent of the Afghan Children's Songbook Project to keep these vibrant poetic songs, and many others, alive for the future generations of Afghan children.

A BRIEF BACKGROUND
ON AFGHANISTAN

Afghanistan is known for its rugged history of fierce warring tribes who, after sweeping through and conquering parts of Afghanistan, left a turbulent countryside. Today, the Pashtun tribe is the largest and the greatest of these tribes. At the same time, even after hundreds of years of later occupations, the blonde hair and blue eyes of descendants of Alexander the Great's army still dominate in the features of many of the faces of Afghanistan.

Before leaving Afghanistan in 328 B.C., Alexander the Great married Roxanne, a daughter of a Sogdin-Bactrian tribal leader. Her ancestors the Sogdins were an ancient Iranian people. The Bactrian ancestries of her father were the noblemen of the Persian Empire until Alexander conquered them in 331 B.C. After their marriage, Roxanne accompanied Alexander on his conquest of India; she was pregnant with their son. Injured in battle and

facing revolt among his troops who wanted to go home, Alexander returned to Baluchistan, fell ill, and died at the age of 32. Roxanne returned to Alexander's home in Macedonia to give birth to their son. Later, both she and her son, Alexander IV, were murdered.

Buddhism had a great impact on Afghanistan. It was introduced in the third century B.C. by Menender, the greatest king of the Mauryan Dynasty (273-232B.C.). Soon, Afghanistan became devoutly Buddhist. King Menender is one ruler about whom some facts are known because we have found the Bactrian Gold near the Greek town of Aï Khanum, which was a large city in Northern Afghanistan. It was thoroughly destroyed by Scythians and the Parthians. Then came the Kushans, originally of Chinese descent, who established a great empire that stretched from the Sea of Aral in present day Russia to the northwestern frontiers of

India, including Afghanistan. Their art uses Indian motifs, but it is their Greek influenced techniques that can be seen in the Buddha statues. The Sassanids, who in turn conquered them, ruled Persia (now modern Iran), but allowed the Afghans to continue practicing Buddhism.

The statues of Buddha at Bamiyan were considered the largest stone statues in the world at 177 feet. They were carved toward the beginning of the Gupta Empire, and Buddhism continued to flourish in Afghanistan until the Arabs invaded in 642 A.D.—and introduced the Afghans to Islam—300 years before Mahmud became the de facto ruler of Afghanistan and founder of the Ghaznavid Empire. Mahmud converted any remaining Hindus and Buddhists to Islam through aggressive and cruel domination.

In the 12th century (1167 to 1227) Genghis Khan and his fierce mounted warriors destroyed the food basket of Western Afghanistan by demolishing the country's elaborate irrigation and water systems. To this day, much re-mains a desert. Genghis Khan's descendants during the last century sat on the thrones of China, Russia, and India. In 1504 Zahir-ud-Din Muhammad, known as Babur, a descendant of Genghis Khan through Tamerlain, founded the Moghul empire. Babur ruled parts of Afghanistan; Kabul was his capital. Babur's Afghan warriors had great endurance because they traveled carrying a compound paste of dried mulberries and walnuts to eat. After some 11 years, Babur went on to conquer parts of India. A superb General, organizer and leader, Babur remained in India until his death, at which time he left instructions to be taken back to Kabul for burial in his beloved garden. His beautiful gardens in Kabul became the pattern for the famous gardens in Versailles and throughout the world.

In 1747, after the assassination of Nabirsah of Persia, Ahmad Shah Durrani established his rule, supported by Pashtun tribal councils. Afghanistan was controlled by the Pashtuns from then until the communists seized power in 1978.

CREDITS

ACKNOWLEDGEMENTS:

I am grateful to the following people who have contributed to this endeavor—I would like to honor their dedication in helping Afghanistan, they have been selfless in the giving of their time to the deep needs of the Afghan people.

My assistant, Charlotte Mixon, for the long hours she has put in. Dr. Peter Saleh, Dr. Gary Davis, Omar Sultan, Joanne Herring, Mitty Beal, and Kate Friedrich, without whom this book would never have appeared; my grandchildren: Caroline Dean, Andre Dean, and Alexandria Lynch; Case and Edmund Lynch, my sons, for their advice; the photographers Beth Wald, Andrew Xenios and Thierry Ollivier; for the original graphics and innovative designs, Patti Manzone; and Jamie Johnson, my editor, for her tireless work.

THE ROSES

Roses are mentioned from as far back as Biblical times, when they were called the flower of the desert. Afghans, whenever possible, have roses and have such pride showing their rose bushes. If you are there for a meal you will see cut roses placed somewhere in the rooms. With the heat of the day and the chill of the evening settling over the sands, roses put roots down six or seven feet to reach water. Roses survive the dry desert and can even endure ten to twenty years of neglect.

THE BUTTERFLIES

The butterfly seen on several pages in this book is the Micropsychae Arinae. These are the smallest butterflies in the world and are indigenous to Afghanistan only; they are shown actual size in this book.

PHOTOGRAPH CREDITS

Unless otherwise indicated, all photos on page are by same photographer.

... a little help 128, 129, 130.
Afghan Institute of Learning 154, 155, 156b.
American University of Afghanistan 99, 102, 171a, 193, 255.
Arghand 231, 232, 233.
Arnoldy, Ben ©2009 The Christian Science Monitor 64, 65, 66.

ARZU 104, 105, 106.
Ayenda 100b.
Barker, Bill 113a, 114b.
Bayat Foundation 192, 194.
Biro, Peter 198b.
Bolz, Julia 150, 152, 171b, 209.
Briggs, Eleanor 167, 202, 262b, 263c.
Counterpart International 210.
CURE International 75, 76.
Davis, Gary 86b.
Direct Relief International 103.
Dupree Foundation 142, 143, 144.
Dunya, Khalida 111.
Firestone, Caroline H. 49a.
Firestone, Gay 249, 250.
Georgetown University 97a.
Gilbert, Captain Russell 86a, 181.
Global Partnership for Afghanistan 39b, e, g, 40, 42, 45f.
HOPE worldwide 203, 216, 217, 218, 219, 220, 222, 223.
Initiative to Educate Afghan Women 109, 114a.
International Assistance Mission 161.
International Rescue Committee 198a.
Johnson, Jamie © 2004 138, 139, 153a, 166, 169a, 189.
Khan, Sarfraz 147, 148, 149.
Marigold Fund 204, 207.
McCloy, Rush 174, 175.
Mobile Mini Circus for Children 245, 246.
National Solidarity Program 196, 197.
Nooristan Foundation 199, 200, 201.
Ollivier, Thierry x, 1, 2, 3, 4, 5, 6, 7.
Organization for the Advancement of Afghan Women 153b, c.
Pasquale, Louise 257, 258, 259, 260, 261.

Quail, Louis 48, 49b, 51, 53a, 54, 55, 59.

Rebuilding Afghanistan Foundation 162, 163, 164, 165.

Roots of Peace 224, 225, 226, 227.

Safi, Dr. Najibullah 89.

Sanayee Development Organization 78, 79.

Saruk, Jonathan © 2009 International Medical Corps 80, 82.

Shelter for Life International 208.

Sherjan, Hassina 158, 159, 160.

Sirat, Taj 112.

Soto, Lena L. 87.

Smile Train 70, 71, 72, 73, 74.

Stars & Stripes 178.

Sulgrave Club 107.

Terre des hommes 133, 134, 135.

Thompson, Suzanne 39a, c, d, f, 41, 43, 44, 45a, c, d, e.

Thunderbird School of Global Management 115, 116a, 117.

TriWest Healthcare Alliance 93.

Turquoise Mountain Foundation 46, 52.

U.S.-Afghan Women's Council 97b, 98, 100a, 110, 116b, 156a, 206.

Wafiq, Muzhgan 113b.

Wald, Beth

 © 2002 i, ii, 239.

 © 2004 vii, vix, 27, 28a, 29, 30, 31, 36a, 125.

 © 2007 inside front cover, 8, 11, 13, 14, 24, 26, 28b, 32, 33, 34, 36b, 37, 63, 67, 68, 91, 92, 141, 173, 179, 189, 190, 247, 248, 233c, 262a, c.

 © 2008 50, 53b, 56, 60, 61, 119, 120, 136, 179.

 © 2009 16, 17, 18, 19, 20, 77, 83b, 84, 85, 94, 123, 124, 132, 140, 157, 169b, 170, 176, 184, 185, 186, 187, 212, 214, 234, 235, 236, 237, 240, 241, 242, 254.

Women for Afghan Women 126, 127.

Xenios, Andrew iv, 22, 23, 45b, 83a, 90, 95, 108, 122, 195, 211, 228, 263a, inside back jacket flap.

NEWS REPORTING

We wish to acknowledge the excellent reporting on Afghanistan by the following news organizations.

AFP

The Associated Press

Athens Banner-Herald

BBC News

The Canadian Press, CanWest News Service

CNN

Dawn

EurasiaNet

Fayob Server

The Guardian

IRIN

The Los Angeles Times

The New York Times

New Zealand Herald

NPR

PAN

Quqnoos.com

Radio Free Europe/ Radio Liberty

ReliefWeb

Reuters, Reuters AlertNet.UK, Reuters Life!, Reuters UK

The Sunday Times

The Telegraph UK

TIME.com

Times London

UPI

Washington TV

Women's enews

Xinhua

... A LITTLE HELP
241 W. Blaine St.
McAdoo, PA 18237
United States of America
http://www.stasek.com/alittlehelp/index.shtml
Rosemary Stasek (rosemary@stasek.com)

AFGHAN CHILDREN'S SONGBOOK PROJECT
The Folk Arts Center
42 West Foster Street
Melrose, MA 02176-3811
1-781-662-7475
www.facone.org
Marcie Van Cleave, Executive Director
(fac@facone.org)

AFGHAN INSTITUTE OF LEARNING
AIL
MAIL: Creating Hope International, "For AIL Project"
PO Box 1058
Dearborn, MI 48121
United States of America
(313) 278-5806
http://afghaninstituteoflearning.org/
www.creatinghope.org/aboutail
chi@creatinghope.org

AFGHAN RED CRESCENT SOCIETY
ARCS
PO Box 3066
Central Post Office
Kabul, Afghanistan
0093 752014446
http://www.icrc.org/eng/afghanistan

AFGHAN TEACHER EDUCATION PROJECT
ATEP
MAIL : Center for Afghanistan Studies
University of Nebraska at Omaha
Omaha, NE 68182
United States of America
(402) 554-2376
www.unomaha.edu
world@unomaha.edu

AFGHAN WOMEN LEADERS CONNECT
MAIL: c/o Rockefeller Philanthropy Advisors
6 West 48th Street, 10th Floor
New York, NY 10036
United States of America
(212)812-4344
www.afghanwomenconnect.org

AFGHAN WOMEN JUDGES TRAINING
IAWJ
600 New Jersey Ave., NW
Gewirz Building, Room 110
Washington D.C., 20001
United States of America
(202) 661-6501
www.iawj.org
office@iawj.org

AGA KHAN DEVELOPMENT NETWORK
AGDN
House 297, Street 17,
Wazir Akbar Khan Road,
Kabul, Afghanistan.
Tel: +93 799 300 082;
www.akdn.org/afghanistan
info@akdn-afg.org

AID AFGHANISTAN FOR EDUCATION
AAE
PO Box 1850
Kabul, 25000
Afghanistan
+ 93 (0) 799 428 512
http://www.aidafghanistan.net/
aid@aidafghanistan.net

THE AMERICAN UNIVERSITY OF AFGHANISTAN
P.O.Box 458
Central Post Office
Kabul, Afghanistan
+93 (0) 797 20 04 00
+93 (0) 799 54 19 83
www.auaf.edu.af
info@auaf.edu.af

ARGHAND COOPERATIVE
Mail: c/o Chayes
3 Hubbard Pk.
Cambridge, MA 02138
United States of America
http://www.arghand.org/
info@arghand.org

ARZU
MAIL : Arzu, Inc.
875 N. Michigan Avenue, Suite 2250
Chicago, IL 60611
United States of America
(312) 321-8663
www.arzurugs.org
arome@arzurugs.org

ASCHIANA FOUNDATION
P.O. Box 9512
Washington, DC 20016
United States of America
(202) 337-8129
www.aschiana-foundation.org
info@aschiana-foundation.org

AYENDA FOUNDATION
2341 Wyoming Avenue, NW
Washington, DC 20008
United States of America
(202) 292-4296
www.ayendafoundation.org
contact@ayendafoundation.org

BAYAT FOUNDATION
P.O. Box 2777
Ponte Vedra Beach, FL 32004
United States of America
(904) 686-1470
www.bayatfoundation.org
info@bayatfoundation.org

CENTRAL ASIA INSTITUTE
P.O. Box 7209
Bozeman, MT 59771
United States of America
(877) 585-7841
www.ikat.org
info@ikat.org

CHURCH WORLD SERVICE
CWS
NY Headquarters:
475 Riverside Drive, Suite 700
New York, NY 10115
United States of America
(212) 870-2061
http://www.churchworldservice.org
info@churchworldservice.org

COMBINED SECURITY TRANSITION COMMAND— AFGHANISTAN
CSTC – A
MAIL: Public Affairs
APO AE 09356
http://www.cstc-a.com/
cstc-apao@swa.army.mil

CURE INTERNATIONAL
CURE
701 Bosler Avenue
Lemoyne, PA 17045
United States of America
www.cureinternational.org
info@cureinternational.org

FUTURE GENERATIONS FOR CHILDREN
FFGC
North Mountain
Franklin, WV 26807
United States of America
304.358.2000
www.future.org
info@future.org

GLOBAL PARTNERSHIP FOR AFGHANISTAN
GPFA
P.O.Box 1237
New York, NY 10276
United States of America
Afghanistan contact info:
Wazir Akbar Khan
Street 11, House 96, Kabul
Afghanistan
www.gpfa.org
info@gpfa.org

GOVERNMENT OF AFGHANISTAN MINISTRY OF COMMUNICATIONS AND INFORMATION TECHNOLOGY
CIT
MAIL: 6th Floor
ICT Directorate
Ministry of Communications and Information Technology
Mohammad Jan Khan Watt
Kabul, Afghanistan
+93-20-2101113
www.mcit.gov.af

THE GROSSMAN BURN FOUNDATION
23679 Calabasas Road, Suite 270
Calabasas, CA 91302-1502
United States of America
(818) 783-6884
www.grossmanburnfoundation.org
stacy@grossmanburnfoundation.org

HELP THE AFGHAN CHILDREN
HTAC
MAIL: 3900 Jermantown Road, Suite 300
Fairfax, VA 22030
United States of America
(888)403-0407
www.htac.com
info@htac.org

HOPE WORLDWIDE
HOPE
353 West Lancaster Avenue, Suite 200
Wayne, PA 19087
United States of America
(610) 254-8800
www.hopeww.org
hope_worldwide@hopeww.org

INSTITUTE FOR ECONOMIC EMPOWERMENT OF WOMEN
IEEW
www.ieew.org

INTERNATIONAL ASSISTANCE MISSION
IAM
www.iam-afghanistan.org
hq@iamafg.org

INTERNATIONAL COMMITTEE OF THE RED CROSS
ICRC
1100 Connecticut Ave. N.W., Suite 500
Washington D.C. 20036
United States of America
(202) 587-4600
www.icrc.org
webmaster.gva@icrc.org

INTERNATIONAL MEDICAL CORPS
IMC
1919 Santa Monica Blvd., Suite 400
Santa Monica, CA 90404
United States of America
(310) 826-7800
www.imcworldwide.org
imc@imcworldwide.org

INTERNATIONAL ORGANIZATION FOR MIGRATION
IOM
Ansari Wat, House 1093
Behind UNICA
Guest House Shari-Naw
Kabul, Afghanistan
+932. 02 20 10 22
www.iom.int
iomkabul@iom.int

INTERNATIONAL RESCUE COMMITTEE
IRC
122 East 42nd Street, 12th Floor
New York, NY 10168
United States of America
(877) 733-8433
www.theirc.org
advocacy@theirc.org

INTERNATIONAL SCHOOL OF KABUL— ISK
P.O.Box 5084
Kart-e-Char
One street north of District 3 Police Headquarters
Kabul, Afghanistan
0700 684 895
www.iskafghan.org
info@iskafghan.org

JOURNEY WITH AN AFGHAN SCHOOL
MAIL: The American Friendship Foundation
P.O. BOX 611
Bothell, Washington 98041
United States of America
www.affhope.org
info@affhope.org

LOUIS AND NANCY HATCH DUPREE FOUNDATION
954 Lexington Avenue, Suite 118
New York, NY 10021
United States of America
(718) 440-6189
www.dupreefoundation.org
dupreefoundation@gmail.com
Afghanistan.centre@gmail.com

MARIGOLD FUND
6221 Blue Grass Ave.
Harrisburg, PA 17112
United States of America
(413) 259-6878
www.marigoldfund.org
info@marigoldfund.org

MOBILE MINI CIRCUS FOR CHILDREN
MMCC
MMCC c/o Settlement
Dybbolsgade 41
1721 Copenhagen V
Denmark
www.afghanmmcc.org
circus@afghanmmcc.org
David Mason (+93-700-280-140)
(for calls within Afghanistan 0700-280-140)

NATIONAL GEOGRAPHIC
104 West 40th Street
New York, NY 10018
(212) 790-9020
www.nationalgeographic.com
adventure@ngs.org

NATIONAL SOLIDARITY PROGRAMME
www.nspafghanistan.org

NEW HUDSON FOUNDATION
825 Fifth Avenue, 2c
New York, NY 10065
United States of America
(212) 838-0800
www.newhudsonfoundation.org
Mrs. Caroline Firestone, President
(cfirestone@newhudsonfoundation.org)

ORGANIZATION FOR THE ADVANCEMENT OF AFGHAN WOMEN
P.O. Box 946
New York, NY 10024
United States of America
(212) 861-6663
www.oaawonline.org
Operation Smile Train
41 Madison Avenue, 28th Floor
New York, NY 10010
United States of America
1-800-932-9541
www.smiletrain.org
info@smiletrain.org

PROJECT ARTEMIS, THUNDERBIRD UNIVERSITY
MAIL: Thunderbird for Good
1 Global Place
Glendale, AZ 85306
United States of America
www.thunderbird.edu

REBUILDING AFGHANISTAN FOUNDATION
RAF
MAIL: RAF c/o Elizabeth Hartnett
220 East 57th Street, Apt 3H
New York, NY 10022
United States of America
www.rebuildingafghanistan.org

ROOTS OF PEACE
ROP
MAIL: ROP – U.S. Headquarters
1299 Fourth Street., Ste 200
San Rafeal, CA 94901
United States of America
(415)-455-8008
1(888)-ROOTS-31
www.rootsofpeace.org
info@rootsofpeace.org

SANAYEE DEVELOPMENT ORGANIZATION
SDO
MAIL (main office): Chahrai Ansari,
Street 5
Near Mohd Alam Faizad High School,
Shahr-e-naw, Kabul
Afghanistan
0093 (0) 220 1693
sdf@ceretechs.com
sdfkabul@ceretechs.com

THE SUNSHINE LADY FOUNDATION
4900 Randall Parkway, Suite H
Wilmington, NC 28403
United States of America
www.sunshinelady.org

TERRE DES HOMMES
TDH
31 Chemin Franck Thomas
CH-1223 Cologny/Geneva
Switzerland
+41 22 736 33 72
www.terredeshommes.org
info@terredeshommes.org

TRIWEST HEALTHCARE ALLIANCE
MAIL : U.S. Office of SOZO International
P.O. Box 436967
Louisville, KY 40253
United States of America
(502) 253-4308
Afghanistan office:
House 23, Street 5
Taimani Main Road
Kabul, Afghanistan
0093 75 200 1120
www.sozointernational.org
info@sozointernational.org

TURQUOISE MOUNTAIN FOUNDATION
TMF
MAIL: Turquoise Mountain Foundation,
Emma Shercliff
4504 Macomb St. NW
Washington DC 20016
United States of America
Tel (Kabul) +93(0) 798 149 173
Tel (UK) +44(0) 1764 650 888
www.turquoisemountain.org
contact@turquoisemountain.org

UNITED NATIONAL CHILDREN'S FUND
UNICEF
MAIL: UNICEF
P.O.Box 54
Kabul, Afghanistan
(93) 7 9050.7000
www.unicef.org
Kabul@unicef.org

UNITED NATIONS ASSISTANCE MISSION IN AFGHANISTAN
UNAMA
Compound B, Peace Street
Kabul, Afghanistan
(Afghanistan) +93 0790 00 6121
(USA) 212-963-2668
www.Unama.unmissions.org
Dominic Medley, Public Information
Officer (medleyd@un.org)

U.S. AGENCY FOR INTERNATIONAL DEVELOPMENT
USAID
USAID Afghanistan
Great Masood Road
Kabul, Afghanistan
0093(0) 700-234-233
www.afghanistan.usaid.gov
kabulinformation@usaid.gov
William Frej, Mission Director
(202)216-6288

U.S. AFGHAN WOMEN'S COUNCIL
USAWC
Media queries : (202) 312-9663
http://usawc.state.gov

VOICE OF WOMEN'S ORGANIZATION
VOWO
Badmorghan, across from Masjidui Reza,
Heart City, Afghanistan
(0093) (0) 799 209 386
www.vwo.org.af
info@vwo.org.af
Suraya Pakzad, Executive Director
(suraya@vwo.org.af)

WORLD HEALTH ORGANIZATION
WHO
Avenue Appia 20
1211 Geneva 27
Switzerland
+41 22 791 21 11
www.who.int
info@who.int

WOMEN FOR AFGHAN WOMEN—WAW
32-17 College Point Blvd.
Room 206
Flushing, NY 11354
United States of America
718-321-2434
www.womenforafghanwomen.org
office@womenforafghanwomen.org